GCSE

Collins

KU-546-302

# Total Revision

# GCSE German

WANDSWORTH PUBLIC LIBRARIES

Ken Wheeler

500 560 514 9X

Series editor: Jayne de Courcy

# Contents

500 560 514

# How this book will help you...

It doesn't matter whether you're heading for mocks in Year 11, or in the final run-up to your GCSE exam – **this book will help you to produce your very best.**

Whichever approach you decide to take to revision, this book will provide everything you need:

1. Total revision support
2. Quick revision check-ups
3. Exam practice

## 1 Total Revision Support

### Everything you need to know

This book contains all the topics you'll have studied at school. **It covers all the main topics set by all the Exam Boards.**

### Short sections of vocabulary and grammar

The vocabulary and grammar you need to know are divided between the 13 topic chapters. This fits with how you are taught German at school. **It also means you won't have to wade through pages and pages of grammar and vocabulary to find what you need.**

The 'What you need to know section' in each chapter contains the vocabulary and structures you need to get a **Grade C**. The 'Going Further' section gives additional language which will help you **move up the grades to an A or an A\*.**

### Revising the 'four skills'

Reading, Writing, Listening and Speaking are in every chapter. But we've also included one whole chapter on each skill. **Read through each of these as revision before each of your specific skill exams.**

...Turn over for QUICK REVISION CHECK-UPS and EXAM PRACTICE... →

# **2** Quick Revision Check-ups

## *Check yourself questions*

It can be really hard knowing where to start when you're revising. Sitting down and wading through pages of text isn't easy. You're probably asleep before the third page! This book makes it easy to stay awake – **because it makes revising ACTIVE.**

We came up with the idea of putting '**Check yourself**' questions into each chapter. **The questions test your understanding of all the important vocabulary and structures** in each chapter. In this way, you can find out quickly and easily just how much you know. You don't need to read through all the chapter first – just try the questions. If you get all the questions right, you can move straight on to the next section. If you get several of the questions wrong, you know you need to read through the vocabulary and grammar sections carefully. **This really cuts down on revision time – and helps you focus on where you need to put most effort.**

## *Answers and Tutorials*

If you want the 'Check yourself' questions to be a genuine test of how much you know, then you need to cover up the answers. But, if you'd rather, you can read through a question, then the answer and then the '**tutorial**'. This will still do you a lot of good – and doesn't require quite as much effort!

**We've included 'tutorials', as well as answers, to give you even more help with your revision.** The tutorials point out common mistakes that the author knows candidates make, and give you hints on answering similar questions in exams.

# Exam technique

Knowing your vocabulary and grammar is important. But **it's even more important to know how to use them to answer exam questions properly.** The author sees hundreds of exam scripts a year and students very often lose marks because **they haven't understood how to tackle exam questions.**

# Foundation and Higher

You will be sitting either the Foundation or Higher tier papers. If you are doing **Foundation**, practise the questions marked **F** and **F/H**; if you are doing **Higher**, practise the questions marked **F/H** and **H**.

# The audio CD

This contains the Listening questions and sample answers for the Speaking questions. We use this symbol ⊠ in the book to show when you need to use the CD.

# Questions to Answer and Examiner's comments

We've included **lots of past exam questions from different Exam Boards for you to have a go at**. The answers are at the back of the book so it's easy not to cheat. Have a go at the questions yourself and then compare them with the answers.

**We've provided comments on the answers to give you extra help.** The comments highlight what is good about the answers and what an examiner looks for in order to award a high grade.

## Three final tips:

1. Work as consistently as you can during your whole GCSE German course. If you don't understand something, ask your teacher straight away, or look it up in this book. You'll then find revision much easier.

2. Plan your revision carefully and focus on the areas you know you find hard. The 'Check yourself' questions in this book will help you do this.

3. Try to do some exam questions as though you were in the actual exam. Time yourself and don't cheat by looking at the answers until you've really had a good go at working out the answers.

v

# About your GCSE German course

## Exam Boards

This book has been produced to help you to study and revise for the German exams set by all the Exam Boards of England, Northern Ireland and Wales.

## Grammar

The grammatical content of all the German syllabuses is very similar. The final chapter of the book is a summary of the grammar required in the GCSE exam. This can be used as a reference section to help you find the answer to any problems you may have in the exercises in the rest of the book. It can also form the basis of a revision programme, as each grammar point refers you to the appropriate chapter, where you will find further examples as well as *Check yourself* exercises that test your recall and understanding.

## Vocabulary

The core vocabulary defined by each board as a minimum for the lower grades differs between boards. There is no upper limit on the amount of vocabulary, and therefore no guide can give a comprehensive list of what might be in any given exam paper. However, if you learn all the vocabulary in this guide you are likely to encounter relatively few unknown words in the exam, and for this reason the use of a dictionary is now allowed by all boards for some parts of the exam.

## Types of questions

The *Exam practice* sections include examples of the types of questions set by all the groups. In Listening and Reading, many of the question-types are very similar for all the groups. In the Speaking and Writing chapters, a note has been included to tell you which group is likely to use each type of task.

All the groups use role-plays and conversation in the Speaking test. NEAB and MEG (and Edexcel in the coursework option) also require candidates to give a prepared presentation.

## Use of dictionaries

All Exam Boards allow the use of dictionaries during Reading and Writing tests and for the preparation of the Speaking test. You will need to consult your board's syllabus for the exact details regarding the use of a dictionary in the Listening test. NEAB and WJEC allow the use of a dictionary for part of the test, while other boards do not.

## Foundation and Higher tiers

All Exam Boards offer the GCSE papers at Foundation and Higher tiers, and candidates can choose – in consultation with their teachers – to enter at either of the two levels in each of the four skills. You can, for example, take Higher level papers in Listening and Reading, but Foundation level papers in the Speaking and Writing tests.

The arithmetic of the points awarded on papers and their conversion to grades goes like this: on each of the four Foundation papers you can score up to 5 points; on each of the four Higher papers you can score between 4 and 8 points. You can 'mix and match' the papers you take

| Number of Foundation papers taken | Number of Higher papers taken | Maximum number of points that this can give you | Best overall grade that you can get |
|---|---|---|---|
| 4 | 0 | 20 | C |
| 3 | 1 | 23 | B |
| 2 | 2 | 26 | A |
| 1 | 3 | 29 | A |
| 0 | 4 | 32 | A* |

Candidates who take all four Foundation papers can reach a maximum of a Grade C, while those who take all four Higher papers will normally be awarded a minimum of a Grade D.

## WHAT YOU NEED TO KNOW

Ich besuche eine Gesamtschule.
In der Schule lerne ich Informatik.
Ich finde Erdkunde sehr interessant.
Ich mache gern Biologie.
Ich mag lieber Physik als Musik.
Mein Lieblingsfach ist Chemie. }
Ich lerne am liebsten Chemie. }
Ich finde Mathe schwer/langweilig.
In Deutsch bin ich eine Eins.
Ich habe die Prüfung bestanden.
Ich bin in Musik durchgefallen.
Wir arbeiten in der Bibliothek.

I go to a comprehensive school.
At school I learn IT.
I find geography interesting.
I like biology.
I prefer physics to music.
My favourite subject is chemistry.

I find maths difficult/boring.
I get top marks in German.
I passed the exam.
I failed (the exam) in music.
We work in the library.

### Die Schulroutine

Ich fahre mit dem Rad zur Schule.
Wir haben fünf Unterrichtsstunden jeden Tag, drei vor der Pause und zwei nach der Pause.
Jede Stunde dauert siebzig Minuten.
Die erste Stunde beginnt um Viertel vor neun.
Die Mittagspause dauert eine Stunde.
In der Mittagspause esse ich Butterbrote/warm in der Kantine.
Die Schule ist um 3.30 Uhr aus.
Nach der Schule treibe ich Sport.
Ich bekomme drei Stunden Hausaufgaben.

### School routine

I come to school by bike.
We have five lessons each day, three before lunch and two after it.

Each lesson lasts 70 minutes.
First lesson begins at 8.45.

The lunch break is an hour long.
At lunch I eat sandwiches/a hot meal in the canteen.
School finishes at 3.30.
I do sport after school.
I get three hours' homework.

### Die Schuluniform

Ich trage...
einen grauen Pullover
eine rote Kràwatte
eine dunkle Hose/einen dunklen Rock
ein weißes Hemd/eine weiße Bluse

### School uniform

I wear ...
a grey pullover
a red tie
dark trousers/a dark skirt
a white shirt/a white blouse

### DIE SCHULFÄCHER

| | |
|---|---|
| Betriebswirtschaft | business studies |
| Fremdsprache(n) | foreign language(s) |
| Handarbeit/ Nähen | needlework/ sewing |
| Holzarbeit | woodwork |
| Sozialkunde | social studies |
| Technik | technical studies |
| Turnen | gymnastics |
| Wirtschaftslehre | economics |

### DIE NOTEN

| | | |
|---|---|---|
| 1 | sehr gut | very good |
| 2 | gut | good |
| 3 | befriedigend | satisfactory |
| 4 | ausreichend | adequate |
| 5 | mangelhaft | weak |
| 6 | ungenügend | unsatisfactory |

### DIE ZIMMER

| | |
|---|---|
| die Aula | hall |
| das Klassenzimmer | classroom |
| das Lehrerzimmer | staffroom |
| die Turnhalle | gym |
| die Werkstatt | workshop |

### DIE SCHULEN

| | |
|---|---|
| der Kindergarten | nursery, kindergarten |
| die Grundschule | primary school |
| das Gymnasium | grammar school |
| die Realschule | type of secondary school |
| die Hauptschule | secondary modern school |

## QUESTIONS/PROMPTS

Wann beginnt die Schule/der Unterricht?

Welche Fächer lernst du in der Schule?

In welchen Fächern bist du gut?

In welchem Fach bist du am schwächsten?

Was ist dein Lieblingsfach/sind deine Lieblingsfächer?

Welches Fach hast du nicht gern?

# *Check yourself*

## QUESTIONS

**Q1** **How would you say in German?**

a) My favourite subject is history.
b) I get good marks in maths.
c) We do PE in the gymnasium.
d) I come to school by bus every day.
e) Each lesson lasts an hour.

**Q2** **Choose the set of symbols which matches each sentence below.**

*Write the number after the appropriate sentence.*

a) Ich bekomme immer gute Noten in Kunst.
b) Ich stehe ziemlich schlecht in Naturwissenschaften.
c) Ich bin eine Eins in Deutsch.
d) Sport macht mir Spaß.
e) Am Mittwoch haben wir nach der vierten Stunde Schluß.

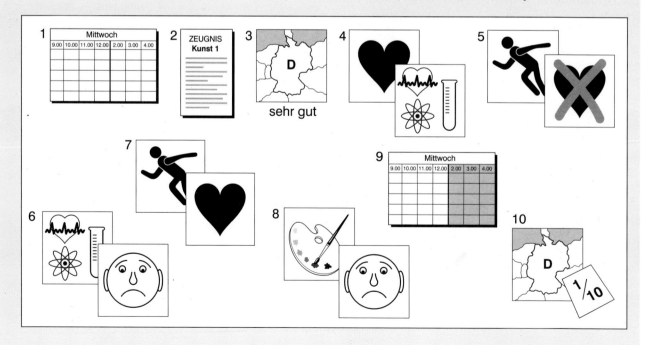

**REMEMBER! Cover the answers if you want to.**

## ANSWERS

**A1**
a) Mein Lieblingsfach ist Geschichte.
b) Ich bekomme gute Noten in Mathe.
c) Wir turnen in der Turnhalle.
d) Ich fahre jeden Tag mit dem Bus zur Schule.
e) Jede Stunde dauert sechzig Minuten.

**A2**
a) 2
b) 6
c) 3
d) 7
e) 9

## TUTORIAL

**T1**
a) *Take care not to confuse* Geschichte *with* das Gesicht.
b) *Don't be misled by* Noten, *meaning 'marks'. It also means 'musical notes'.*
c) *German speakers use* turnen *for any sort of* PE *in the gym. Take care not to use* Gymnasium *for anything to do with sport.*
d) *Remember the order of adverb phrases: Time, Manner, Place.*
e) *Avoid* Jede Stunde dauert eine Stunde.

**T2**
*Exam boards are making increasing use of visual materials, including standardised icons to represent many everyday objects and also feelings such as liking or disliking something. You need to familiarise yourself with the sort of visual material that is available. Most of it should be obvious, since it is widely used in language teaching books, but there may be subjects or items beyond your experience. Don't be afraid to ask your teacher what is meant.*

# GOING FURTHER

You need to be able to describe your school and your routine in some detail. It is expected that Higher Level candidates will always look for opportunities to express their opinions about what they do. It helps if you are positive, so say what you do like about school and why.

### Meine Schule

Meine Lehrer sind in Ordnung, besonders der Mathelehrer.
Er ist jung und sehr lustig.
Französisch macht mir Spaß, weil wir oft Spiele machen.
Ich treibe gern Sport und spiele Fußball/Hockey in der Schulmannschaft.
Ich bin ziemlich gut in Kunst, weil ich gern zeichne und male.
Naturwissenschaften finde ich schwer, aber ich versuche mein Bestes.

### My school

My teachers are OK, especially the maths teacher.
He is young and very funny.
French is fun because we often play games.
I enjoy sport and play football/hockey for the school team.
I'm quite good at art, because I like drawing and painting.
I find science difficult but I do my best.

### Meine Schulroutine

Ich komme normalerweise zu Fuß in die Schule, außer wenn es regnet.
Meine Mutter bringt mich mit dem Auto dahin, wenn es regnet.
In der Mittagspause treffe ich mich mit Freunden auf dem Schulhof.
Ich lerne Deutsch seit vier Jahren.

Ich mache meine Hausaufgaben, sobald ich nach Hause komme.

### My school routine

I usually walk to school, except when it rains.
My mother brings me to school, when it rains.
At lunchtime I meet my friends in the playground.
I've been learning German for four years.
I do my homework as soon as I come home from school.

3

**Die Zukunft**

Ich möchte in den Sommerferien arbeiten, um Geld zu verdienen.

Ich werde im September in die Oberstufe gehen.

Ich werde Deutsch, Geschichte und Englisch studieren.

Ich möchte Elektriker(in) werden. Im Juli werde ich die Schule verlassen und im September werde ich die Berufsschule besuchen.

Ich möchte auf die Uni gehen, aber ich weiß noch nicht, was ich studieren werde.

Ich möchte Schauspieler(in) werden.

**Future plans**

I would like to work in the summer holidays to earn some money.

I shall go into the sixth form in September

I shall study German, history and English.

I'd like to be an electrician. I shall leave school in July and go to technical college in September.

I'd like to go university but don't yet know what I will study.

I'd like to be an actor/actress.

## HOW THE GRAMMAR WORKS

## POSSESSIVE ADJECTIVES

Possessive adjectives look like this:

| **Singular** | | **Plural** | |
|---|---|---|---|
| *mein* | my | *unser* | our |
| *dein* | your (familiar) | *euer* | your (familiar) |
| *Ihr* | your (formal/polite) | *Ihr* | your (formal/polite) |
| *sein* | his | *ihr* | their |
| *ihr* | her | | |
| *sein* | its | | |

**Note:** There should be no confusion about which *sein* or *ihr* is being used. Simply look back to see which noun or person it refers to, for example:

> *Der Junge hat seine Hausaufgaben vergessen.* - **his** homework
> *Das Kaninchen hat sein Futter gefressen.* - **its** food

Similarly:

> *Die Lehrerin hat ihren Schirm mitgebracht.* - **her** umbrella
> *Die Mädchen haben ihre Taschen verloren.* - **their** bags

Always look carefully at Ihr and ihr. With a capital letter, it nearly always means 'your', unless it comes at the beginning of a sentence, in which case it could mean 'her', 'their' or 'your'.

Unlike the other adjectives you will meet, the possessives follow the pattern of the indefinite article: *ein, eine, ein.*

| Case* | Masculine | Feminine | Neuter | Plural |
|---|---|---|---|---|
| **Nominative** | mein Hund | meine Katze | mein Pferd | meine Tiere |
| **Accusative** | meinen Hund | meine Katze | mein Pferd | meine Tiere |
| **Genitive** | meines Hundes | meiner Katze | meines Pferdes | meiner Tiere |
| **Dative** | meinem Hund | meiner Katze | meinem Pferd | meinen Tieren |

*Further explanation of cases and their uses follows in Chapter 5.

This pattern is easy to follow for *dein* and *sein*, but less so for *ihr, unser, euer,* etc. Just remember to add the same ending to each one, as if it were *mein*.
**That includes adding no ending:**

> *Mein Hund heißt Kim. Wie heißt euer Hund?*
> *Ich spiele mit meinen Freunden Tischtennis. Was macht ihr mit euren Freunden?*
> *Das Zimmer unserer Klasse ist im Erdgeschoß. Wo ist das Zimmer eurer Klasse?*

Note that the second *e* is sometimes omitted from *euer*.

# Check yourself

## QUESTIONS

**Q1** **How would you say in German?**

a) What's your sister called?
b) I'll bring my brother with me.
c) That is my mother's car.
d) The girl is going for a walk with her friend.
e) Have you forgotten your bags, Mrs Wenzler?

**Q2** **Correct the errors in the English.**

a) Sie ist die Schwester meiner Freundin.
   She is my sister's friend.
b) Meine Freunde sind böse, weil ich unseren Hund nicht finden kann.
   My friends are annoyed because I can't find their dog.
c) Bitte nehmen Sie ihre Tasche mit und geben Sie sie ihr.
   Please take your bag with you and give it to them.
d) Die Mädchen haben ihre Mütter im Kaufhaus getroffen.
   The girl met her mother in the department store.

---

**REMEMBER! Cover the answers if you want to.**

---

## ANSWERS

**A1**

a) Wie heißt deine/eure/Ihre Schwester?
b) Ich bringe meinen Bruder mit.
c) Das ist das Auto meiner Mutter.
d) Das Mädchen geht mit seinem Freund/seiner Freundin spazieren.
e) Haben Sie Ihre Taschen vergessen, Frau Wenzler?

**A2**

a) She is my friend's sister.
b) My friends are annoyed because I can't find our dog.
c) Please take her bag with you and give it to her.
d) The girls met their mothers in the department store.

## TUTORIAL

**T1**

a) Use eure *if you are talking to two friends as* ihr, *and* Ihre *if you are using the polite form* Sie *in a formal situation.*
b) *Remember to add the* mit. *This translates the English 'with me'.*
c) Meiner Mutter *is obviously feminine, although it refers to* das Auto.
d) *This is a tricky one, but it comes up frequently. The German word for girl is* das Mädchen, *and therefore the possessive must be* sein.
e) *You need the polite forms* Sie *and* Ihr *when talking to this woman.*

**T2**

a) *Take extra care where two people are involved. It may be confusing, but you need to be clear about the difference between my 'teacher's brother' and 'my brother's teacher'.*
b) *Don't assume an automatic connection between a person mentioned and the possessive adjective which follows.*
c) *Again, the formal* Sie *is likely to lead you astray with the* ihre *which follows, just as the* sie *in the second clause might lead you to believe that the bag has something to do with 'them'.*
d) *Remember that* Mädchen *is a neuter word and that therefore* Die Mädchen *must be plural. Similarly, the umlaut on* Mütter *shows you that it is plural. Higher Level candidates are expected to know the plurals of common nouns.*

# EXAM PRACTICE

**F H LISTENING**

*You will find the transcript and answers, with examiner's comments, on page 172.*

**1** Find Chapter 1 – Exam Practice Listening on the CD and listen to the German (Track 1) twice.

 Anna beschreibt ihren Stundenplan. Füllen Sie den folgenden Stundenplan auf deutsch aus.

(Anna is describing her timetable. Complete the timetable below in German.)

*Annas Stundenplan*

| Stunde | Montag | Dienstag | Mittwoch | Donnerstag | Freitag | Samstag |
|--------|--------|----------|----------|------------|---------|---------|
| 1 | Englisch | Deutsch | Mathe | | Biologie | |
| 2 | Geschichte | | Deutsch | Englisch | Deutsch | Englisch |
| | P | A | U | S | E | |
| 3 | | Kunst | | Informatik | | |
| 4 | Musik | Physik | | | | |
| | P | A | U | S | E | |
| 5 | Deutsch | | Chemie | Sozialkunde | Englisch | |
| 6 | | Mathe | Latein | Mathe | Latein | |
| 7 | | Turnen | | | | |
| 8 | | Turnen | | | | |

[10 marks]

**H SPEAKING**

*You will find the transcript and examiner's comments on page 173.*

**2** **Presentation/Narrative situation**
Sie haben letztes Jahr einen Schüleraustausch gemacht. Erzählen Sie, was Sie an einem typischen Schultag in Deutschland gemacht haben. (You went on a school exchange to Germany last year. Describe what you did on a typical school day there.)

**Aufstehen**
Um wieviel Uhr?

**Frühstück**
Wo? Was?

**Schulweg**
Wie?

**Wetter**

**Schultag/ Stundenplan**
Fächer? Wo? Was gemacht?

**Pausen**
Freunde?
Was gemacht?

**Nach Hause**
Wann?
Schöner Tag?

**Am Nachmittag**
Was gemacht?

*You may now like to try and narrate the story yourself. Think about how you can use all you know about your timetable, lessons and teachers to make this narrative interesting. Remember that the examiner is going to ask you questions about what you say, so in the examination you need to be prepared to listen and respond.*

 Find Chapter 1 – Exam Practice Speaking on the CD and listen to how a candidate might tackle this Higher Level narrative (Track 2). When you have finished, think about what you have heard before reading the examiner's comments. Did any of these points occur to you?

Then listen to the better version of the narrative twice and try to memorise some of the phrases used.

**3** Read the passage, then answer the question below.

Lesen Sie das folgende Stück über die Schule in Deutschland. Jürgen freut sich auf den Sommer.

(Read the following passage about school in Germany. Jürgen is looking forward to the summer.)

Nach den Osterferien gibt es viel mehr Sport bei uns in der Schule, was mir natürlich sehr gefällt. In den Turnstunden gehen wir im Sommer meistens auf den Schulhof oder auf die Spielwiese, wenn es geht. Das macht uns allen mehr Spaß als immer in der Halle an den Geräten zu turnen. Jemand hatte die Idee, einige Tennisplätze bei uns an der Schule anzulegen, aber es soll sehr teuer sein, und es können immer nur so wenig Leute auf einmal spielen. Ich glaube, es lohnt sich nicht.

Volleyball ist in meiner Klasse der Lieblingssport, und ein paar von uns organisieren im Juni ein Turnier für alle zehnten Klassen an unserer Schule. Hoffentlich gewinnt unsere Klasse!

Wir haben auch eine Arbeitsgemeinschaft für Rudern, und ab der neunten Klasse darf man auf dem Rhein rudern. Wir leihen die Boote vom Ruderverein in der Stadt, und es kommt immer jemand vom Verein, der mit uns trainiert. Dieses Jahr bereiten wir eine längere Fahrt vor, denn in den Sommerferien wollen wir eine Moseltour machen. Klasse! Darauf freue ich mich besonders.

In den nächsten Wochen schreiben wir in einigen Fächern Klausuren, und danach bekommen wir unsere Zeugnisse. Manche aus meiner Klasse haben Angst vor den Klassenarbeiten, aber ich glaube, es sind meistens nur die faulen Schüler. Ich denke, wenn man einigermaßen gut gearbeitet hat, sollte man die Prüfungen bestehen. Außerdem sind meine Eltern sehr vernünftig und verlangen immer nur, daß ich mein Bestes tue. Es gibt einen Elternabend im Juli, aber ich schaffe die Versetzung in die Oberstufe ohne Probleme. Leider glaubt meine Freundin Beate schon, daß sie sitzenbleiben wird.

Der Höhepunkt unseres Sommers ist das Schulfest im Juli mit der Disco abends in der Aula und draußen auf dem Schulhof. Es gibt Würstchen vom Grill, verschiedene Salate mehrere Brotsorten und genug zu trinken, versteht sich! Normalerweise macht das einen Riesenspaß.

Richtig oder falsch? Kreuzen Sie die Sätze an.

(True or false? Put a cross by the sentences.)

*You will find the answers, with examiner's comments, on page 174.*

| | richtig | falsch |
|---|---|---|
| 1 In den Osterferien treibt man viel Sport in der Schule. | | |
| 2 Jürgen interessiert sich sehr für Sport. | | |
| 3 Das Volleyballturnier ist für alle Klassen. | | |
| 4 Der Wassersport ist nicht für die jüngeren Schüler. | | |
| 5 Im Sommer macht Jürgen eine Moselfahrt. | | |
| 6 Jürgen hat keine Lust, Klassenarbeiten zu schreiben. | | |
| 7 Jürgen fürchtet, daß Beate sitzenbleibt. | | |
| 8 Jürgen findet das Klassenfest toll. | | |
| 9 Die Disco läuft den ganzen Tag. | | |
| 10 Es gibt immer genug zu essen und zu trinken. | | |

F H **WRITING** ➔ **4** Write a letter of 110-130 words to your pen-friend, describing your school.

Schreiben Sie einen Brief an Ihren Brieffreund, in dem Sie Ihre Schule beschreiben. Schreiben Sie 110-130 Wörter.

## Sample Student's Answer

Newbury, den 13. Mai

Liebe Gabi,

Deine Schule scheint sehr groß zu sein. Im Vergleich ist unsere viel kleiner. Wir haben nur etwa fünfhundert Schüler und Schülerinnen. Wir haben auch sechs Unterrichtsstunden jeden Tag, aber wir sind den ganzen Tag in der Schule, weil wir viel später anfangen.

Ich komme zu Fuß in die Schule und treffe mich so gegen 8.15 Uhr mit meinen Kameraden auf dem Schulhof. Die Schule beginnt mit einer Klassenversammlung um 8.40 Uhr, und die erste Stunde beginnt um neun Uhr.

Ich lerne zwei Fremdsprachen, Französisch und Deutsch, Französisch seit vier und Deutsch seit drei Jahren. Ich bin viel besser in Mathe als in den Naturwissenschaften, aber mein Lieblingsfach ist trotzdem Sport.

Bis bald,
Tschüß

### EXAMINER'S COMMENTS

- This is a straightforward question and the better candidate need have no fear of writing such a short letter. The same candidate will, of course, need to know more for a Speaking Test presentation.

- The skill here is to get as many good pieces of German into this short space as possible. The following items of language are particularly impressive:

  scheint ... zu sein instead of the simple ist.
  Im Vergleich ... kleiner: good use of the comparative.
  Subordinate clause introduced by weil.
  Ich komme …: this sentence contains five adverbial phrases in the correct order.
  Ich treffe mich ... mit.
  Correct use of seit.
  besser als: good use of the comparative.

- The trick is to use the letter to show what you can do in German, regardless of whether this is actually true or simply fantasy. This is a common topic and you must always expect it in your exam in some form or other.

*You may now like to try writing your own letter, using this sample and other material from this chapter.*

## WHAT YOU NEED TO KNOW

**Ich wohne...**
   in einem Einfamilienhaus
   in einem Doppelhaus
   in einem Reihenhaus
   in einem Bungalow
   in einer Wohnung
   auf einem Bauernhof
Das Haus ist ziemlich alt.
Die Wohnung ist relativ modern.

**Im Wohnzimmer haben wir...**
   einen Tisch
   einen Fernseher
   ein Sofa
   zwei Sessel

**In der Küche gibt es...**
   einen Elektroherd/Gasherd
   einen Mikrowellenherd
   einen Kühlschrank
   eine Waschmaschine
   viele Schränke
Wir haben (keine) Zentralheizung.
Wir haben einen großen/kleinen Garten.

**Im Garten gibt es...**
   Gemüse
   einige alte Bäume
   schöne Blumen
   einen Rasen
Meine Eltern arbeiten
gern im Garten.
Ich finde das Haus/die Wohnung schön.
Ich habe mein Zimmer selbst
angestrichen/tapeziert.
Mein Zimmer ist blau angestrichen.

**I live...**
   in a detached house
   in a semi-detached house
   in a terraced house
   in a bungalow
   in a flat
   on a farm
The house is quite old.
The flat is relatively modern.

**In the living room, we have...**
   a table
   a TV
   a sofa
   two armchairs

**In the kitchen, there is/are...**
   an electric/gas cooker
   a microwave
   a fridge
   a washing machine
   lots of cupboards
We have (no) central heating.
We have a large/small garden.

**In the garden, there is/are...**
   vegetables
   some old trees
   lovely flowers
   a lawn
My parents enjoy working
in the garden
I like the house/flat.
I painted/papered my room myself.

My room is (painted) blue.

### QUESTIONS/PROMPTS

Wie ist dein/Ihr Haus?

Wie sieht dein/Ihr
Schlafzimmer aus?

Kannst du deine Wohnung
beschreiben?

Können Sie Ihre Wohnung
beschreiben?

Erzähl' mir etwas über dein Haus.

Erzählen Sie mir etwas über
Ihr Haus.

### DIE FARBEN

schwarz    rosa

weiß    grau

rot    lila

gelb    orange

grün

## MEIN ZIMMER

In meinem Zimmer habe ich...

einige Poster/Bilde
einen Computer
eine Stereoanlage
einen Stuhl
einen Schreibtisch
einen Fernseher
eine Kommode
ein Bett

# Check yourself

## QUESTION

`Q1` **How would you say in German?**

a) I live in a semi-detached house.
b) We have a new kitchen.
c) In my room I have a desk and a chair.
d) My parents work in the garden.
e) We have a sofa and two chairs in the living room.

---

**REMEMBER! Cover the answers if you want to.**

---

## ANSWER

`A1`
a) Ich wohne in einem Doppelhaus.
b) Wir haben eine neue Küche.
c) In meinem Zimmer habe ich einen Schreibtisch und einen Stuhl.
d) Meine Eltern arbeiten im Garten.
e) Wir haben ein Sofa und zwei Stühle im Wohnzimmer

## TUTORIAL

`T1`
*b)* *Remember the feminine agreements are 'eeeasy'.*
*c)* *Remember to turn round the subject and verb after a phrase at the beginning of the sentence.*
*d)* *Use the contraction* im *whenever possible.*
*e)* *Remember that not all plurals of common nouns are as straightforward as those of feminine nouns, where you simply add -n or -en.*

## GOING FURTHER

You need to be able to describe your house in a little more detail and to say what you do in each room. In addition you should be able to say something about the daily routine at home, who does what jobs around the house, and most importantly, what you think about it all.

### Mein Haus, mein Zimmer

Ich finde unser Wohnzimmer ziemlich gemütlich.

I think our living room is very cosy.

Wir haben ein großes, bequemes Sofa und zwei große Sessel.

We have a large comfortable couch and two large armchairs.

In der Ecke steht eine moderne Stereoanlage mit CD-Spieler.

In the corner there is a modern music centre with a CD-player.

Wir haben kein Eßzimmer und essen fast immer in der Küche, die sehr groß ist.

We have no dining room and almost always eat in the kitchen, which is very large.

Dort haben wir einen enormen, alten Eßtisch.

We have an enormous old dining table.

Ich verbringe ziemlich viel Zeit in meinem Zimmer.

I spend quite a lot of time in my bedroom.

Ich mache dort meine Hausaufgaben, höre Musik, lese oder faulenze.

I do my homework there, listen to music, read or just laze about.

Meine Eltern sagen, es ist immer unordentlich, aber das stimmt nicht.

My parents say it's always untidy, but that's not true.

Ich mache mein Bett jeden Morgen.

I make my bed every morning.

Ich decke den Tisch und räume nach dem Essen ab.

I lay the table and clear away after the meal.

Mein Bruder spült nicht gern.

My brother doesn't like washing up.

Ich muß jeden Samstag mein Zimmer aufräumen, und im ganzen Haus staubsaugen.

I have to tidy up my room every Saturday and vacuum the whole house.

**Meine tägliche Routine**

Although this can be a simple list of verbs in the present tense, it becomes much more valuable with the addition of a few extra words, especially time phrases.

| | |
|---|---|
| Ich stehe normalerweise um 7 Uhr auf. | I normally get up at 7 o'clock. |
| Ich gehe ins Badezimmer. | I go to the bathroom. |
| Ich wasche mich. | I wash. |
| Ich dusche. | I shower. |
| Ich ziehe mich schnell an | I quickly get dressed. |
| Ich gehe in die Küche, und ich frühstücke mit meiner Schwester. | I go into the kitchen and I have my breakfast with my sister. |
| Ich esse gewöhnlich Toast mit Marmelade und trinke eine Tasse Tee oder ein Glas Orangensaft. | I usually have toast and jam and a cup of tea or a glass of orange juice. |
| Ich packe meine Bücher/Sachen zusammen und ich verlasse das Haus so gegen acht Uhr. | I get my books/things together and I leave the house at about 8 o'clock. |

**Note:** It is better to avoid English names for breakfast cereals and, whatever you do, don't use *Getreide* for 'cereals'.

## HOW THE GRAMMAR WORKS

## PRESENT TENSE

It is very important to realise that German has only one form of the present tense, whereas English has three.

He enjoys school/ He is enjoying himself/ He does enjoy a good walk.

### Regular verbs (also known as weak verbs)

**machen** – to make (known as the infinitive)

| | | stem – **mach-** |
|---|---|---|
| **singular** | | |
| 1st person | I | ich mach -**e** |
| 2nd person | you (familiar) | du mach -**st** |
| 2nd person | you (formal/polite) | Sie mach -**en** |
| 3rd person | he, she, it | er, sie, es mach -**t** |
| **plural** | | |
| 1st person | we | wir mach -**en** |
| 2nd person | you (familiar) | ihr mach -**t** |
| 2nd person | you (formal/polite) | Sie mach -**en** |
| 3rd person | they | sie mach -**en** |

So, if you find yourself writing any part of the verb *sein* and getting stuck for what to write next, look again. If what you are trying to use is the present tense of a verb, one word is all you need. For example:

> I am going – *ich gehe*
> we are sending – *wir senden*

If you find that the stem ends in a *-t*, *-d* or *-n*, you will need to add an 'e' in the *du*, *er/sie/es*, and *ihr* forms:

> *Du öffnest die Tür.*
> *Er arbeitet in der Küche.*
> *Ihr findet den Film bestimmt gut.*

### Irregular verbs (also known as strong verbs)

These verbs follow the regular pattern except in the *du* and *er/sie/es* forms.

> *fahren, tragen, schlafen* and some others add an umlaut to these parts:
> | | |
> |---|---|
> | *du* | *fährst, trägst, schläfst* |
> | *er, sie es* | *fährt, trägt, schläft* |

> *lesen, sehen, geben* and some others change their vowel:
> | | |
> |---|---|
> | *du* | *liest, siehst, gibst* |
> | *er, sie, es* | *liest, sieht, gibt* |

Some of these verbs are very common indeed and must be memorised. A more detailed list of the strong and irregular verbs appears in the Grammar Summary on pages 170–171.

## QUESTIONS

The question or interrogative form of the verb is formed by simply turning round the subject and verb.

> *Machst du dein Bett jeden Tag?*
> *Gehen Sie in die Stadt?*
> *Kommt sie bald nach Hause?*

There will be more notes on interrogatives in Chapter 8.

## SEPARABLE VERBS

Talking about your daily routine means using a number of separable verbs. Remember to take off the separable prefix – that short part at the front of the infinitive – and put it at the end of the clause.

> | | |
> |---|---|
> | *aufstehen* | Ich **stehe** morgens um sieben Uhr **auf.** |
> | *einkaufen* | Ich **kaufe** im Supermarkt **ein.** |
> | *abwaschen* | Ich **wasche** immer nach dem Frühstück **ab.** |

**Note:** You will need to use these same verbs in the perfect tense, for example when you are talking or writing about what happened last weekend. Remember to form the past participle like this:

> *Ich **bin** sehr früh **aufgestanden.***
> *Ich **habe** in der Stadt **eingekauft.***
> *Ich **habe** nach dem Mittagessen **abgewaschen.***

## REFLEXIVE VERBS

You will need some of the most common reflexive verbs when talking or writing about your daily routine. You can use them in two different ways, and it is a good idea to decide which you are going to do before the day of the exam!

Either: *Ich wasche mich.* – I wash (myself).
Or: *Ich wasche mir die Hände.* – I wash my hands.
Either: *Ich kämme mich.* – I comb my hair.
Or: *Ich kämme mir die Haare.* – I comb my hair.

Learn to handle the two common verbs which are both reflexive and separable – *sich anziehen* and *sich ausziehen*.

*Ich ziehe mich an/aus.* – I get dressed/undressed.
But: *Ich ziehe mir eine Jacke an.* – I put on a jacket.
*Ich ziehe mir die Schuluniform aus.* – I take off my school uniform.

Again, you will need these in the perfect tense:

*Ich habe mich angezogen/ausgezogen.*
*Ich habe mir eine Jacke angezogen.*

# *Check yourself*

## QUESTIONS

**Q1** **How would you say in German?**

a) We have a very cosy kitchen, where we always eat.
b) I have a cupboard with lots of cassettes in it.
c) I go into the kitchen and have breakfast with my sister.
d) I usually get up at 6.30.
e) I am putting on my shoes.

**Q2** **Correct the errors in the English.**

a) Wir haben keinen Garten.
We have a small garden.
b) Zum Frühstück esse ich Toast mit Marmelade.
I have toast and marmalade for breakfast.
c) Ich verlasse das Haus um halb acht.
I leave home at half past eight.
d) Ich habe drei Geschwister.
I have three sisters.

---

**REMEMBER! Cover the answers if you want to.**

---

## ANSWERS

**A1**
a) Wir haben eine sehr gemütliche Küche, wo wir immer essen.
b) Ich habe einen Schrank mit vielen Kassetten drin.
c) Ich gehe in die Küche und frühstücke mit meiner Schwester.
d) Ich stehe gewöhnlich um halb sieben auf.
e) Ich ziehe mir die Schuhe an.

**A2**
a) We have no garden.
b) I have toast and jam for breakfast.
c) I leave home at half past seven.
d) I have three brothers and sisters.

## TUTORIAL

**T1**
a) *Remember that the verb goes to the end in this subordinate clause after* wo.
b) *Dative endings after* mit.
c) *in + accusative shows movement.* mit *+ dative.*
d) *The verb is separable.*
e) *This verb is both separable and reflexive.*

**T2**
a) *Watch out for the kein/klein trap!*
b) *Marmelade is a 'false friend'.*
c) *Remember that verlassen must have a place mentioned after it.*
d) *The most obvious of 'false friends'.*

# EXAM PRACTICE

**F H LISTENING**

**1** Find Chapter 2 – Exam Practice Listening on the CD. Listen to the German (Track 3) twice, then answer the following question.

 Vier junge Leute sagen, wo und wie sie wohnen möchten. Füllen Sie die Tabelle aus. Kreuzen Sie die richtigen Kästchen an.

(Four young people are describing where and how they would like to live. Complete the table below by ticking the appropriate boxes.)

| Name | auf dem Land | in der Stadt | Haus | Wohnung | Garten | Hund | Katze |
|---|---|---|---|---|---|---|---|
| Cornelia | | | | | | | |
| Uwe | | | | | | | |
| Thomas | | | | | | | |
| Eva | | | | | | | |

[15 marks]

*You will find the transcript and answers, with examiner's comments, on page 174.*

**F H SPEAKING**

**2** Find Chapter 2 – Exam Practice Speaking on the CD and listen to the conversation (Track 4). When you have finished, think for a moment about what you have heard, then read the examiner's comments. Did any of these points occur to you?

*You will find the transcript and examiner's comments on page 175.*

---

*You may now like to try answering the questions yourself:*

*1. Was machst du morgens, bevor du in die Schule kommst?*
*2. Kannst du dein Haus beschreiben?*
*3. Wie hilfst du zu Hause?*

*Look back at the examples in previous sections of this chapter for help.*
*You may also want to play the CD again or look at the transcript.*

**3** Read the letter, then fill in the gaps in the sentences below.

Beate hat einen Brief über ihr neues Haus geschrieben. Lesen Sie den Brief.

> Düsseldorf, den 26. Februar
>
> Hallo Katherine!
> Wir sind umgezogen und ich muß Dir unbedingt von
> unserem neuen Haus erzählen. Also, das neue Haus
> ist einfach toll – nicht nur größer als das letzte,
> sondern auch viel gemütlicher. Ich habe jetzt ein
> eigenes Zimmer, und meine Schwester Monika auch.
> Das war im letzten Haus einfach nicht möglich, denn
> mein Bruder braucht ein Zimmer für sich, und meine
> Eltern natürlich auch. Außerdem haben meine Eltern
> eine eigene Dusche, was sehr praktisch ist. Meine
> Schwester und ich brauchen nämlich morgens nicht so
> lange warten, bis das Badezimmer frei ist. Und mit
> dem Fernsehen abends ist es jetzt viel besser, denn
> wir haben im Erdgeschoß eine Küche und noch zwei
> Zimmer. Also, wenn ich meine Hausaufgaben an dem
> großen Tisch im Eßzimmer machen will, stört mich
> der Fernseher im Wohnzimmer gar nicht.
> Meine Eltern sind froh, daß sie endlich einen richtigen
> Garten haben, denn sie arbeiten beide ganz gern
> draußen. Das heißt, mein Vater mag seine Blumen sehr
> gerne, Rasenmähen nicht so sehr. Vielleicht kann ich
> ein bißchen mehr Taschengeld verdienen, wenn ich es
> mache. 'Mal sehen
>
> Beate

1 Beates neues Haus hat .............. Schlafzimmer.

drei     vier     fünf

2 Sie teilt ihr Schlafzimmer .............................................

mit ihrer Schwester     mit ihrem Bruder     nicht mehr

3 Beates Eltern haben .........................................................

keine Dusche     eine separate Dusche     ein Badezimmer im Erdgeschoß

4 Beate macht ihre Hausaufgaben ........................................

immer auf ihrem Zimmer     manchmal unten     immer in der Küche

5 Beates Eltern freuen sich .................................................

auf den Garten     aufs Badezimmer     aufs Rasenmähen

*You will find the answers and examiner's comments on page 176.*

4  Schreiben Sie einen Brief an Ihren Brieffreund, in dem Sie Ihr Haus beschreiben. Schreiben Sie 110-130 Wörter.
(Write a letter to your pen-friend describing your home. Write between 110-130 words.)

## Sample Student's Answer

Reading, den 3. März

Lieber Martin,

Heute schreibe ich Dir etwas über unser Haus.

Wir haben zwei große Schlafzimmer und ein kleines Schlafzimmer, wo ich schlafe. Unser Wohnzimmer ist schön und bequem, unser Eßzimmer ist relativ klein. Wir haben unsere Küche modern eingerichtet, und mein Vater findet die Spülmaschine besonders toll!

Mein Zimmer ist klein, aber ich finde es gemütlich. Ich habe viele Poster an den Wänden und einen CD-Spieler in der Ecke. Unter dem Fenster steht mein kleiner Schreibtisch, wo ich meine Schulaufgaben mache.

Draußen haben wir einen großen Garten, wo meine Eltern beide gern arbeiten. Auf dem Rasen haben wir Platz genug, um Federball zu spielen. Das Haus ist in der Nähe der Schule, aber auch nicht weit von der Stadtmitte entfernt. Das ist ganz praktisch, wenn man sich mit Freunden treffen will.

Viele Grüße
Tschüß
Peter

### EXAMINER'S COMMENTS

- The letter is of the correct length and covers the topic well. Most of the rooms in the house are mentioned and there are some pleasing details about the kitchen, Peter's bedroom and the garden.

- There is good use of prepositions: über unser Haus; an den Wänden; Unter dem Fenster.

- The candidate has mastered the verb inversion; Heute schreibe ich; Draußen haben wir, and uses correct adjective endings: mein kleiner Schreibtisch; zwei große Schlafzimmer.

- The three simple subordinate clauses with wo show that this is the work of a good candidate who would score at least a Grade C.

- You must use the letter to show what you can do in German, regardless of whether this is actually true or simply fantasy. This is a common topic and you must always expect it in your exam in some form or other. Sometimes the question will require you to include specific details, and it is important to do so because some of the marks are likely to be related to each point. The information contained in the letter would be equally impressive in the Speaking Test.

*You may now like to try writing your own letter, using this sample. Remember to use the German material which you have practised, and don't be tempted to work out what you want to say in English and then try to translate it.*

## WHAT YOU NEED TO KNOW

### ESSEN UND TRINKEN

| | |
|---|---|
| Ich habe (großen) Hunger. | I'm (very) hungry. |
| Ich habe Durst. | I'm thirsty. |
| Ich esse gern... | I like (eating) ... |
| Ich trinke gern... | I like (drinking) … |
| Ich esse nicht gern... | I don't like (eating) ... |
| Was ißt du/trinkst du gern? | What do you like to eat/drink? |
| Was möchtest du essen/trinken? | What would you like to eat/drink? |
| Ich möchte... | I would like... |

| die Getränke | drinks | das Essen | food |
|---|---|---|---|
| der Apfelsaft | apple juice | der Aufschnitt | cold meat |
| das Bier | beer | die Bockwurst (¨e) | frankfurter |
| das Cola | cola | das Brathähnchen | roast chicken |
| die Flasche | bottle | die Bratwurst (¨e) | fried sausage |
| der Kaffee | coffee | die Currywurst (¨e) | curried sausage |
| der Kakao | chocolate drink | das Ei | egg |
| das Kännchen | pot | der Fisch | fish |
| die Limo(nade) | lemonade | das Fleisch | meat |
| das Mineralwasser | mineral wate | die Gulaschsuppe | goulash soup |
| der Orangensaft | orange juice | das Kotelett (s) | chop, cutlet |
| das Pils | lager | die Leberwurst | liver sausage |
| der Rotwein | red wine | das Omelett | omelett |
| der Sprudel | sparkling drink | das Rindfleisch | beef |
| der Tee | tea | das Rührei | scrambled egg |
| der Weißwein | white wine | der Schinken | ham |
| | | das Schweinefleisch | pork |
| **das Gemüse** | **vegetables** | das Spiegelei | fried egg |
| die Bratkartoffeln (pl.) | fried potatoes | das Steak | steak |
| der Kartoffelsalat (e) | potato salad | die Tomatensuppe | tomato soup |
| die Pommes Frites | chips | das Wiener Schnitzel | veal cutlet in breadcrumbs |
| der Reis | rice | | |
| der Salat (e) | salad | **die Nachspeisen** | **desserts** |
| die Salzkartoffel (n) | boiled potatoes | der Eisbecher (−en) | ice-cream sundae |
| das Sauerkraut | pickled cabbage | der Jogurt | yoghurt |
| die Tomate (n) | tomato | das Kompott | stewed fruit |
| der Wurstsalat (e) | sausage salad | der Obstsalat | fruit salad |
| | | der Pudding (s) | instant whip |
| | | die Sahne | cream |
| | | die Schlagsahne | whipped cream |

**das Obst**

der Apfel (Äpfel)

die Apfelsine (n)

die Banane (n)

die Erdbeere (n)

die Himbeere (n)

die Kirsche (n)

der Pfirsich (e)

die Traube (n)

die Zitrone (n)

*(Phrases you will hear in a restaurant)*

| | |
|---|---|
| Ich komme sofort. | I'm just coming/I'm on my way. |
| Haben Sie schon gewählt? | Have you chosen? |
| Was möchten Sie? | What would you like? |
| Sonst noch etwas? | Anything else? |
| Darf ich … empfehlen? | May I recommend … ? |
| Möchten Sie …probieren? | Would you like to try … ? |

*(Phrases you will need in a restaurant)*

| | |
|---|---|
| Herr Ober! Fräulein! | (to call the waiter or waitress) |
| Haben Sie einen Tisch frei? | Have you a table free? |
| Haben Sie einen Tisch für drei/vier? | Have you a table for three/four? |
| Ich möchte in der Ecke/am Fenster/auf der Terrasse sitzen. | I'd like to sit in the corner/by the window/on the terrace. |
| Ich möchte die Speisekarte. | I'd like the menu. |
| Was ist die Tagessuppe? | What is the soup of the day? |
| Ich bin Vegetarier(in). | I'm a vegetarian. |
| Ich möchte bestellen, bitte. | I'd like to order, please. |
| Zweimal Bratwurst mit Pommes Frites. | Sausage and chips twice. |
| Ich möchte Menü drei. | I'd like set menu 3. |
| Ich möchte eine kleine Portion… | I'd like a small portion (of…) |
| Das ist genug, danke./Das reicht, danke. | That's enough, thank you. |
| Ich nehme als Vorspeise/Nachspeise… | I'll have … as a starter/dessert. |
| Darf ich Salz und Pfeffer haben? | May I have the salt and pepper? |
| Das war lecker/prima/ausgezeichnet! | That was delicious/great/excellent! |
| Das hat sehr gut geschmeckt. | That tasted very good. |
| Zahlen, bitte!/Die Rechnung, bitte! | The bill, please. |
| Danke, das stimmt so. | Keep the change. |
| Ist die Mehrwertsteuer/die Bedienung inbegriffen? | Is VAT/service included? |

## WHAT YOU NEED TO KNOW

## GESUNDHEIT

| | |
|---|---|
| Mir tut der Finger/das Bein weh. | My finger/leg hurts. |
| Ich habe mir am Bein/an der Hand weh getan. | I have hurt my leg/my hand. |
| Ich bin krank/ich fühle mich unwohl. | I'm ill./I don't feel well. |
| Mir ist heiß/kalt/übel/schwindlig. | I feel hot/cold/sick/dizzy. |
| Ich habe Kopfschmerzen/Kopfweh. | I have a headache. |
| Ich habe Ohrenschmerzen/Zahnschmerzen. | I have ear/toothache. |
| Ich habe eine Magenverstimmung. | I have a stomach upset. |
| Ich habe eine Erkältung/einen Schnupfen. | I have a cold. |
| Ich habe Verstopfung. | I'm constipated. |
| Ich habe seit zwei Tagen Fieber. | I've had a temperature for two days. |
| Ich blute. | I'm bleeding. |
| Kann ich einen Termin haben? | Can I have an appointment? |
| Haben Sie Tabletten gegen Zahnschmerzen? | Have you any tablets for toothache? |
| Wie oft muß ich sie einnehmen? | How often must I take them? |

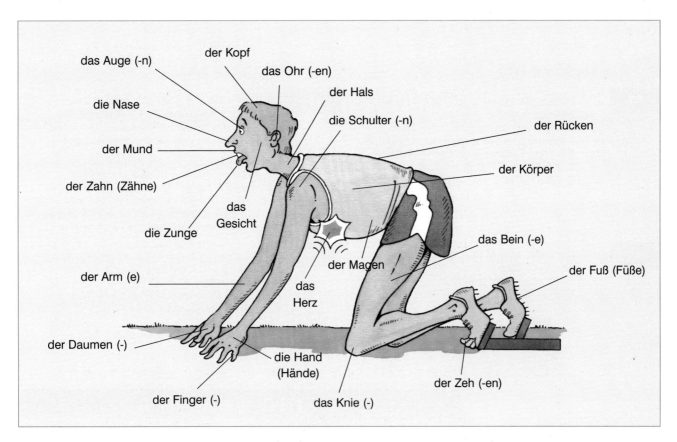

das Auge (-n)
der Kopf
das Ohr (-en)
die Nase
der Hals
die Schulter (-n)
der Rücken
der Mund
der Körper
der Zahn (Zähne)
das Gesicht
die Zunge
das Bein (-e)
der Arm (e)
der Magen
der Fuß (Füße)
das Herz
der Daumen (-)
die Hand (Hände)
der Zeh (-en)
der Finger (-)
das Knie (-)

| Beim Arzt | At the doctor's |
|---|---|
| Was ist los?/Was haben Sie? | What's wrong? |
| Wie lange haben Sie schon…? | How long have you had…? |
| Ich schreibe Ihnen ein Rezept. | I'll give you a prescription. |
| Nehmen Sie eine Tablette/einen Teelöffel dreimal täglich/vor dem Essen. | Take one tablet/one teaspoonful three times a day/before a meal. |
| Legen Sie sich hin. | Lie down. |
| Ruhen Sie sich aus. | Have a rest. |

# Check yourself

## QUESTIONS

**Q1**  **Im Restaurant** (Foundation role-play)

a) Ask for a table for six at the window.

b) Ask for the menu.

c) Order sausage and chips twice.

d) Order a glass of white wine and a pot of tea.

e) Ask for the bill.

**Q2**  *Complete the following interview.*

**Beim Arzt**
**Arzt:** Was fehlt Ihnen?
**Patient:** [a) Tell him you have an upset stomach.]
**Arzt:** Wie lange haben Sie das schon?
**Patient:** [b) Tell him for three days.]
**Arzt:** Ist Ihnen auch schwindlig?
**Patient:** [c) Say no, but you feel hot.]
**Arzt:** Also, ich gebe Ihnen ein Mittel.
**Patient:** [d) Ask how often you must take it.]
**Arzt:** Dreimal täglich nach dem Essen.

## ANSWERS

**A1**
a) Haben Sie einen Tisch für sechs am Fenster, bitte?
b) Ich möchte die Speisekarte, bitte.
c) Zweimal Bratwurst mit Pommes Frites.
d) Ein Glas Weißwein und ein Kännchen Tee, bitte.
e) Zahlen, bitte.

**A2**
a) Ich habe eine Magenverstimmung.
b) Seit drei Tagen.
c) Nein, aber mir ist heiß.
d) Wie oft muß ich es einnehmen?

## TUTORIAL

**T1**
*This is the usual sort of role-play which you are expected to be able to conduct in a restaurant. You should get used to interpreting what you are required to do by following the sequence of pictures or diagrams.*

*Don't forget that the examiner – in this case the waiter – is part of the dialogue. He may go along with everything you say, but he may offer you alternatives, or indeed say that you can't have what you are asking for. Look at the examiner as he/she speaks, so that you become aware of any problems you need to deal with.*

**T2**
b) German uses *seit* with the present tense to convey the English idea 'I have had it for three days'.
c) Resist the temptation to say Ich bin heiß.
d) Use *es* for das Mittel.

# GOING FURTHER

### Essen

| | |
|---|---|
| Haben Sie reserviert? | Have you made a reservation? |
| Das haben wir leider nicht mehr da. | We have no more of that. |
| Geht das zusammen oder getrennt? | Do you want to pay the bill altogether or separately? |
| Das Glas/der Teller ist nicht sauber! | The glass/plate is not clean. |
| Es fehlt ein Löffel. | There's a spoon missing. |
| Warum dauert es so lange? | Why is it taking so long? |
| Das Essen ist kalt. | The food is cold. |
| Die Rechnung stimmt nicht. | The bill is not correct. |

### Gesundheit

| | |
|---|---|
| Meinem Freund/Meiner Freundin geht es nicht gut. | My friend is not feeling well. |
| Er/Sie hat die Grippe. | He/She has the 'flu. |
| Der Junge/Das Mädchen hat sich am Bein verletzt. | The boy/girl has hurt his/her leg. |
| Er/Sie ist auf dem Schulhof hingefallen. | He/She fell over in the playground. |

# HOW THE GRAMMAR WORKS

## NOUNS, ARTICLES AND GENDERS

Nouns are the naming words of the language. To find out if a word is a noun try saying 'the' in front of it.

Unlike English, all German nouns are written with a capital letter, not just the names of people and places (proper nouns). If you don't follow this convention in your writing at Higher Level you will almost certainly lose some marks.

All German nouns are masculine, feminine or neuter:

|  | **Masculine** | **Feminine** | **Neuter** |
|---|---|---|---|
| *Singular* | der Vater | die Mutter | das Kind |
| *Plural* | die Väter | die Mütter | die Kinder |
|  | ein Vater | eine Mutter | ein Kind |

*Der, die* and *das* are definite articles and mean 'the'. In the plural the word for 'the' is always *die*. *Ein, eine* and *ein* are indefinite articles and mean 'a' or 'an'.

Whenever you come across a new word in German, you need to note its gender and its plural form, so that you will be able to use the word correctly in your work.

## PLURAL NOUNS

All feminine nouns form their plural by adding *-n* or *-en* to the singular. That's the easy part! Most masculine and neuter nouns do fall into groups which form their plurals in a similar way, but until you have learnt those you need, it's safer to check them in a text book or dictionary.

Most text books show only the plurals of masculine and neuter nouns, but when you find the masculine and neuter nouns in the German–English side of your dictionary they usually have some more letters in a bracket after them:

Kind (**-es, -er**)

The first letters are used for the genitive case (more about this in Chapter 5); the next letters show you the plural, and it is this which you need to remember.

## ARTICLE ENDINGS

It is very useful to remember some other words which follow the same pattern of endings as the definite and indefinite articles.

These all follow the pattern of *der, die, das*:

*dieser* – this
*jener* – that
*jeder* – each, every
*welcher* – which ?

Examples:

*Dieser Wagen ist schnell, jener Wagen ist langsamer.*
*Jede Mutter mag den Film.*
*Welches Kind war das?*

The possessive adjectives *mein, dein, sein,* etc. follow the pattern of *ein, eine, ein* (see Chapter 1), as does the word *kein* which means 'not a' or 'no':

*Ich habe kein Geld.* – I have no money.
*Ich habe keine Bücher.* – I have no books.

# Check yourself

## QUESTIONS

**Q1** Here are some common examples of words in the plural which you will need. Some of them are rarely seen in the singular. See if you know them already. Some are listed in the singular to jog your memory. Watch out for a few well-known words which are plural in English but singular in German!

*Give the German for the following:*

**Q2** *How would you say in German?*

a) Which car is faster, this one or that one?
b) Every girl likes this pop group.
c) I don't like these shoes. Which do you like?
d) Everyone knows the answer.

grapes

..........................

peas

..........................

carrots

..........................

potatoes

..........................

drinks

..........................

trousers

..........................

shoes

..........................

socks

..........................

glasses

..........................

buses

..........................

school subjects (*das Fach*)

..........................

school books

..........................

exercise books (*das Heft*)

..........................

friends (masc) (*der Freund*)

..........................

friends (feminine) (*die Freundin*)

..........................

3 pounds (weight)

..........................

2 kilos

..........................

teeth

..........................

fingers

..........................

feet

..........................

## ANSWERS

**A1**

| | |
|---|---|
| grapes | school subjects (*das Fach*) |
| Trauben | Schulfächer |
| peas | school books |
| Erbsen | Schulbücher |
| carrots | exercise books |
| Karotten | Hefte |
| potatoes | friends (masc) (*der Freund*) |
| Kartoffeln | Freunde |
| drinks | friends (feminine) (*die Freundin*) |
| Getränke | Freundinnen |
| trousers | 3 pounds (weight) |
| eine Hose (sing.) | 3 Pfund (not plural) |
| shoes | 2 kilos |
| Schuhe | 2 Kilo |
| socks | teeth |
| Socken | Zähne |
| glasses | fingers |
| eine Brille (sing.) | Finger (plural = sing) |
| buses | feet |
| Busse | Füße |

## TUTORIAL

**A2**

a) Welches Auto ist schneller, dieses oder jenes?
b) Jedes Mädchen mag diese Popgruppe.
c) Ich mag diese Schuhe nicht. Welche magst du?
d) Jeder weiß die Antwort.

**T1** *Just as in English, the definite article is not always required; indeed it sometimes makes nonsense of the sentence. If you say* Ich mag die Bohnen, *it implies that the listener knows which beans you are talking about. Perhaps you simply mean* Ich mag Bohnen, *which implies that you like beans in general. Think carefully before using* die, *every time you use a noun in the plural.*

**T2**

a) Jenes *is almost always used to contrast with* dieser. *However,* **dieser** *is frequently used to mean 'that' on its own, even when the article or person in question is not close at hand.*
b) *Don't forget:* das Mädchen. *She is not feminine!*
d) *Unless there is a clear reason to use another gender, for instance in a class of girls, we assume that 'everyone/everybody' is masculine.*

# EXAM PRACTICE

H **LISTENING** ➤

**1** Find Chapter 3 – Exam Practice Listening on the CD, and listen to the German (Track 5) twice.

Schreiben Sie jetzt auf, was jeder zu essen und zu trinken bekommt. Sie brauchen nicht in jedes Kästchen schreiben.

(Now write out the orders for each person. You need not write in every box.)

*You will find the transcript and answers, with examiner's comments, on page 177.*

|  | Vorspeise | Hauptgericht | Nachspeise | Getränke |
|---|---|---|---|---|
| Herr Kolbitz |  |  |  |  |
| Frau Kolbitz |  |  |  |  |
| Herr Radler |  |  |  |  |
| Frau Radler |  |  |  |  |

[20 marks]

F H **SPEAKING** ➤

**2** Look at these two role-plays. The pictures suggest what you need to do. There are a number of ways to phrase the questions/requests.

You will notice that Number 2 contains a question which you cannot prepare. In the exam you will need to look at the examiner as this question is asked. See if you can write down two or three questions which would fit into the role-play at this point.

---

**1 Im Restaurant**

1

2  **?**

3 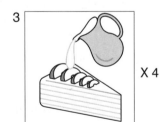 X 4

4 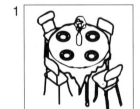 X 2

 X 2

5 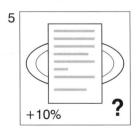 +10% **?**

---

**2 Beim Arzt in München**

**4 Beantworten Sie die Frage.**

Now find Chapter 3 – Exam Practice Speaking on the CD and listen to how a candidate might tackle these role-plays (Track 6).

*You will find the transcripts and examiner's comments on page 178.*

**3** Sie schreiben einen Brief aus Österreich an Ihren Brieffreund/Ihre Brieffreundin in Deutschland. Sagen Sie ihm/ihr, daß es Ihnen nicht gut geht, nachdem Sie in einem Restaurant gegessen haben. Schreiben Sie nicht mehr als 150 Wörter.

WRITING H

(You write a letter from Austria to your penfriend in Germany. Tell him/her that you are not well at the moment, after going out to eat at a restaurant. Write no more than 150 words.)

## Sample Student's Answer

Salzburg, Dienstag, den 15. März

Liebe Sabine,
Wie geht's Dir? Ich bin gerade in Österreich, wie Du weißt. Mir geht's im Moment leider nicht so gut. Ich habe fürchterliche Bauchschmerzen.

Ich war gestern beim Arzt, und er fragte, ob ich etwas Besonderes gegessen hätte. Ich habe gestern nicht viel gegessen, aber am Sonntagabend bin ich mit Freunden in eine Gaststätte gegangen. Dort haben wir ein Käsefondu bestellt und zusammen gegessen.

Der Arzt meinte, es hat mit dem Essen und Trinken nichts zu tun, denn im Moment sind viele Schüler krank. Das ist wahrscheinlich richtig, denn einer von meinen Kameraden ist zur Zeit auch krank.

Der Arzt sagte, ich sollte bis morgen im Bett liegen bleiben und nicht in die Schule gehen. Naja, in England würde ich mich freuen, aber hier bin ich im Urlaub, und ich möchte lieber gesund bleiben.

Hoffentlich geht es Euch allen gut.

Tschüß

Peter

*You might like to try and write your own version of the letter, using some of the sentences from the sample.*

**4** Read the letter, then complete the sentences below with the appropriate words or phrases.

> An den Geschäftsführer
> des Restaurants „Zum Adler"
>
> den 26. Februar
>
> Sehr geehrter Herr Vogel,
>
> Ich war am Montag mit meinen Kollegen bei Ihnen im Restaurant und wollte sie zu einem schönen Mittagessen einladen. Folgende Sachen waren nicht in Ordnung:
>
> Wir mußten leider zehn Minuten warten, obwohl meine Sekretärin einen Tisch für ein Uhr reserviert hatte.
> Der Kellner brachte uns zu einem Tisch für vier Personen und begann erst dann, das schmutzige Geschirr abzuräumen und für uns neues Besteck und weitere Stühle zu bringen. Für sechs Leute war es wirklich sehr eng.
> Mit dem Essen wurde die Sache erst recht ärgerlich. Meine Sekretärin bekam ihr Hauptgericht um Viertel vor zwei, der letzte von uns eine gute Viertelstunde später. Als die Beilagen endlich kamen, war das Fleischgericht schon kalt. Unverschämt!
> Man hat uns als Nachtisch die „frisch gebackene Obsttorte" empfohlen, aber sie hat nicht besonders geschmeckt. Außerdem habe ich draußen den Lieferwagen vom Supermarkt gesehen. War die Torte wirklich aus Ihrer Küche?
> Als wir endlich zahlen wollten, war die Bedienung nirgends zu sehen, und als sie dann doch kam, dauerte es sehr lange, bis sie mit der Rechnung fertig war.
>
> Ich habe selbstverständlich kein Trinkgeld hinterlassen, und außerdem werde ich Ihre Küche in meinem Bekanntenkreis nicht weiter empfehlen. Sie sehen mich natürlich nie wieder in Ihrem Restaurant.
>
> Ihr
>
> Rainer Nußbaum

Wählen Sie die passenden Wörter.

**Beispiel:**

Herr Nußbaum schreibt einen Brief _an den Chef_ des Restaurants.
an den Koch/an die Bedienung/an den Chef.

1 Herr Nußbaum wollte.................................................essen.
Frühstück/zu Mittag/zu Abend

2 Herr Nußbaum hatte im voraus..........................................................
einen Tisch reserviert/keinen Tisch reserviert/
einen Tisch reservieren lassen

3 Am Eßtisch hatte man .............................................................
viel Platz/genug Platz/wenig Platz

4 Die Beilagen kamen ....................... an den Tisch.
zuerst/pünktlich/zu spät

5 Als Nachspeise aßen sie das, ..............................................
was man ihnen empfohlen hat/was sie nicht bestellt hatten/
was auf dem Tisch stand

6 Herr Nußbaum fand die Bedienung ...................................
sehr langsam/sehr nett/sehr lustig

7 Herr Nußbaum schrieb am Ende, ......................................
daß er äußerst zufrieden war/
daß er das Restaurant nie wieder besuchen wollte/
daß er Herrn Vogel bald wieder sehen würde.

*You will find the answers and examiner's comments on page 178.*

## WHAT YOU NEED TO KNOW

### FAMILIE UND VERWANDTEN

| | |
|---|---|
| das Baby (s) | baby |
| das Einzelkind (er) | only child |
| die (Groß)Eltern (*pl*) | (grand)parents |
| der/die Erwachsene (n) | adult (*m/f*) |
| die Frau (en) | woman/wife |
| der Freund (e) | friend (*m*) |
| die Freundin (nen) | friend (*f*) |
| die Geschwister (*pl*) | brothers and sisters |
| die Großmutter (mütter) | grandmother |
| der Großvater (väter) | grandfather |
| der Junge (n) | boy |
| das Kind (er) | child |
| die Kusine (n)/die Cousine (n) | cousin (*f*) |
| die Leute (*pl*) | people |
| das Mädchen (–) | girl |
| der Mann (Männer) | man/husband |
| der Mensch (en) | person |
| Mutti | mum |
| der Neffe (n) | nephew |
| die Nichte (n) | niece |
| die Person | person |
| der Sohn | son |
| die Tochter (Töchter) | daughter |
| der/die Verwandte (n) | relative |
| der Vetter (–)/der Cousin (s) | cousin (*m*) |
| die Ehefrau (en) | wife |
| der Ehemann (Ehemänner) | husband |
| das Ehepaar (e) | married couple |
| das Geschlecht (er) | sex |
| der/die Jugendliche (en) | youth/young person |
| der Schwager | brother-in-law |
| die Schwägerin | sister-in-law |
| der Schwiegersohn | son-in-law |
| die Schwiegertochter | daughter-in-law |
| der/die Verlobte (n) | fiancé(e) |
| die Witwe (n) | widow |
| der Witwer (–) | widower |

### QUESTIONS/PROMPTS

Wie heißt du?
Wann bist du geboren?
Wann hast du Geburtstag?
Hast du Geschwister?
Wie alt ist er/sie?
Wie sieht er/sie aus?

### WIE SIND SIE?

| | |
|---|---|
| ledig/ verheiratet | single/married |
| geschieden | divorced |
| verlobt | engaged |
| männlich/ weiblich | male/female |
| allein | alone |
| arm | poor |
| böse | angry, naughty |
| dumm | stupid |
| faul | lazy |
| fleißig | hard-working |
| freundlich | friendly |
| glücklich | happy |
| intelligent | intelligent |
| lustig | cheerful, funny |
| klug | clever |
| reich | wealthy |
| unfreundlich | unfriendly |

| | |
|---|---|
| Er ist 1960 geboren. | He was born in 1960. |
| Ich bin 1982 geboren. | I was born in 1982. |
| Ich habe am vierten (4). März Geburtstag. | My birthday is on March 4th. |
| Mein Geburtstag ist im Januar. | My birthday is in January. |

## MEINE FAMILIE

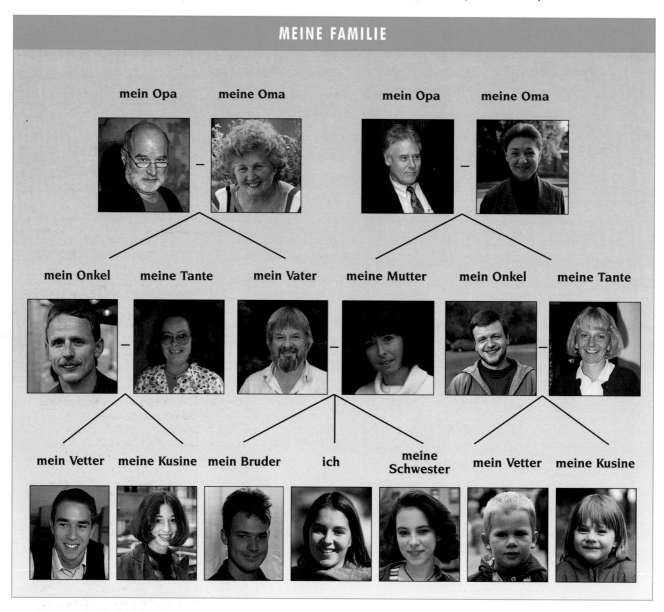

Mein Bruder interessiert sich für Fußball und Briefmarken.
My brother is interested in football and stamps.

Meine Mutter ist Journalistin von Beruf.
My mother is a journalist.

Mein Bruder arbeitet als Maurer.
My brother works as a bricklayer.

Meine Schwester hat eine Stelle bei der Bank/bei Lloyds.
My sister has a job in the bank/at Lloyds.

Ich komme gut mit meiner Schwester aus.
I get on well with my sister.

Ich verstehe mich gut mit meinem Onkel.
I get on well with my uncle.

Meine Eltern sind sehr tolerant.
My parents are very tolerant.

Ich streite mich mit meinem Bruder.
I argue with my brother.

**Note:** Many jobs and occupations are listed in Chapter 10.
There is a wider variety of sport and leisure pursuits in Chapter 5.

# Check yourself

## QUESTIONS

**Q1** **How would you say in German?**

a) I get on well with my grandparents.
b) My brothers and I do not get on very well.
c) My aunt works at Waitrose/at the supermarket.
d) My mother has no brothers or sisters. She is an only child.
e) My sister and I are interested in birds.

**Q2** **You are Charles. Write five sentences introducing your family. Make sure you mention everyone.**

**Meine Familie**

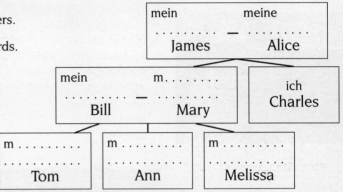

mein . . . . . . . . . . meine . . . . . . . . . .
James — Alice

mein . . . . . . . . . . m. . . . . . . .
Bill — Mary

ich
Charles

m . . . . . . . .
Tom

m . . . . . . . .
Ann

m . . . . . . . . . .
Melissa

---

## REMEMBER! Cover the answers if you want to.

---

## ANSWERS

**A1**
a) Ich komme mit meinen Großeltern gut aus.
b) Meine Brüder und ich verstehen uns nicht sehr gut.
c) Meine Tante arbeitet bei Waitrose/im Supermarkt.
d) Meine Mutter hat keine Geschwister. Sie ist Einzelkind.
e) Meine Schwester und ich interessieren uns für Vögel.

**A2**
a) Ich heiße Charles.
b) Meine Schwester Mary ist verheiratet und hat drei Kinder.
c) Meine zwei Nichten heißen Ann und Melissa, und mein Neffe heißt Tom.
d) Ich komme mit meinem Schwager Bill sehr gut aus.
e) Meine Eltern, James und Alice, sind sehr tolerant, und ich verstehe mich gut mit ihnen.

## TUTORIAL

**T1**
*a/b)* *Decide which of the phrases you can best remember. One contains a separable verb, the other a reflexive verb. You need to master one of them; you are bound to need it in the Speaking Test.*
*c)* *Both bei and im can mean 'at' and 'at the'.*
*d)* *Remember that Geschwister means 'brothers and sisters'. It is frequently mistaken for Schwester.*
*e)* *If you have difficulty with the reflexive pronoun, look back to Chapter 2.*

**T2** *You can combine the information on the family tree in a number of different ways. Try to make these family descriptions interesting by the addition of adjectives and short pieces of additional information such as interests. You will learn more about these in the next chapter.*

## GOING FURTHER

You can talk about pocket money or earnings from your part-time job and how you use it.

| | |
|---|---|
| Ich bekomme fünf Pfund Taschengeld pro Woche/die Woche. | I get five pounds a week pocket money. |
| Ich arbeite im Supermarkt/im Geschäft am Samstag und ich verdiene ... | I work in the supermarket/in the shop on Saturday and I earn ... |
| sehr gut | very good money |
| zwanzig Pfund pro Tag | £20 a day |
| drei Pfund pro Stunde | £3 an hour |
| Ich brauche es für ... | I need it for ... |
| Ich spare für ... | I am saving for ... |
| Ich gebe es für ... aus. | I spend it on ... |
| Platten/CDs/Kassetten | records/CDs/cassettes |
| Zeitschriften/Comics | magazines/comics |
| neue Kleidung | new clothes |
| den Urlaub | my holiday |
| das Kino | the cinema |

## HOW THE GRAMMAR WORKS

### COMPARISON

**Comparative of adjectives**

Regular adjectives form their comparative, as in English, by adding *-er*. In German an umlaut is added to the vowels *a, o,* and *u* where possible. The resulting word still needs to agree with its noun as normal.

Note the use of *als* to make comparisons:
> *Ich bin größer als er.* – I am taller than him.
> *Er ist älter als ich.* – He is older than me.

The people or things being compared are in the same case, usually the nominative.

Note also the use of *so ... wie* for the English 'as ... as':
> *Er ist so groß wie sie.* – He is as tall as her.

**Superlative of adjectives**

Again, this is similar to the English: *-st* or *-est* is added to the adjective. An umlaut is added where possible, as in the comparative.

Adjectives ending in *-d, -s, -ß, -sch, -t, -tz* add *-est*.

Because they are superlatives (the fastest, the largest, etc.), these words will naturally have the definite article in front of them and take the corresponding adjective endings.

Note that these words often become adjectival nouns and are therefore written with a capital letter:
> *Sie ist die schnellste Läuferin.* – She is the fastest runner.
BUT *Sie ist die Schnellste.* – She is the fastest.
> *Das ist das schönste Bild.* – That is the most beautiful picture.
BUT *Das ist das Schönste.* – That is the most beautiful.

| Adjective | Comparative | Superlative |
|---|---|---|
| **Regular** | | |
| klein | kleiner | kleinst- |
| jung | jünger | jüngst- |
| schön | schöner | schönst- |
| schnell | schneller | schnellst- |
| sauber | sauberer | sauberst- |
| wichtig | wichtiger | wichtigst- |
| **-est** | | |
| alt | älter | ältest- |
| nett | netter | nettest- |
| interessant | interessanter | interessantest- |
| **Irregular** | | |
| gut | besser | best- |
| groß | größer | größt- |
| hoch | höher | höchst- |
| nah | näher | nächst- |
| viel | mehr | meist- |
| | | **Note:** die meisten Leute |

## Comparative of adverbs

The comparative of adverbs is formed in exactly the same way as that of adjectives:

*Sie läuft schnell.* – She runs fast.
*Sie läuft schneller als ich.* – She runs faster than me.

## Superlative of adverbs

The superlative is also similar, with the addition of *am* and *-en*:

*Er zeichnet am schönsten.*

| Adverb | Comparative | Superlative |
|---|---|---|
| **Regular** | | |
| schön | schöner | am schönsten |
| schnell | schneller | am schnellsten |
| **-est** | | |
| schlecht | schlechter | am schlechtesten |
| oft | öfter | am öftesten |
| spät | später | am spätesten |
| **Irregular** | | |
| gern | lieber | am liebsten |
| gut | besser | am besten |
| bald | früher | am frühsten |
| hoch | höher | am höchsten |
| nah | näher | am nächsten |
| viel | mehr | am meisten |

*Beispiele*:

| | |
|---|---|
| Er *schreibt besser als ich, aber sie schreibt am schönsten.* | – He writes better than I (do), but she writes best of all. |
| *Ich kam später als ich wollte, aber er kam am spätesten.* | – I came later than I intended, but he arrived the latest (last) of all. |

# Check yourself

## QUESTIONS

**Q1** *Complete the following sentences.*

a) Mein Bruder gewinnt viele Preise im Hochsprung. Er kann ......................... springen als alle anderen in seiner Schule.
hoch   höher   am höchsten

b) Mein Freund ist nie pünktlich. Er kommt immer .............................. der Lehrer in den Unterricht.
am spätesten   spät   später als

c) Ich trinke gern Kaffee, aber ich trinke manchmal ............................. Tee.

d) Diese Jacke steht mir nicht; die andere gefällt mir ............................

e) Meine Schuhe sind recht dreckig, aber die Schuhe meines Bruders sind noch
.............................................

**Q2** *How would you say in German?*

a) My eldest brother plays volleyball more often than me.

b) Most pupils in the class run faster than me.

c) The easiest subject is English.

d) I find technology the hardest.

e) My sister finds English (just) as difficult as technology.

---

**REMEMBER! Cover the answers if you want to.**

---

## ANSWERS

**A1**
a) höher
b) später als
c) lieber
d) besser
e) dreckiger

**A2**
a) Mein ältester Bruder spielt Volleyball öfter als ich.
b) Die meisten Schüler in der Klasse laufen schneller als ich.
c) Das leichteste Schulfach ist English
d) Ich finde Technologie am schwersten.
e) Meine Schwester findet Englisch (genau) so schwer wie Technologie.

## TUTORIAL

**T1**
a/b) Because a direct comparison is being made with other people, the comparative plus *als* is needed in both sentences.

c) You can create interest in your Speaking Test by showing your preferences, not simply your likes and dislikes.

d) The superlative is also possible, because it implies that you have looked at more than the two jackets.

e) *Noch* almost always introduces the comparative - 'even bigger', 'even faster'.

**T2**
a) The adjective needs -est plus the masculine ending -er.

b) Die meisten *translates as 'most of the' and is very common.*

c) You might also use *einfachste.*

d) Das Schwerste *is also possible here.*

e) Genauso *is written as one word in phrases such as* Ich bin genauso gut wie du!

# EXAM PRACTICE

**1** Look at the following role-play. You spend a day with your exchange partner's relations. Tell the examiner about the day. The pictures show some of the things you may wish to mention.

SPEAKING H

Find Chapter 4 – Exam Practice Speaking on the CD and listen to how a candidate might tackle this role-play (Track 7).

*You will find the transcript and examiner's comments on page 179.*

**2** Ihre Brieffreundin hat Ihnen einen Brief geschickt und ein Bild von einem Familientreffen mit allen Namen darauf. Verbinden Sie den richtigen Namen mit jeder Beschreibung.

(Your pen-friend has sent you a picture of a family gathering with all the people named. Look at the picture. Write the correct name alongside each description on page 35.)

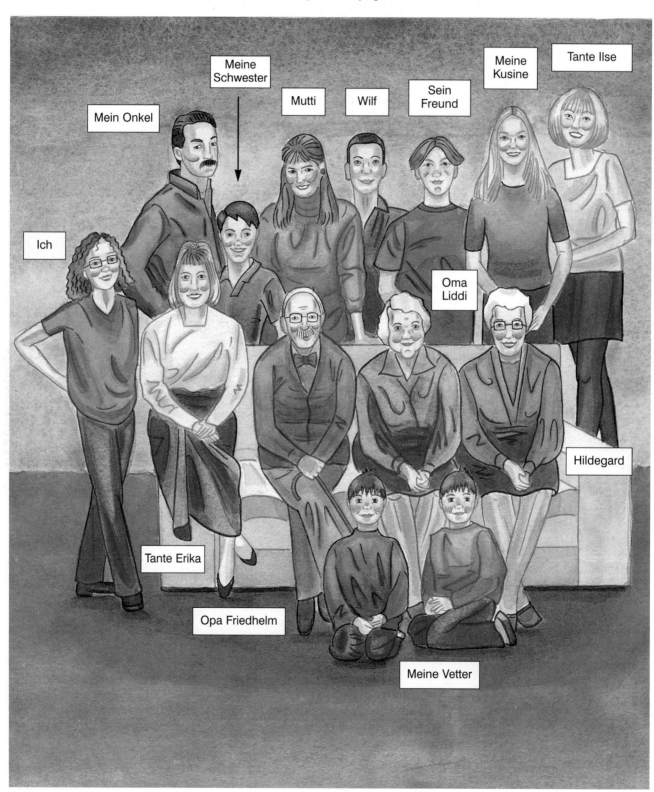

1 .................................. hat lange, braune Haare und blaue Augen, lächelt oft. Trägt einen alten Rollkragenpulli.

2 .................................. habe eine runde Nase, bin relativ klein und schlank. Habe braune, lockige Haare und trage eine Brille.

3 .................................. hat kurze, glatte Haare, trägt oft eine Hose und sieht eher wie ein Junge aus. Sie ist etwas größer als ich.

4 .................................. sind erst sieben Jahre alt, beide etwas rund im Gesicht aber nicht dick. Sie haben blaue Augen und braune Haare. Sie sind immer lustig.

5 .................................. sieht meiner Mutter ähnlich, hat die gleiche Nase. Ist ein bißchen ernst. Hat einen Schnurrbart.

6 .................................. ist sehr hübsch mit langen, blonden Haaren und blaue Augen. Sie ist fast so groß wie ihre Mutter.

7 .................................. ist relative groß, sieht noch jung aus. Lacht gerne und trägt gern modische Kleider, kurze Röcke sogar!

8 .................................. sitzt ganz vorne neben ihrer jüngeren Schwester Hildegard. Hildegard trägt eine Brille. Beide sind weißhaarig.

*You will find the answers and examiner's comments on page 180.*

**3** Find Chapter 4 – Exam Practice Listening on the CD. Listen to the German (Track 8) twice, then fill in the grid.

**LISTENING F H**

Deutsche Schüler stellen sich vor. Kreuzen Sie die richtigen Kästchen an!

|  | Einzelkind | 1 Br. | 2 Br. | 1 Schw. | 2 Schw. | Haustiere | mag Sport | Briefmarken | Münzen |
|---|---|---|---|---|---|---|---|---|---|
| Norbert |  |  |  |  |  |  |  |  |  |
| Edith |  |  |  |  |  |  |  |  |  |
| Margret |  |  |  |  |  |  |  |  |  |
| Martin |  |  |  |  |  |  |  |  |  |

[12 marks]

*You will find the transcript and answers, with examiner's comments, on page 180.*

**4** Write the letter to your penfriend, then compare your version with the sample answer on page 181.

**WRITING H**

Sie schreiben einen Brief an Ihren Brieffreund/Ihre Brieffreundin in Österreich. Erzählen Sie ihm/ihr über Ihre Familie. Schreiben Sie nicht mehr als 150 Wörter.

(You write a letter to your penfriend in Austria. Tell him/her all about your family. Write no more than 150 words.)

*You will find the sample answer, with examiner's comments, on page 181.*

# CHAPTER 5

# FREIZEIT UND FERIEN

LEISURE AND HOLIDAYS

## WHAT YOU NEED TO KNOW

| | |
|---|---|
| Ich gehe ins Kino/in die Disco/ins Theater. | I go to the cinema/disco/theatre. |
| Ich gehe zum Jugendklub/zum Stadion. | I go to the youth club/stadium. |
| Ich spiele gern Fußball/Tischtennis. | I like playing football/table tennis. |
| Ich treibe gern Sport. | I like doing sport (in general). |
| Ich gehe gern ... | I like going ... |
| angeln | fishing |
| baden/schwimmen | swimming |
| joggen | jogging |
| Ich fahre gern Rad. | I like cycling. |
| Ich höre gern Musik. | I like listening to music. |
| Ich höre gern die Popmusiksendungen im ersten Programm. | I like listening to the pop music programmes on Radio One. |
| Ich höre lieber Popmusik als klassische Musik. | I prefer listening to pop music than classical music. |
| Ich spiele Klarinette in einem Orchester. | I play the clarinet in an orchestra. |

| | |
|---|---|
| die Aufführung (en) | performance |
| die Disco (s) | disco |
| das Eintrittsgeld (er) | entrance fee/cost |
| der Fan (s) | fan |
| der Film (e) | film |
| der Jugendklub (s) | youth club |
| die Karte (n) | ticket |
| die Kasse (n) | box office, cash desk |
| die Kirmes (sen) | fair |
| das Kino (s) | cinema |
| der Klub (s) | club |
| das Konzert (e) | concert |
| das Museum (Museen) | museum |
| das Schauspiel (e) | play |
| das Schloß (Schlösser) | castle |
| das Stadion (Stadien) | stadium |
| das Theater (–) | theater |
| das Theaterstück (e) | play |
| die Vorstellung (en) | performance |
| der Zoo (s) | zoo |

## MUSIK

| | |
|---|---|
| die CD(s) | CD |
| der CD-Player | CD player |
| der Kassettenrecorder | cassette recorder |
| die Platte (n) | record |
| das Radio | radio |
| die Stereoanlage | stereo system |
| das Videogerät (e) | video player |

## QUESTIONS/PROMPTS

Was machst du am Wochenende?
Spielst du ein Instrument?
Wieviel Taschengeld bekommst du?
Was machst du mit dem Taschengeld?
Wann/Wohin fährst du in Urlaub?

## SPORT

Ich gehe gern spazieren.

Ich reite gern.

Ich segele gern.

Ich laufe gern.

Ich tauche gern.

Ich fahre gern ski.

Ich wandere gern.

Ich trainiere gern.

der Computer — computer
das Hobby (s) — hobby
das Interesse (n) — interest
die Karten (pl) — cards
das Magazin — magazine
der Roman (e) — novel
die Sammlung (en) — collection
das Taschenbuch (–bücher) — paperback
die Zeitschrift (en) — magazine
basteln — to make things/make models
fotografieren — to take photographs
malen — to paint
zeichnen — to draw

Ich bekomme 5 Pfund pro Woche. — I get £5 a week.
Ich spare für … — I am saving for …
Ich gebe das Geld für … aus. — I spend the money on …
Ich brauche das Geld für … — I need the money for …

Ich fahre … in Urlaub. — I go away on holiday …
   in den Osterferien/zu Ostern — in the Easter holidays/at Easter
   in den Pfingstferien — in the Whitsun holidays
   in den Sommerferien/im Sommer — in the summer holidays/in summer
Wir (Meine Familie und ich) — We (My family and I)
fahren meistens … — usually go …
   an die Küste — to the coast
   ans Meer — to the sea
   in die Berge — to the hills/mountains
   nach Schottland/Wales/Irland, usw. — to Scotland/Wales/Ireland, etc.

auspacken — to unpack
bleiben — to stay
einpacken — to pack up
fahren — to travel
organisieren — to organise
planen — to plan
verbringen — to spend (time)
vorhaben — to plan, intend
zelten — to camp (in a tent)

**INSTRUMENT**

Geige

Blockflöte

Klavier

Trompete

Gitarre

Schlagzeug

Flöte

# Check yourself

## QUESTIONS

**Q1** *Answer the questions in German.*
a)  Was machst du abends?
b)  Wie oft gehst du ins Kino?
c)  Wann triffst du dich mit deinen Freunden?
d)  Was für Sport treibst du?
e)  Was liest du gern?

**Q2** *Answer the questions in German.*
a)  Was gibt es für Jugendliche in der Stadt?
b)  Wo ist das nächste Hallenbad?
c)  Was kostet der Eintritt im Theater?
d)  Was für ein Instrument spielst du?
e)  Wo arbeitest du?

## ANSWERS

**A1** For example:

a)   Ich sehe gern fern.
b)   Ich gehe einmal im Monat ins Kino.
c)   Ich treffe mich am Wochenende mit meinen Freunden.
d)   Ich spiele gern Volleyball.
e)   Ich lese gern Romane.

**A2** For example:

a)   Es gibt zwei Discos und einen Jugendklub.
b)   Das nächste Hallenbad ist zwei Kilometer von zu Hause entfernt.
c)   Der Eintritt kostet zwei Pfund fünfzig.
d)   Ich spiele kein Instrument – aber ich höre gern Musik.
e)   Ich arbeite in einem Supermarkt/in einem Schuhladen.

## TUTORIAL

**T1**
a)   *Remember to separate the verb (see Chapter 2).*
b)   *Frequency (per week/per month) is expressed either by* pro *or* in: einmal pro Woche, zweimal im Jahr.
c)   *Note the reflexive verb* sich treffen.
d/e) *Add* gern *to the present tense of the verb to express liking.*

**T2**
a)   *Be prepared to say more than one item.*
b)   Von ... entfernt *means 'away from'.*
c)   *Don't forget to say the price in pounds, not marks.*
d)   *Use the question to lead into something you do like.*
e)   *Don't forget to use* in einem *not* im *here, because the examiner doesn't know which shop you are talking about.*

## GOING FURTHER

In the Higher Level Speaking and Writing Tests, you need to be able to talk about your holidays in greater depth. Here are some model answers which you can modify for your needs.
Here are the key questions you should be able to answer :

| | | |
|---|---|---|
| 1 | Wann? | When? |
| 2 | Wo? Wohin? | Where? Where to? |
| 3 | Wie? | How? |
| 4 | Mit wem? | With whom? |
| 5 | Wo gewohnt? | Stayed where? |
| 6 | Das Wetter? | The weather? |
| 7 | Was gemacht? | Did what? |
| 8 | Gut/nicht gut? | Was it good/not so good? |

You can answer each question simply, then follow that basic sentence with another sentence or clause to give a little more detail. For example, here are two different sets of answers to the questions above:

**1+2+4**   In den letzten Sommerferien war ich mit meiner Familie in Nordwales. Das ist das zweite Mal, daß wir nach Wales gefahren sind.

**3**   Wir sind mit dem Auto dahin gefahren, aber es war ziemlich viel Urlaubsverkehr auf der Straße, und die Fahrt hat sehr lange gedauert.

**5**   Wir haben in einer Pension an der Küste gewohnt. Es war nicht sehr teuer, aber auch nicht besonders bequem.

**6+7**   Das Wetter war einigermaßen gut, und wir haben viele Ausflüge in die Berge gemacht. Wir haben auch einige Museen besucht.

**8**   Meine Eltern fanden es schön, aber ich fand es ziemlich langweilig. Die Landschaft dort ist ganz herrlich, vor allem die Küste und die Strände waren ganz toll.

1+2 Letztes Ostern bin ich (für) vierzehn Tage mit meinen Freunden nach Frankreich gefahren.

3+4 Wir waren zwei Mädchen und zwei Jungen und sind mit dem Zug und mit der Fähre gereist.

5 Wir haben in einer Jugendherberge gewohnt. Es war extrem billig dort, aber ganz nett und sauber. Die Herbergseltern waren auch ziemlich freundlich. Die Jugendherberge war in einem alten Schloß.

8 Es hat uns dort sehr gut gefallen, und das Essen war prima.

6 Wir hatten herrliches Wetter, und wir haben die meisten Tage am Strand verbracht.

7 Die Stadt um das Schloß war sehr interessant, und wir sind jeden Tag zum Marktplatz gelaufen, um zu sehen, was dort los war.

# HOW THE GRAMMAR WORKS

## CASES

The definite and indefinite article alter their form according to their function in the sentence.

When you learn the gender of a new word, you are given the nominative case *der, die, das* of the definite article 'the'. The following table shows how the article changes according to its function in the sentence.

| | **Masculine** | **Feminine** | **Neuter** | **Plural** |
|---|---|---|---|---|
| **Nominative** (subject) | der | die | das | die |
| | ein | eine | ein | – |
| **Accusative** (direct object) | den | die | das | die |
| | einen | eine | ein | – |
| **Genitive** ('of') | des | der | des | der |
| | eines | einer | eines | – |
| **Dative** ('to'/'for') | dem | der | dem | den |
| | einem | einer | einem | – |

### Nominative

The nominative is used for the subject of the verb:

**Der Wagen** *fährt schnell.*  **Ein Wagen** *ist teuer.*
**Die Straßenbahn** *kommt gleich.*  **Eine Straßenbahn** *erscheint.*
**Das Flugzeug** *landet gleich.*  **Ein Flugzeug** *ist schneller.*
**Die Theaterkarten** *sind teuer.* (plural)

### Accusative

The accusative is used for the direct object of the verb:

*Ich brauche* **den Kuli.**  *Sie sucht* **einen Lehrer.**
*Ich nehme* **die Tasche.**  *Ich kaufe* **eine Theaterkarte.**
*Wir essen* **das Brot.**  *Sie kaufen* **ein Auto.**

### Genitive

The genitive denotes possession, and is used where we frequently use an apostrophe in English:

*Die Farbe* **des Wagens** *ist grün.* – The colour of the car is green.
*Der Wagen* **der Krankenschwester** *war neu.* – The nurse's car is new.
*Die Bilder* **des Hauses** *sind alt.* – The pictures of the house are old.
*Die Jacken* **der Kinder** *sind dreckig geworden.* – The children's jackets got dirty.

### Dative

The dative expresses the idea of 'to' or 'for' in English.

| | |
|---|---|
| Ich gab **dem Lehrer** meine Hausaufgaben. | – I gave my homework to the teacher. (I gave the teacher my homework.) |
| Wir kauften **der Frau** einen Blumenstrauß. | – We bought a bouquet for the lady. |
| Ich schenkte **dem Mädchen** eine Kassette. | – I gave a cassette to the girl. (I gave the girl a cassette.) |

## PREPOSITIONS

The definite and indefinite articles alter their form when following prepositions. The following table sets out which case follows each of the prepositions.

| Accusative | | Dative | | Acc/Dat | | Genitive | |
|---|---|---|---|---|---|---|---|
| bis | until | aus | out of | an | at, on | trotz | despite |
| durch | through | bei | at (someone's house) | auf | on | während | during |
| entlang* | along | gegenüber** | opposite | hinter | behind | wegen | because of |
| für | for | mit | with | in | in | | |
| gegen | against | nach | after | neben | near | | |
| um | around | seit | since | über | over, above | | |
| wider | against | von | from | unter | under, below | | |
| | | zu | to | zwischen | between | | |

\* usually follows the noun    \*\* sometimes follows the noun

| | |
|---|---|
| **Accusative:** | Ich spiele Volleyball für eine Mannschaft. |
| **Dative:** | Die Katze springt aus dem Fenster. |
| **Genitive:** | Während der Kunststunde bleiben wir ruhig. |
| | Trotz des Regens gehen wir in den Park. |

The prepositions in the third column take either the accusative or the dative according to their meaning. With the dative they answer the question wo? and tell you where someone or something is. With the accusative they answer the question wohin? and tell you where someone or something is moving to. Here are some of the most common verbs which imply movement or no movement. They should act as a trigger for you when you write a preposition after them.

| | |
|---|---|
| **Accusative** | gehen, fahren, fallen, fliegen, kommen, reisen, sich setzen, springen, treten |
| **Dative** | sich befinden, bleiben, liegen, sein, sitzen |
| **Accusative for movement:** | Wir gehen in den Park. Der Hund springt auf das Sofa. |
| **Dative for position:** | Wir sitzen in dem Park. Der Hund liegt auf dem Sofa. |

# Check yourself

## QUESTIONS

**Q1** *Answer the questions with the prepositions indicated.*

a) Wie kommst du zur Schule?
   **mit** (say 'by bike')
b) Wohin gehst du?
   **zu** (say 'to the market')
c) Für wen kaufst du das?
   **für** (say 'for my friend')
d) Wo ist der Park?
   **gegenüber** (say 'opposite the bank')
e) Wohin fährst du ?
   **in** (say 'into town')

**Q2** *Complete the sentences with the correct phrase.*

a) Der Hund jagt die Katze ......................
   um das Haus/um dem Haus
b) Wir treffen uns ......................
   ins Theater/im Theater
c) Wir bringen die Teller ......................
   ins Eßzimmer/im Eßzimmer
d) Wir kommen ......................
   von die Schule/von der Schule
e) Die Vase fällt ......................
   aus das Fenster/aus dem Fenster

---

**REMEMBER! Cover the answers if you want to.**

---

## ANSWERS

**A1**
a) Ich komme mit dem Rad.
b) Ich gehe zu dem/zum Markt.
c) Ich kaufe es für meinen Freund.
d) Der Park liegt gegenüber der Bank.
e) Ich fahre in die Stadt.

**A2**
a) um das Haus
b) im Theater
c) ins Eßzimmer
d) von der Schule
e) aus dem Fenster

## TUTORIAL

**T1**
a) *Most forms of transport use* mit. Zu Fuß *is a common exception.*
b) *Try to use the common contractions where possible:* am/ans, beim, im/ins, vom, zum/zur.
c) *The possessive adjective follows the form of the indefinite article* ein.
d) *Nowadays,* gegenüber *is increasingly found in front of the noun, but still follows pronouns:* er stand mir gegenüber.
e) *This is such a common phrase that you could learn to add another simple one before it for the transport –* mit dem Bus, mit dem Rad.

**T2**
a) Um *is always used with the accusative, whether or not there is movement implied.*
b) *'We will **go to** the theatre, but we will **be in** the theatre when we meet' – no movement, therefore dative.*
c) *'Where did we take the plates?' – movement is obviously implied, so accusative.*
d) *Even though there is movement,* von *is **only** used with the dative.*
e) *Similarly with* aus, *despite the obvious movement.*

# EXAM PRACTICE

You will find the
transcript and answers,
with examiner's comments,
on page 182.

**H LISTENING**

**1** Find Chapter 5 – Exam Practice Listening on the CD. Listen to the German (Track 9) twice, and fill in the names of the people in the first column of the grid.

Wer ist das? Schreiben Sie die folgenden Namen in die fünf richtigen Kästchen. Drei Kästchen werden leer bleiben.

| Peter   Gerd   Martin   Norbert   Jürgen |

Schreiben Sie die Namen.

| Schreiben Sie die Namen ↓ | | | | | | | |
|---|---|---|---|---|---|---|---|
| 1 | | ✓ | ✓ | | | | ✓ |
| 2 | ✓ | ✓ | | | | ✓ | |
| 3 | ✓ | | | ✓ | | ✓ | |
| 4 | | | ✓ | | ✓ | ✓ | |
| 5 | ✓ | ✓ | | | ✓ | | |
| 6 | | | ✓ | ✓ | | | ✓ |
| 7 | ✓ | | | | ✓ | ✓ | |
| 8 | | ✓ | | ✓ | | | ✓ |

**F H SPEAKING**

You will find the
transcript and examiner's
comments, on page 182.

**2** **Topic-based conversations**

You need to be able to talk at greater length about some of the following topics. The suggestions which follow in English show you what you need to do in order to score the B, A and A* grades.

**Freizeitmöglichkeiten in meiner Stadt**
- describe the leisure facilities in your area and express a range of opinions about them

**Theater und Filme**
- talk about a film, TV programme, sporting event or theatre performance you have seen, comment on it and ask the examiner's opinion

**Was würden Sie machen, wenn Sie könnten?**
- describe what you would do if you had the opportunity and the necessary money

**Ein besonderer Tag**
- give a detailed account of a special occasion, e.g. birthday or wedding

**Mein Urlaub**
- give details of places you visited, make comparisons, and express your opinions about what you did
- give similar details and opinions to a tourist visiting your area

 Find Chapter 5 – Exam Practice Speaking on the CD and listen to how a candidate might tackle one of these topics (Track 10).

**3** Read the descriptions, and choose the most suitable penfriend for each of the British students.

Finden Sie eine passenden Partnerin für jede englische Schülerin. Schreiben Sie den richtigen Namen neben jede Schülerin.

| | |
|---|---|
| **Heidi** | Ich wünsche mir Brieffreunde aus der Schweiz oder aus England. Meine Hobbys sind Laufen, Hochsprung, Schwimmen, Popmusik und Kochen. |
| **Birgit** | Ich bin gar nicht sportlich, aber ich mag gern Musik aller Art. Ich spiele Geige im Schulorchester und lerne neuerdings auch Gitarre. Ich möchte gern nach England. |
| **Paula** | Ich bin 16 und wohne in Kiel. In meiner Freizeit gehe ich oft segeln oder manchmal auch tauchen. Ich bin sonst nicht sehr sportlich. Ich lese gern Romane oder höre klassische Musik. |
| **Hannalore** | Ich reise sehr gern und sammle ausländische Münzen. Wer hat Lust, im Sommer mit mir nach Südfrankreich zu fahren? |
| **Susi** | Ich würde gern Amerikaner und Engländer brieflich oder persönlich kennenlernen. Meine Hobbys sind Kochen, Reisen und Sprachen. Ich lese gern Modezeitschriften. |
| **Margret** | Ich bin sportlich (Handball, Reiten, Wandern) und mag Musik, Klavierspielen und Reisen. |
| **Lies** | Ich bin 15 Jahre alt. Gehe gern ins Kino und ins Theater. Sammle auch Briefmarken aus Europa. |

1 Helen – likes reading and enjoys all sorts of water sports.

.........................................................................................

2 Lorna – is very athletic and also listens to a lot of pop music.

.........................................................................................

3 Michelle – prefers indoor hobbies, enjoys going to plays and films.

.........................................................................................

4 Charlotte – enjoys cooking. Has ambitions to travel and likes to keep up with fashions.

.........................................................................................

5 Victoria – her main hobby is horse-riding. She enjoys classical music and plays the piano.

.........................................................................................

*You will find the answers and examiner's comments on page 183.*

**4**  Sie schreiben einen Bericht über Ihre Sommerferien für die Schülerzeitschrift in Ihrer Partnerschule. Sie können den Familienurlaub erwähnen, und das, was Sie sonst in der Freizeit gemacht haben. Schreiben Sie nicht mehr als 150 Wörter.

(You write a report about what you did in the summer holidays for the magazine of your exchange school. You may like to mention the family holiday and other things you did in your spare time. Write no more than 150 words.)

## Sample Student's Answer

### Meine Sommerferien

Ich habe die ersten drei Wochen auf einem Bauernhof gearbeitet, um Geld zu verdienen. Der Bauer und seine Frau sind Freunde meiner Eltern, und es machte mir Spaß, die Tiere zu füttern. Ich mußte jeden Morgen sehr früh aufstehen, aber ich bin meistens gegen Mittag nach Hause gekommen.

Am zweiten August haben wir den Wagen gepackt und sind am Sonntag, dem dritten, losgefahren. Wir haben am ersten Abend auf einem Campingplatz im Lake District übernachtet und am Montag sind wir nach Fort William gefahren. Dort haben wir unsere Zelte auf einem tollen Campingplatz in den Bergen aufgeschlagen. Wir sind zwei Wochen da geblieben und haben viele Ausflüge in die Berge gemacht.

Das Wetter war meist sonnig und klar, eigentlich ganz schön, aber ich mußte abends immer einen Pullover tragen. Das schottische Hochgebirge — Highlands genannt — ist sehr sehenswert, aber außer Wandern gibt es für Jugendliche recht wenig zu tun.

## EXAMINER'S COMMENTS

- Notice the use of the imperfect tense in the first and third paragraphs. Any scene-setting, such as talking about the weather or feelings, will involve the imperfect tense. However, as soon as you start relating the individual events or actions, you will of course use the perfect tense.

- The greatest difficulty for you, the competent candidate, is restricting yourself to about 150 words. Sometimes you scarcely seem to have started when you have to bring the text, story or letter to a close. If you do find that you have written a few sentences too many, return to what you have written and remove something.

*You might like to try and write your own version of the report, using some of the sentence patterns from the one above. If you are unsure about the tenses, look ahead to Chapters 10 and 12.*

## WHAT YOU NEED TO KNOW

**Leute treffen, Freunde vorstellen, Abschied nehmen**

Grüß Gott!
Servus!
Tschüß!
Darf ich …vorstellen?
Das ist …
Es freut mich (Sie kennenzulernen)!
Gute Fahrt!
Gute Heimfahrt!
Guten Appetit!
Schlaf gut!
Komm' gut nach Hause!

**Meeting people, introducing friends and saying goodbye**

Hello! (regional)
Hello! (regional)
Bye!
May I introduce … ?
This is …
I'm pleased/A pleasure (to meet you).
Have a good journey
Have a good journey home!
Enjoy your meal!
Sleep well!
Get home safely!

**Pläne machen**

Wollen wir ins Kino/Schwimmbad, usw?
Wann treffen wir uns?
Wann wollen wir uns treffen?
Es ist mir egal.
Es macht nichts.
Bis dann.
Bis gleich.
Bis morgen.
Bis nachher.
Bis später.

am Montag
montags, usw.
den ganzen Tag
eine halbe Stunde
Endlich!
heute
heute vormittag/morgen
heute nachmittag
im Mai/Juni, usw.
jeden Tag
jede Woche
morgen (früh)

**Making arrangements to meet**

Shall we go to the cinema/pool, etc?
When shall we meet?
When shall we meet?
I don't mind./It's all right by me.
It doesn't matter.
See you then.
See you soon.
See you tomorrow.
See you later.
See you later.

on Monday
on Mondays/every Monday
the whole day
(for) half an hour
At last!
today
this morning
this afternoon
in May/June, etc.
every day
every week
tomorrow (morning)

### WÜNSCHE

| | |
|---|---|
| Herzlichen Glückwunsch! | Congratulations! |
| Prost! | Cheers! |
| Zum Wohl! | Cheers! |
| Viel Glück! | Good luck! |
| Viel Spaß! | Have fun! |
| Entschuldigung! | Excuse me! (Sorry!) |
| Hoffentlich! | I hope so |
| Klasse! | great! |
| Alles Gute zum Geburtstag! | Happy Birthday! |
| Frohe Ostern! | Happy Easter! |
| Frohe/fröhliche Weihnachten! | Happy Christmas! |
| Ein frohes/ glückliches neues Jahr! | Happy New Year! |

### QUESTIONS/PROMPTS

Wann gehst du meistens mit Freunden aus?

Wann fährst du?

Wie lange bleibst du?

Wie lange dauert das?

Wann kommst du wieder?

# Check yourself

## QUESTIONS

**Q1** **Underline the odd-one-out.**

a) Guten Tag! Servus! Tschüß! Grüß Gott!
b) Prost! Gute Reise! Guten Appetit! Zum Wohl!
c) Viel Spaß! Quatsch! Viel Gluck! Schönen Abend!
d) am Montag morgen früh gestern heute abend
e) Prima! Toll! Schade! Klasse!

**Q2** **Complete the following dialogue with suitable expressions.**

| | |
|---|---|
| Anton | ............................................. |
| Bodo | Hallo Anton ! |
| Anton | ............................................. |
| Bodo | Ganz gut, danke. Und Dir ? |
| Anton | ............................................. |
| Bodo | Darf ich meinen Vetter Hans vorstellen ? |
| Anton | ............................................. ............................................? |
| Hans | Ich komme aus Dresden. Ich bin schon seit einer Woche hier. |
| Anton | Wann wollen wir ins Kino gehen ? |
| Bodo | ............................................. |
| Anton | Dann sagen wir am Montag gegen acht Uhr. |
| Bodo | OK. ................................. Tschüß! |

---

**REMEMBER! Cover the answers if you want to.**

---

## ANSWERS

**A1**
a) Tschüß!
b) Gute Reise!
c) Quatsch!
d) gestern
e) Schade!

**A2** Suggested dialogue:

| | |
|---|---|
| Anton | Servus! |
| Bodo | Hallo Anton! |
| Anton | Wie geht's dir? |
| Bodo | Ganz gut, danke. Und dir? |
| Anton | Mir geht's ausgezeichnet, danke. |
| Bodo | Darf ich meinen Vetter Hans vorstellen? |
| Anton | Es freut mich, dich kennenzulernen. Wo kommst du denn her? |
| Hans | Ich komme aus Dresden. Ich bin schon seit einer Woche hier. |
| Anton | Wann wollen wir ins Kino gehen? |
| Bodo | Ich weiß nicht. Es ist mir egal. |
| Anton | Dann sagen wir am Montag gegen acht Uhr. |
| Bodo | OK. Bis dann. Tschüß! |

## TUTORIAL

**T1**
a) All the rest are greetings you use when you meet.
b) You would use the others at mealtimes.
c) You would use the others to wish people a good time.
d) The other expressions are for making arrangements in the future.
e) The others exclamations are happy and positive.

**T2**
● Although Servus is often regarded as regional, you must not be surprised to hear it in any area of Germany. People do move house, after all!
● Notice that the du form is most common among teenagers, even when meeting for the first time. You can keep the Sie form for meeting older people you don't know or for formal situations, such as at the doctor's, or when talking to your teacher.
● Ich komme aus tells people where you live, i.e. originate from. Ich komme vom Arzt, von der Schule tells someone where you have just been, i.e. where you have just been.
● Anton uses Wann wollen wir ...? to ask 'When shall we ... ?', but don't forget that you should usually use werden to introduce a future idea. (See Chapter 10 for more examples of the future tense.)

## GOING FURTHER

**Vorschläge**

Wie wäre es mit einem Fußballspiel?

Wollen wir nicht lieber ins Kino?


Ich habe (keine) Lust, in die
Stadt zu gehen.

Hast du Lust dazu?

**Suggesting meetings**

How about a game of football?

Why don't we go to the cinema?
(alternative suggestion)

I (don't) fancy going into town.


Do you feel like it?

**Schwierigkeiten**

Ich verstehe nicht.

Ich habe das nicht verstanden.

Ich weiß nicht.

Könnten Sie das buchstabieren, bitte?

Noch 'mal, bitte.

Was bedeutet das (auf englisch)?

Könnten Sie bitte langsamer sprechen?

Wie sagt man … auf deutsch?

**Handling difficulties**

I don't understand.

I didn't understand that.

I don't know.

Could you spell that, please?

Could you repeat that, please?

What does that mean (in English)?

Could you speak more slowly, please?

How do you say … in German?

## HOW THE GRAMMAR WORKS

## CONJUNCTIONS

Conjunctions are words which join main clauses together. There are two kinds:
coordinating and subordinating. Coordinating conjunctions are easy to use
because they don't affect the word order and the verb remains the second
idea in the clause.

| | |
|---|---|
| *und* – and | *aber* – but |
| *denn* – for, because, | *sondern* – but rather (used to make a |
| *oder* – or | contrasting statement) |

**z.B.** *Ich nahm meine Kusine mit, **und** ich stellte sie meinem Lehrer vor.*
*Sie fand die Englischstunde nicht interessant, **sondern** langweilte sich.*
*Wir konnten nicht in die Stadt fahren, **denn** wir hatten kein Geld.*

Subordinating conjunctions join a main clause to a subordinate clause, i.e the
clause after the conjunction. The word order in the subordinate clause is
altered and the finite verb goes to the end of the clause.

| | |
|---|---|
| *als* – when | *ob* – whether |
| *bevor* – before | *obgleich/obwohl* – although |
| *bis* – until | *so daß* – with the result that |
| *damit* – so that, in order that | *während* – while |
| *daß* – that | *weil* – because |
| *nachdem* – after | *wenn* – if, when |

**z.B.** *Sie kann nicht kommen, weil sie sich das Bein gebrochen **hat.***
*Er bleibt heute zu Hause, damit er sein Rad reparieren **kann.***
*Ich weiß nicht, ob ich morgen so früh **aufstehe.****
*Notice how the separable verb and its prefix join up at the end of the clause.

Your work will be even more impressive if you can master the art of beginning
a sentence with the subordinate clause. Look closely at the word order:
**Weil** *sie sich das Bein gebrochen **hat, kann** sie nicht kommen.*
**Ob** *ich morgen so früh **aufstehe, weiß** ich nicht.*

The word order in the subordinate clause is as before, but the subject and verb
in the main clause turn round. This is called inversion, and it brings the two
finite verbs together in the middle of the sentence, separated only by a comma.

So, if you begin with a subordinating conjunction, remember:
**VERB COMMA VERB** in the middle of the sentence.

# *Check yourself*

## QUESTIONS

**Q1** **Add a suitable conjunction to these sentences.**

a) Er geht heute nicht ins Kino, … er kein Geld hat.
b) Sie blieben im Geschäft, … der Regen endlich aufhörte.
c) Sie kommt schnell nach Hause, … sie ,,EastEnders'' sehen kann.
d) Wir dürfen ausgehen, … Mutti nach Hause kommt.
e) Ich kann die neue Platte kaufen, … ich mein Taschengeld bekomme.

**Q2** **Complete the following sentences by using a clause from the list below. You will not need to use all the clauses.**

a) Weil es stark regnet,
b) Sobald meine Freundin vorbeikommt,
c) Peter besucht morgen seine Großeltern,
d) Ich bleibe morgen mit meinem Bruder zu Hause,
e) Meine Eltern kommen uns abholen,

1 weil sie kein Geld hat.
2 denn meine Mutter muß arbeiten.
3 ist es sehr sonnig.
4 obwohl er zu Fuß gehen muß.
5 gehen wir auf keinem Fall spazieren.
6 nachdem sie von der Stadt zurückkommen.
7 können wir zusammen schwimmen gehen.

---

**REMEMBER! Cover the answers if you want to.**

---

## ANSWERS

**A1**
a) weil
b) bis, *or possibly* obgleich/obwohl
c) damit
d) sobald/wenn, *or possibly* obgleich/obwohl
e) wenn/sobald

**A2**
a) Weil es stark regnet, gehen wir auf keinem Fall spazieren.
b) Sobald meine Freundin vorbeikommt, können wir zusammen schwimmen gehen.
c) Peter besucht morgen seine Großeltern, obwohl er zu Fuß gehen muß.
d) Ich bleibe morgen mit meinem Bruder zu Hause, denn meine Mutter muß arbeiten.
e) Meine Eltern kommen uns abholen, nachdem sie von der Stadt zurückkommen.

Unused:
1 weil sie kein Geld hat.
3 ist es sehr sonnig.

## TUTORIAL

**T1**
c) *Beware of using* so daß *as often as you would use 'so that' in English. Make sure you can tell the difference between the clauses which imply result and those which imply intent.*
d/e) *Wenn would imply the conditional 'if', whereas sobald implies that the action in the following clause is bound to happen.*

**T2**
*Apart from making the best sense of the sentences, the following might have helped you to put the clauses together:*
a) and b) *both began with subordinating conjunctions and you therefore had to create the 'verb, verb' pattern in the middle of the sentence. Only 3, 5 and 7 could do this.*
c), d) and e) *began with main clauses and needed either another main clause or a subordinate clause to complete them. 1, 2, 4 and 6 could do this.*

# EXAM PRACTICE

**1** Find Chapter 6 – Exam Practice Listening on the CD. Listen to the German (Track 11) twice and complete the sentences.

Ergänzen Sie die folgenden Sätze!

1  Bernd will nicht gleich Fußball spielen, weil .......................................

2  Er will mitgehen, wenn.................................................................

3  Bernd geht ins Kino, nachdem.........................................................

4  Ralf bekommt den ‚Gameboy', bevor ................................................

5  Bernds Familie macht jetzt Urlaub, damit ...........................................

*You will find the transcript, with answers and examiner's comments, on page 184.*

 LISTENING H

**2** Look at this role-play and think what you might say.

Sie gehen ans Telefon. Der Lehrer/die Lehrerin spielt die Rolle eines Klassenkamerades/einer Klassenkameradin. Sie wollen heute abend etwas zusammen machen.

> **Am Telefon**
>
> 1  Melden Sie sich.
>
> 2  Sagen Sie, daß Sie ins Kino möchten.
>
> 3  Beantworten Sie die Frage. (Sagen Sie, was für ein Film läuft.)
>
> 4  Fragen Sie, wer mitgeht.
>
> 5  Beantworten Sie die Frage. (Sagen Sie, wann und wo Sie sich treffen wollen.)

SPEAKING F H

*You will find the transcript and examiner's comments on page 184.*

Find Chapter 6 – Exam Practice Speaking on the CD and listen to how a candidate might tackle this role-play (Track 12).

**3** Read the text on page 50, then choose the right word or phrase to complete each of the sentences which follow.

READING H

**Im Stadtpark**

Einige junge Leute spielen Volleyball auf einer Wiese. Am Rande sitzen zwei Mädchen und gucken zu. Ein Junge geht auf die zwei Mädchen zu.

**Peter** Wollt ihr zwei mitmachen? Wir brauchen noch zwei Mitspieler.

**Suzanne** Was meinst du, Ingrid? Sollen wir?

**Ingrid** Meinetwegen, gerne. Also, ich heiße Ingrid, und das ist die Suzanne. Wie heißt du?

**Peter** Ich bin der Peter. Das sind Leute aus meiner Klasse. Wir haben heute schulfrei. Ihr werdet sie alle gleich kennenlernen. Aber laßt uns zuerst das Spiel zu Ende machen.

Eine Stunde später ...

**Peter** Also, ihr zwei. Was macht ihr hier in Düsseldorf?

**Suzanne** Wir machen eine Klassenfahrt und haben heute einen freien Tag. Wir wollten uns die Stadt ein bißchen anschauen.

**Peter** Wir zeigen euch gern unsere Stadt. Wollt ihr denn mitkommen? Wir gehen zu Mittag in die Imbißstube, und dann machen wir einen Stadtbummel.

**Ingrid** Wir müssen bloß zuerst anrufen und die Lehrerin fragen, aber ich glaube, das geht in Ordnung. Sag' uns, wie wir zur Imbißstube kommen, und wir treffen uns alle dort.

**Suzanne** So viel Zeit haben wir heute nachmittag nicht, denn wir müssen bis fünf wieder in der Jugendherberge sein. Heute abend gehen wir ins Theater, um ein Stück von Brecht zu sehen. Wir haben „Mutter Courage" in der Schule gelesen, und die Aufführung soll sehr gut sein.

**Peter** OK. Aber in der Stadt gibt es auch schöne Sachen zu sehen. Es gibt ein ganz berühmtes Glockenspiel, das einmal in der Stunde läutet, und dann gibt es natürlich das Heinrich-Heine Haus, wenn ihr euch für so 'was interessiert.

**Ingrid** Bloß nicht zu viel Kultur an einem Tag. „Allzuviel ist ungesund" wie man sagt! Gehen wir lieber ein bißchen am Rhein entlang spazieren, oder auf den Rheinturm.

**Peter** Fein! Bis nachher also. Tschüß!

Wählen Sie die richtigen Wörter.

1 Peter .................................................................., Volleyball zu spielen.

    hatte Lust     lud die Mädchen ein     wollte bald beginnen

2 Suzanne .............................................. sie spielen will.

    sagt sofort, daß     ist nicht so sicher, ob     ist ganz sicher, daß

3 Peter stellt seine Klassenkameraden vor, ...................................

    bevor sie zu spielen beginnen     während sie spielen

    nachdem sie spielen

4 Ingrid und Suzanne sind ....................................... in Düsseldorf.

    allein     mit ihren Familien     mit einer Schülergruppe

5 Peter möchte ................................................... essen gehen.

    gleich     gar nicht     nach dem Stadtbummel

6 Die zwei Mädchen müssen zuerst ...........................................

    um Geld bitten     Hunger haben     um Erlaubnis bitten

7 Die zwei Mädchen müssen zurück in die Jugendherberge, weil ............................................................................... .

    sie dort eine Aufführung machen     sie dann abends ausgehen

    sie ein Buch lesen müssen

**8** Peter will den Mädchen …….....................……...................… .

ein Essen ausgeben     sein Glockenspiel vorspielen

die Sehenswürdigkeiten zeigen

**9** Ingrid findet seine Idee ………...........…............…..……………

nicht so gut     ganz toll     interessant

*You will find the answers and examiner's comments on page 185.*

---

**4** Answer the following question in German.

Schreiben Sie einen Brief an Ihren Brieffreund/an Ihre Brieffreundin, in dem Sie einige Freunde beschreiben, und auch die Sachen, die Sie mit ihnen unternehmen. Schreiben Sie nicht mehr als 150 Wörter.

**WRITING** **H**

## Sample Student's Answer

Kingston, den 22. April

Liebe Irene,

Wie geht's? Du hast gefragt, was ich mit meinen Freundinnen so unternehme, also erzähle ich Dir ein bißchen, was wir so machen.

Mein Freund, Kevin, und ich kennen uns schon seit der 5. Klasse. Damals konnte ich ihn nicht ausstehen, weil er immer so egoistisch war. Lebhaft ist er aber auch, und mit der Zeit habe ich ihn näher kennengelernt. Er ist wirklich nicht so gemein und frech, wie er früher war, und wir gehen gern miteinander ins Kino oder einfach spazieren.

Meine Freundinnen sind meistens in meinem Alter, nur Mary ist ein Jahr älter als ich. Ich habe sie in der Reitschule kennengelernt, und wir verstehen uns sehr gut. Jackie und Georgie sind in meinem Jahrgang. Wir arbeiten oft zusammen nach der Schule, oder gehen zusammen in die Disco. Kevin hat nichts dagegen, daß ich ihn nicht einlade, denn er ist vom Tanzen nicht so begeistert.

Laß bitte bald von Dir hören,

Lynsey

### EXAMINER'S COMMENTS

- Notice the excellent use of *was* in the first sentence.

- How many conjunctions can you spot? *Und, aber, denn* and *oder* are easy to use, but try to use at least two or three subordinating conjunctions as well, such as *daß, weil* and *wenn*.

- The ending is quite colloquial: literally, 'Let me hear from you soon'. You may like to use it for a change.

*Try writing your own version of the letter, using some of the sentence patterns from this one. Remember that a good candidate can express feelings, and describe emotions.*

# CHAPTER 7

# DIE STADT, DIE UMGEBUNG, DAS WETTER

HOME TOWN, LOCAL ENVIRONMENT AND WEATHER

## QUESTIONS/PROMPTS

Wo wohnst du?

Wo liegt das?

Wie war das Wetter am Wochenende?

## WHAT YOU NEED TO KNOW

| | |
|---|---|
| Ich wohne ... | I live ... |
| in Newbury | in Newbury |
| in einem Dorf | in a village |
| in einer Stadt | in a town |
| in einer Großstadt | in a city |
| in einer Siedlung | on an estate |
| auf dem Lande | in the country |
| Newtown liegt ... | Newtown is ... |
| im Norden/Süden/Osten/Westen | in the north/south/east/west |
| in Nordengland/Südengland, usw. | in the north/south of England, etc. |
| nicht weit von London | not far from London |
| in der Nähe von Birmingham | near Birmingham |
| an der (Süd)küste | on the (south) coast |
| in den Bergen | in the hills |
| an der Themse | on the Thames (but 'am' for all other rivers: am Trent) |
| Die Stadt/Das Dorf ist ... | The town/village is ... |
| relativ klein | relatively small |
| ziemlich groß | quite large |
| etwas ruhig | rather quiet |
| sauber/schmutzig | clean/dirty |
| angenehm | pleasant |
| Das Wetter ist herrlich/toll/prima. | The weather is fine/great/marvellous. |
| Das Wetter ist furchtbar/schrecklich. | The weather is terrible/dreadful. |
| Es ist heiter. | It's bright. |
| Es ist regnerisch. | It's rainy. |
| Es ist trocken. | It's dry. |
| Es ist naß. | It's wet. |
| Der Wind kommt aus dem Süden. | The wind is from the south/southerly. |

## DIE WETTERVORHERSAGE

| | | | |
|---|---|---|---|
| die Aufheiterung (en) | brighter period | das Hochdruckgebiet | high pressure system |
| das Gewitter | thunderstorm | der Tiefdruckgebiet | low pressure system |
| 20 Grad Celsius | 20 degrees centigrade | die Höchsttemperatur (en) | highest temperature |
| der Hagel | hail | die Tiefsttemperatur (en) | lowest temperature |
| der Niederschlag (äge) | rainfall, precipitation | der Schauer (—) | shower |
| der Wetterbericht (e) | weather report | die Kälte | (the) cold |
| die Hitze | heat | niederschlagsfrei | dry, i.e. no rain or showers |
| zeitweise | from time to time | zunehmend | increasing(ly) |

## DAS WETTER

| | | | |
|---|---|---|---|
| Es ist sonnig.  | Es ist neblig.  | Es regnet.  | Es friert.  |
| Es ist bewölkt/ wolkig.  | Es ist stürmisch.  | Es schneit.  | kalt / kühl / warm / heiß  |

# Check yourself

## QUESTIONS

**Q1** **How would you say in German?**

a) I live in a large town in the north-east.
b) It's a bit dirty, but quite pleasant.
c) There is always lots to do.
d) The village is quite a long way from the nearest town.
e) There's a lot to see in the vicinity.

**Q2** **How would you say in German?**

a) Tomorrow (it) will be cold and cloudy.
b) The weather is bright, if somewhat cool.
c) There's a northerly wind and it's freezing.
d) It's quite wet and rather foggy.
e) The lowest temperatures will be around 5 degrees.

## REMEMBER! Cover the answers if you want to.

## ANSWERS

**A1**
a) Ich wohne in einer großen Stadt im Nordosten.
b) Es ist ein bißchen dreckig, aber ganz angenehm.
c) Es gibt immer viel zu tun.
d) Das Dorf ist ziemlich weit von der nächsten Stadt.
e) Es gibt viel Sehenswertes in der Umgebung.

**A2**
a) Morgen wird es kalt und wolkig sein.
b) Das Wetter ist heiter, wenn auch etwas kühl.
c) Der Wind kommt aus dem Norden, und es friert.
d) Es ist ganz naß und ziemlich neblig.
e) Die Tiefsttemperaturen liegen bei 5 Grad.

## TUTORIAL

**T1**
a) *Notice the difference between this and* in einer Großstadt – 'in a city'.
b) *Compare two aspects of the town using* aber *between the adjectives.*
c) *You could also use* es gibt immer etwas los – *'there's always something on'.*
d) *Notice that* weit *is all you need for 'a long way'.*
e) Sehenswertes *means 'things/places worth seeing' or simply 'sights'.*

**T2**
a) *You can use* bewölkt *for* wolkig.
b) Wenn auch *is a stylish way to make a contrast.*
c) *Compare this with 'I come from ...'* (Ich komme aus ...).
d) *Qualify the adjectives wherever possible.*
e) Liegen bei *is the weather jargon for 'will be around'.*

Wie findest du deine Stadt?
Warum?

Was findest du gut daran, und
was nicht so gut?

Was möchtest du ändern?

# GOING FURTHER

| | |
|---|---|
| Ich wohne sehr gern in Ledbury, weil die Landschaft in der Umgebung so schön ist. | I like living in Ledbury, because the countryside around is so beautiful. |
| Es gibt schöne Wanderwege am Fluß entlang. | There are nice walks along the river. |
| Man kann im Wald spazieren gehen. | You can go for walks in the woods. |
| Das Dorf hat weder Kino/Theater noch Disco/Sportzentrum. | The village has neither cinema/theatre nor a disco/sports centre. |
| Ich finde den Jugendklub auch nicht so gut, aber man kann mit der Bahn/mit dem Bus in die nächste Stadt fahren. | I don't think much of the youth club, but you can catch a train/bus to the next town. |
| Dort gibt es sehr viel zu tun/einen tollen Jugendklub/eine tolle Disco. | There is plenty to do/a great youth club/a fantastic disco there. |
| Der größte Nachteil ist, daß ich meine Freunde in der Stadt nicht so schnell besuchen kann. | The biggest disadvantage is that I can't visit my friends in town so easily. |
| Man sollte hier ein Sportzentrum bauen. | They ought to build a sports centre here. |
| Man könnte hier ein Schwimmbad hinstellen. | They could build a swimming pool here. |
| Wir sollten bessere Bus-/Bahnverbindingen haben. | We ought to have a better bus/train service. |

# HOW THE GRAMMAR WORKS

## ADVERBS AND ADVERB PHRASES

An adverb or adverb phrase usually comes as close as possible to the verb which it qualifies, whether the verb is finite:

> *Er spricht* **langsam.**
> *Kommen Sie* **schnell** *her!*

or in the infinitive form:

> *Ich sollte meine Hausaufgaben* **heute** *machen.*
> *Mein Vater kann* **erst morgen** *kommen.*

## TIME, MANNER, PLACE

Most adverbs and adverb phrases can be put into three main groups: those which describe **when** something happens, those which describe **how** it happens, and those which show **where** it takes place.

When you use more than one adverb together in the sentence, you should write them in the order **Time, Manner, Place:**

> *Ich fahre morgen mit dem Rad in die Stadt.*
> *Wir kommen heute abend mit dem Zug in Düsseldorf an.*

For emphasis, you can put one adverb at the beginning of the sentence:

> *Morgen fahre ich mit dem Rad in die Schule.*

Notice that the subject and verb are inverted when the adverb comes first in the sentence.

The following table shows some more adverbs and phrases which you can use to enhance your writing power, especially at Higher Level.

| Time | Manner | Place |
|------|--------|-------|
| gestern | mit dem Bus | in die/der Stadt* |
| gestern vormittag/ nachmittag/abend | mit der Bahn | in die/der Schule* zur Schule |
| heute | mit dem Wagen/Auto | in den/dem Park |
| heute morgen/ nachmittag/abend | zu Fuß | zum Museum |
| morgen | sehr schnell | ins Kino |
| morgen früh | langsam | die Straße entlang |
| morgen vormittag/ nachmittag/abend | leise | über die Brücke |
| um vier Uhr | laut | |
| zu Mittag | plötzlich | |
| nach einer Weile/einer halben Stunde | | |
| den ganzen Tag/Abend | | |

\* Look back to Chapter 5 for notes on place and movement.

## HIN/HER

These small words are usually found attached to verbs and simply tell you whether the movement of the verb is away from, or towards the speaker. They often correspond to the English 'there' and 'here':

*Gehen Sie hin!* – Go there.
*Kommen Sie her!* – Come here.

They are very frequently attached to other separable prefixes:

„Geh' hinunter in die Küche, hole deine Tasche und komm' wieder herauf."

„Geh' hinauf, hol' deine Sachen und komm' sofort wieder herunter!"

# Check yourself

## QUESTIONS

**Q1** *Pick out the adverbs and adverb phrases in this passage and put them in the correct column of the table.*

Ich bin gestern mit meiner Mutter in die Stadt gefahren. Wir sind um 8 Uhr losgefahren, denn früh am morgen gibt es viel Verkehr auf der Hauptstraße. Wir haben den Wagen hinter dem Rathaus geparkt, und sind dann zu Fuß zum Markt gelaufen, wo man Obst und Gemüse relativ billig kaufen kann. Gegen 1 Uhr sind wir mit vollen Taschen zum Auto zurückgelaufen.

| Time | Manner | Place |
|------|--------|-------|
|      |        |       |
|      |        |       |
|      |        |       |
|      |        |       |
|      |        |       |

**Q2** *Complete the sentences with at least two adverbs or adverb phrases.*

a) Ich habe die Jacke gekauft.
b) Wir sind gereist.
c) Bringen Sie das Buch!
d) Sie kommt mit.
e) Wir können nicht fahren.

**REMEMBER! Cover the answers if you want to.**

## ANSWERS

**A1**

| Time | Manner | Place |
|------|--------|-------|
| gestern | mit meiner Mutter | in die Stadt |
| um 8 Uhr | zu Fuß | auf der Hauptstraße |
| früh am morgen | relativ billig | hinter dem Rathaus |
| dann | mit vollen Taschen | zum Markt |
| gegen 1 Uhr |  | zum Auto |

For example:

**A2** a) Ich habe die Jacke gestern mit meinem eigenen Geld gekauft.
b) Wir sind letztes Jahr mit der ganzen Familie nach Portugal gereist.
c) Bringen Sie das Buch sofort zu Ihrem Mathelehrer!
d) Sie kommt morgen nach der Schule ins Kino mit.
e) Wir können nächste Woche nicht in Urlaub fahren.

## TUTORIAL

**T1** You should build up a list of useful phrases like these, which you can use in a number of different situations. These are particularly good for 'filling', when you check back through your work and find you are 15–20 words short of the required total.

**T2** d) Don't be misled by nach der Schule, which means 'after school' and so is a time phrase.
e) The position of nicht can of course vary according to the meaning you want. For example, Wir können nicht nächste Woche in Urlaub fahren would imply that you could go some time other than next week.

# EXAM PRACTICE

**1** Find Chapter 7 – Exam Practice Listening on the CD and listen to the German twice (Track 13), then put a cross in the correct column for each sentence.

**LISTENING** **H**

Richtig oder falsch? Kreuzen Sie die richtige Kästchen an!

|  | richtig | falsch |
|---|---|---|
| 1 Die Wettervorhersage kommt am Freitag im Radio. |  |  |
| 2 In den letzten Tagen war es etwas kälter als jetzt. |  |  |
| 3 Die erste Nacht bleibt trocken. |  |  |
| 4 Es wird am Samstag Eis auf den Straßen geben. |  |  |
| 5 Das Tiefdruckgebiet kommt vom Süden. |  |  |
| 6 Am Samstag sieht man im Süden keine Sonne. |  |  |
| 7 Am Samstagabend könnte es im Norden stürmisch werden. |  |  |
| 8 Es gibt fast keinen Wind. |  |  |

*You will find the transcript and answers, with examiner's comments, on page 185.*

**SPEAKING** **H**

**2** Look at the situation outlined below, and think what you might say. Then find Chapter 7 – Exam Practice Speaking on the CD (Track 14) and listen to how a candidate might tackle this role-play.

Sie machen eine Fahrradtour in die Berge. Beschreiben Sie den Tag und das Dorf, das Sie besuchen.

*You will find the transcript and examiner's comments on page 186.*

**H READING** ➤

**3** Read the passage, then answer the questions below.

Lesen Sie das folgende Stück über die Stadt Mayrhofen.

---

Das Zillertal ist eines der herrlichsten Täler in ganz Österreich. Hier kann man schön Urlaub machen, die Aussicht aufs Gebirge geniessen und viel Sport treiben, das ganze Jahr lang.

Mayrhofen ist bei den Touristen beliebt, nicht nur weil es tagsüber so viel an Sport- und Wandermöglichkeiten zu bieten hat, sondern auch weil abends so viel los ist. In den zahlreichen, gemütlichen Cafés und Restaurants gibt es leckeres Essen, in den Bars und Discos Musik und Tanz. Dazu gibt es noch Kurkonzerte und weitere kulturelle Veranstaltungen in der Gegend.

Daß Mayrhofen ein bekanntes Ziel für Wintersportfreunde ist, weiß jeder. Aber wußten Sie auch, daß man auch im Hochsommer im hochgelegenen Skiort Hintertux ganz in der Nähe immer noch skifahren kann?

Dazu kann man im Sommerangebot Wandertouren machen, Tennis spielen, radfahren oder im beheizten Freibad schwimmen. Für Ihre Kleinen gibt es auch viel Spaß. Drachenfliegen, Reiten, Malen, Basteln sind alle im Kinderprogramm.

Geniessen Sie einen gesunden Urlaub! Hier können Sie sich ausruhen und entspannen, die herrliche Luft und den Duft der Berge geniessen.

---

Richtig oder falsch? Kreuzen Sie die richtige Kästchen an!

|  | richtig | falsch |
|---|---|---|
| 1 Mayrhofen liegt in der Schweiz. |  |  |
| 2 In der Stadt kann man nicht besonders gut essen. |  |  |
| 3 Musik gibt es nur für kranke Leute. |  |  |
| 4 Die Stadt ist ein bekannter Skiort. |  |  |
| 5 Man kann nur im Winter skifahren. |  |  |
| 6 Der Sommersport findet nur im Freien statt. |  |  |
| 7 Das Kinderprogramm ist nur für schlechtes Wetter gedacht. |  |  |
| 8 Der Ort ist auch wegen der Luft sehr empfehlenswert. |  |  |

*You will find the answers and examiner's comments on page 187.*

**H WRITING** ➤

**4** Answer the following question in German, then compare your answer with the sample on page 188.

Sie schreiben einen Bericht für die Schülerzeitschrift Ihrer Partnerschule, in dem Sie Ihr Dorf bzw. Ihre Stadt und die Umgebung beschreiben.
(You write a description of your village/town and the surrounding area for the magazine of your partner school.)

*You will find the sample answer and examiner's comments on page 188.*

## WHAT YOU NEED TO KNOW

There are two main areas of shopping vocabulary which you should know. The first is food and drink, much of which was dealt with in Chapter 3. The second is clothing. You should also think of a few simple ideas for presents and souvenirs in case you are asked to buy either of these in a role-play.

Ich möchte/Ich hätte gern … — I would like …

- ein Kilo Äpfel — a kilo of apples
- ein Pfund Birnen — 500 grammes (continental pound) of pears
- ein halbes Kilo Bananen — half a kilo (500g) of bananas
- 200 Gramm Wurst — 200 grammes of sausage
- fünf Scheiben Schinken — five slices of ham
- ein Stück Käse — a piece of cheese
- eine Schachtel Pralinen — a box of chocolates
- ein Paket Waschpulver — a packet of washing powder
- ein Päckchen Kaffee — a small packet of coffee
- eine Tube Zahnpasta — a tube of toothpaste
- eine Tafel Schokolade — a bar of chocolate
- eine Flasche Mineralwasser — a bottle of mineral water
- eine Dose Limonade — a can of lemonade
- eine Tüte — a bag
- eine Tragetasche/Plastiktüte — a carrier bag

ein bißchen/etwas — a little/a bit
mehr/weniger — more/less
genug — enough
Ist gut so. — That'll do.
Stimmt so. — That's fine.
die Sandale (n) — sandal
der Schuh (e) — shoe
der Stiefel (–) — boot
der Pantoffel (n) — slipper
der Sportschuh (e) — trainer

aus … — made of …
- Baumwolle/Kunststoff — cotton/man-made fibre
- Leder/Wildleder — leather/suede
- Wolle — wool

die Größe — size
eine Nummer größer/kleiner — a size bigger/smaller

**Finally, here are some useful shopping phrases you might hear:**

Was darf es sein, bitte? — What would you like?
Werden Sie schon bedient? — Are you being served?
Welche Größe haben Sie? — What size are you?
Sonst noch etwas? — Anything else?
Haben Sie sonst noch einen Wunsch? — Would you like anything else?
Ist das alles? — Is that all?

die Kleider — clothes
die Kleidung — clothing
der Anorak (s)
die Socke (n) / der Strumpf (Strümpfe)
der Anzug (züge)
das Kleid (er)
der Badeanzug (züge)
die Badehose (n)
die Bluse (n)
die Krawatte (n) / der Schlips (e)
der Gürtel (–)
der Handschuh (e)
der Pulli (s) / Pullover (–)
das Hemd (en)
der Rock (Röcke)

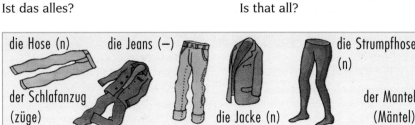

die Hose (n)
die Jeans (–)
die Strumpfhose (n)
der Schlafanzug (züge)
die Jacke (n)
der Mantel (Mäntel)

# Check yourself

## QUESTIONS

*The goods and the quantities have got mixed up. Can you correct the sentences?*

**Q1**
a) Ich möchte eine Tube Schinken.
b) Geben Sie mir ein Kilo Waschpulver, bitte.
c) Haben Sie ein Paket Äpfel, bitte?
d) Und dann hätte ich gern fünf Scheiben Limonade.
e) Ich möchte eine Flasche Zahnpasta, bitte.

*How would you say in German?*

**Q2**
a) Have you the same (thing) in blue?
b) That is too expensive (for me). Have you something cheaper?
c) That is too big (for me). Have you a size smaller?
d) I'm looking for something for my father.
e) Can you wrap it as a present, please?

---

**REMEMBER! Cover the answers if you want to.**

---

## ANSWERS

**A1**
For example:

a) Ich möchte eine Tube Zahnpasta.
b) Geben Sie mir ein Kilo Äpfel, bitte.
c) Haben Sie ein Paket Waschpulver, bitte?
d) Und dann hätte ich gern fünf Scheiben Schinken.
e) Ich möchte eine Flasche Limonade, bitte.

**A2**
a) Haben Sie das gleiche in Blau?
b) Das ist mir zu teuer. Haben Sie etwas Billigeres?
c) Das ist mir zu groß. Haben Sie eine Nummer kleiner?
d) Ich suche etwas für meinen Vater.
e) Können Sie es bitte als Geschenk einpacken?

## TUTORIAL

**T1**
*Notice that there are at least four ways of asking for something when shopping. Make sure that you can use at least one of them successfully every time without a second thought. You will recognise the others, but you don't have to alternate them. After all, you probably stick to the same phrase in English all the time.*
d) *This turn of phrase is for the second or third thing you are asking for.*

**T2**
a) *Change the gender of das gleiche according to the garment.*
b) *The word following etwas must be a noun and therefore has a capital.*
c) *Notice the addition of mir in both b) and c). Use Nummer not Größe for 'size' in this context.*
e) *Notice the alternative place for bitte, instead of leaving it to the end.*

## GOING FURTHER

## BANK UND POST

Of course, shopping means more than just buying items. You'll need to pay, to change money at a bank, and to go to a post office.

| | |
|---|---|
| Nehmen Sie Schecks? | Do you accept cheques? |
| Kann ich mit Kreditkarte bezahlen? | Can I pay by credit card? |
| Ich habe nur einen Hundertmarkschein. | I only have a 100 mark note. |
| Könnten Sie einen Fünzigmarkschein wechseln? | Have you change for a 50 mark note? |

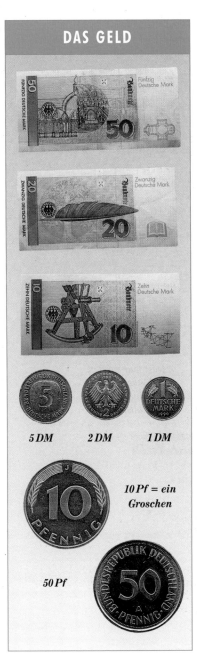

## DAS GELD

5 DM     2 DM     1 DM

10 Pf = ein
Groschen

50 Pf

| | |
|---|---|
| Wo kann man Geld wechseln? | Where can I change some money? |
| Ich möchte Reiseschecks wechseln. | I would like to change some travellers' cheques. |
| Wie steht der Kurs für das Pfund? | What is the exchange rate for the pound? |
| Muß ich eine Gebühr bezahlen? | Do I have to pay a charge? |
| Wo muß ich unterschreiben? | Where do I sign? |
| Haben Sie Ihren Ausweis dabei? | Do you have your passport with you? |
| Was kostet eine Postkarte nach England? | How much is a postcard to England? |
| Ich möchte dieses Paket nach England schicken. | I would like to send this parcel to England. |
| Wie lange dauert es? | How long does it take? |
| Vier Briefmarken zu 80 Pfennig, bitte. | Four stamps at 80 pfennigs, please. |
| Wann ist die nächste Leerung? | When is the next collection? |

# HOW THE GRAMMAR WORKS

## ADJECTIVES

Adjectives in German need no agreement when they come after the noun:

*Mein Zimmer ist klein.*

However, they must show their agreement in gender and case when they come immediately before the noun:

*Ich habe ein kleines Zimmer.*

The following chart will give you all the endings you need. You may have seen it as two separate tables for definite and indefinite articles.

| Case | Gender | | | |
|---|---|---|---|---|
| | Masculine | Feminine | Neuter | Plural |
| Nominative (subject) | der  -e<br>ein  -er | die  -e<br>eine  -e | das  -e<br>ein  -es | die  -en<br>-e |
| Accusative (direct object) | den  -en<br>einen  -en | die  -e<br>eine  -e | das  -e<br>ein  -es | die  -en<br>-e |
| Genitive (possessive) | des  -en<br>eines  -en | der  -en<br>einer  -en | des  -en<br>eines  -en | der  -en<br>-er |
| Dative ('to'/'for') | dem  -en<br>einem  -en | der  -en<br>einer  -en | dem  -en<br>einem -en | den  -en<br>-en |

Notice that, below the heavy line, all the adjectives except one (which you are unlikely to use) end in *-en*.

The adjective endings after *dieser, jener, jeder* and *welcher* follow the same pattern as the endings after the definite article:

*Was ist in diesem kleinen Koffer?*
*Welches rotes Auto magst du am liebsten?*

The adjective endings after *kein* and after possessive adjectives (*mein, dein,* etc.) follow the same pattern as the endings after the indefinite article:

*Wir haben keine roten Äpfel mehr.*
*Unser neues Auto ist grün.*

# Check yourself

## QUESTIONS

**Q1** *Complete the adjective endings in this passage.*

Mein jünger..[1]. Bruder lief durch die offen..[2]. Tür des groß..[3]., weiß..[4]. Gebäude..[5].. und kaufte eine einfach..[6].. Fahrkarte nach Bonn. Mit den beid..[7]. Koffer..[8]. in den Händen ging er den lang..[9].. Bahnstieg entlang, bis er den letzt..[10]. Wagen erreichte. Peter fand ein leer..[11]. Abteil und legte die schwer..[12]. Koffer in das altmodisch..[13]. Gepäcknetz über dem einzig..[14]. freien Platz im ganz..[15]. Zug.

**Q2** *Choose the correct words from the box below to complete each sentence.*

a) Unser VW ist jetzt sehr ................, Vater möchte einen .................. Wagen kaufen.

b) Ich kaufe mir eine ................. Jacke, die ................. kann ich nicht mehr anziehen.

c) Der ................... Bus war zu voll, aber der ................... kommt in fünf Minuten.

d) Die Hose ist nicht in der ....................... Kommode, sondern im ........................ Kleiderschrank.

e) Du bist ein .................. Mädchen, aber mein ..................... Fahrrad leihe ich dir nicht!

| neues | alte | alt | letzte | neuen | neue |
|---|---|---|---|---|---|
| nettes | nächste | modernen | alten | | |

---

**REMEMBER! Cover the answers if you want to.**

---

## ANSWERS

**A1** Mein jüngerer Bruder lief durch die offene Tür des großen, weißen Gebäudes und kaufte eine einfache Fahrkarte nach Bonn. Mit den beiden Koffern in den Händen ging er den langen Bahnstieg entlang, bis er den letzten Wagen erreichte. Peter fand ein leeres Abteil und legte die schweren Koffer in das altmodisches Gepäcknetz über dem einzigen freien Platz im ganzen Zug.

**A2**
a) Unser VW ist jetzt sehr alt, Vater möchte einen modernen Wagen kaufen.

b) Ich kaufe mir eine neue Jacke, die alte kann ich nicht mehr anziehen.

c) Der letzte Bus war zu voll, aber der nächste kommt in fünf Minuten.

d) Das ist nicht in der alten Kommode, sondern im neuen Kleiderschrank.

e) Du bist ein nettes Mädchen, aber mein neues Fahrrad leihe ich dir nicht!

## TUTORIAL

**T1**

| Case required | Function |
|---|---|
| 1 *masculine nominative* | *subject* |
| 2 *feminine accusative* | *following* durch |
| 3 *neuter genitive* | *possessive* |
| 4 *neuter genitive* | *possessive* |
| 5 *neuter genitive* | *(Remember to add -s to the noun.)* |
| 6 *feminine accusative* | *direct object* |
| 7 *dative plural* | *following* mit |
| 8 *dative plural* | *(Remember to add -n to the noun.)* |
| 9 *masculine accusative* | *to agree with the* entlang *following it* |
| 10 *masculine accusative* | *direct object* |
| 11 *neuter accusative* | *direct object* |
| 12 *plural accusative* | *direct object* |
| 13 *neuter accusative* | *following* in |
| 14 *masculine dative* | *following* über |
| 15 *masculine dative* | *following* im |

**T2**
a) 1 *no agreement after the noun;* 2 *masculine accusative*

b) 1 *feminine accusative;* 2 *feminine accusative – noun omitted*

c) 1 *masculine nominative;* 2 *masculine nominative – noun omitted*

d) 1 *feminine dative;* 2 *masculine dative*

e) 1 *neuter nominative – don't forget that girls are not feminine in German!* 2 *neuter accusative – and notice the different word order for emphasis.*

# EXAM PRACTICE

**1** Find Chapter 8 – Exam Practice Listening on the CD. Listen to the German twice (Track 15), then choose the correct word or phrase to complete each sentence below.

LISTENING **F** **H**

**Im Fundbüro**

Ergänzen Sie die Sätze.

*You will find the transcript, with answers and examiner's comments, on page 189.*

1 Das Mädchen ging ins Fundbüro, ....................................................

    um Geld zu holen
    um Information zu bekommen
    um etwas zu finden

2 Sie hatte die Jacke (a) ..........................(b)....................................
    verloren.
    (a)  am Tag davor    (b)  auf der Straße
          letzte Woche           im Kino
          morgen             im Park

3 Die Jacke war..................................und ........................................

    dreckig
    neu
    groß
    teuer
    nicht mehr neu
    hellblau

4 In der Tasche der Jacke hatte das Mädchen ........................... und

.......................................... .

    eine Fahrkarte
    etwas Geld
    ein Foto
    ihre Schlüssel
    Bonbons

5 Das Mädchen hat ............................................... zurückgekriegt.

    alles
    nichts
    nur eine Sache                 [8 marks]

**H SPEAKING**

**2** Look at the situation outlined below and think what you might say. Then find Chapter 8 – Exam Practice Speaking on the CD (Track 16) and listen to a good candidate developing a narrative from the pictures.

Sie sind in Deutschland und gehen mit Ihrem Brieffreund einkaufen. Erzählen Sie, was Sie in der Stadt machen.

*You will find the transcript and examiner's comments on page 189.*

**3** Read the text, then answer the questions below.

## Ein Spaß in der Damenabteilung

Almut und Gabi waren Zwillingsschwestern und gingen gern zusammen einkaufen. Sie trugen oft die gleichen Sachen, und sie sahen sich so ähnlich, daß nur ihre beiden Brüder und die Eltern sie schnell erkennen konnten.

An diesem Samstag hatten sie gerade ihr Taschengeld bekommen und wollten gleich los in die Stadt laufen, um neue Kleider zu suchen. Wie gewöhnlich waren sie identisch gekleidet.

Als sie im zweiten Stock des Kaufhauses waren, wollten sie einen Spaß mit der Verkäuferin machen. Almut ließ sich einen blauen Pulli von der Verkäuferin geben und ging in die Umkleidekabine.

In dem Augenblick kam die Gabi von hinten auf die Verkäuferin zu. Sie hatte den gleichen Pulli in Schwarz in der Hand, und sagte der Verkäuferin, daß sie die Farbe nicht mochte.

Die Verkäuferin war erstaunt, aber gab Gabi einen gelben Pullover. Ein paar Sekunden später, als Gabi in der Umkleidekabine war, kam Almut im blauen Pulli heraus und sagte, sie fand ihn ganz toll.

Die Verkäuferin wußte nicht, was los war, bis Gabi auch wieder erschien. Als die Verkäuferin die beiden Schwestern zur gleichen Zeit sah, lachte sie laut, und schien den Spaß zu verstehen. Sie stand an der Kasse und wollte die Pullis einpacken, aber dann ging die Sache schief, denn Almut und Gabi wollten die Pullover gar nicht kaufen, sondern nur ihren Spaß haben.

,,Wir haben die Sachen nur so anprobiert," meinte Gabi. Aber die Verkäuferin wurde auf einmal böse mit den Mädchen.

,,Das ist eine Unverschämtheit," schimpfte sie. ,,Sie haben meine Zeit verschwendet. So 'was soll man nicht machen."

Die beiden Teenager entschuldigten sich und gingen schnell aus dem Geschäft.

Richtig oder falsch? Kreuzen Sie die richtige Kästchen an!

| | richtig | falsch | nicht im Text |
|---|---|---|---|
| 1 Almut und Gabi waren Freunde. | | | |
| 2 Sie hatten zwei Geschwister. | | | |
| 3 Sie trugen oft die gleiche Kleidung. | | | |
| 4 Sie wollten neue Kleidung für eine Party kaufen. | | | |
| 5 Die Verkäuferin war eine ältere Frau. | | | |
| 6 Almut sprach zuerst mit der Verkäuferin. | | | |
| 7 Die Verkäuferin hatte keinen Sinn für Humor. | | | |
| 8 Sie wurde sofort ärgerlich. | | | |
| 9 Die Schwestern kauften keinen der Pullis. | | | |

*You will find the answers and examiner's comments on page 190.*

**4** Write the letter of complaint outlined below, then compare your letter with the sample on page 191. Before you start, you may find it helpful to re-read the letter of complaint in the Reading section of Chapter 3 (page 26) so that you can use some of the constructions which you find there.

*You will find the sample answer and examiner's comments on page 191.*

Schreiben Sie einen Brief an die Leitung eines Geschäftes, in dem Sie sich über etwas beklagen, das Sie dort gekauft haben.

## NEHMEN SIE ...

| | |
|---|---|
| die erste Straße links | the first on the left |
| die zweite Straße | the second on the left |
| die dritte Straße rechts | the third on the right |
| die nächste Straße rechts | the next on the right |

# WHAT YOU NEED TO KNOW

**You need to know how to give and receive directions to places, both on foot and by means of public transport.**

| | |
|---|---|
| Entschuldigen Sie, bitte. | Excuse me, please. |
| Ich bin hier fremd. | I am a stranger here. |
| Können Sie mir helfen? | Can you help me? |
| Wie komme ich ... ? | How do I get ... ? |
| zum Bahnhof/Museum/ Rathaus, usw (all masculine and neuter nouns) | to the station/museum/ town hall etc. |
| zur Stadtmitte/Post, usw. (all feminine nouns) | to the town centre/ post office, etc. |
| Geht es hier nach Meckenheim? | Is this the way to Meckenheim? |
| Ist es weit nach/zum/zur ... ? | Is it far to ... ? |
| Wie lange braucht man, um zum Markt zu kommen/laufen? | How long does it take to get/walk to the market place? |
| Wo ist der Busbahnhof? | Where is the bus station? |
| Wo ist die nächste Bushaltestelle? | Where is the nearest bus-stop? |
| Gehen Sie hier geradeaus. | Go straight ahead. |
| Gehen Sie die Marktstraße entlang. | Go along Market Street. |
| Gehen Sie die Marktstraße hinunter. | Go down Market Street. |
| bis an die Ampel/bis ans Rathaus bis zur Ampel/bis zum Rathaus } | as far as the traffic lights/town hall, |
| Biegen Sie links/rechts ab. Biegen Sie nach links/nach rechts. } | Turn left/right. |
| dem Rathaus gegenüber | opposite the town hall |
| am Rathaus/an der Galerie vorbei | past the town hall/past the gallery |
| Das Rathaus liegt auf der linken Seite. | The town hall is on the left. |
| Sie können es nicht verfehlen. | You can't miss it. |

**You should be able to deal with a car breakdown, by saying what is wrong with the vehicle and understanding how to get help.**

| | |
|---|---|
| Gibt es eine Reparaturwerkstatt/ eine Tankstelle in der Nähe? | Is there a garage (repairs)/petrol station nearby? |
| Können Sie unser Auto reparieren? | Can you repair our car? |
| Wir haben eine Panne. | We've broken down. |
| Wir haben eine Reifenpanne. | We have a flat tyre. |
| Der Motor springt nicht an. | The engine won't start. |
| Wir haben kein Benzin. | We've run out of petrol. |
| Wir haben ein Problem mit dem Motor/den Bremsen/dem Auspuff. | We have a problem with the engine/the brakes/the exhaust. |
| Unsere Windschutzscheibe ist kaputt. | Our windscreen is smashed. |
| Können Sie einen Mechaniker herausschicken? | Can you send out a mechanic? |
| Können Sie einen Abschleppwagen schicken? | Can you send out a tow vehicle? |
| Wie lange dauert es? | How long will it take? |
| Wir sind auf der Autobahn | We are on the motorway |
| in der Nähe von Neuß | near Neuß |
| zwischen Düsseldorf und Essen. | between Düsseldorf and Essen. |
| Wir fahren Richtung Mainz. | We are travelling in the direction of Mainz. |
| Das Kennzeichen ist .... | The registration number is .... |

**An der Tankstelle**

Können Sie das Öl/das Wasser/
die Luft nachsehen, bitte?
Ich brauche Öl/Wasser/Luft, bitte.
25 Liter bleifrei/Diesel, bitte.

**At the petrol station**

Can you check the oil/
water/air, please?
I need oil/water/air, please.
25 litres of unleaded/diesel, please.

# Check yourself

## QUESTIONS

**Q1**  **How would you say in German?**

a) Go past the bridge and take the third
   on the right.
b) Go as far as the lights and turn left.
c) The gallery is on the left opposite the
   town hall.
d) Take the next left and carry straight on.
e) You can't miss it.

**Q2**  **Complete the dialogue.**

**Am Telefon**

Stimme: Hier Fleischauer.
Sie:    Wir haben eine P.............
Stimme: Was ist dann los?
Sie:    Wir haben ein P.................... mit
        dem M................. .
        Können Sie einen M....................
        s...................?
Stimme: Ja, aber nicht sofort.
Sie:    Wie l............. d................ es?
Stimme: Eine Stunde. Wo sind Sie?
Sie:    Wir sind auf der A........................
        in der N.........:..... von Koblenz.
        Wir fahren R.................. Bonn.

---

**REMEMBER! Cover the answers if you want to.**

---

## ANSWERS

**A1**  a) Gehen Sie an der Brücke vorbei, und
           dann nehmen Sie die dritte Straße rechts.
       b) Gehen Sie bis zur Ampel und dann
           biegen Sie nach links ab.
       c) Die Galerie liegt auf der linken Seite
           dem Rathaus gegenüber.
       d) Nehmen Sie die nächste Straße links
           und gehen Sie immer geradeaus.
       e) Sie können es nicht verfehlen.

**A2**  Stimme: Hier Fleischauer.
        Sie:    Wir haben eine Panne.
        Stimme: Was ist dann los?
        Sie:    Wir haben ein Problem mit
                dem Motor. Können Sie einen
                Mechaniker schicken?
        Stimme: Ja, aber nicht sofort.
        Sie:    Wie lange dauert es?
        Stimme: Eine Stunde. Wo sind Sie?
        Sie:    Wir sind auf der Autobahn in der
                Nähe von Koblenz. Wir fahren
                Richtung Bonn.

## TUTORIAL

**T1**  *These examples are straightforward and you should try
to memorise them. Although you may feel you know the
structures, make sure you are confident with the genders
of all the places in the town, so that you can get the
zum/zur and am/an der etc. correct every time.*
        c)    Gegenüber dem Rathaus *is also correct.*

**T2**  *This dialogue contains the key phrases to remember and
is typical of the sort you may be expected to take part
in for the Speaking Test role-play. The exam will not
be testing your mechanical knowledge or skills, so
you are unlikely to be asked to produce any
specialist vocabulary.*

## ÖFFENTLICHE VERKEHRSMITTEL

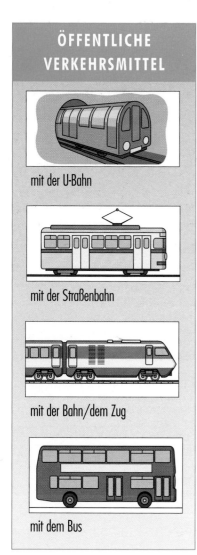

mit der U-Bahn

mit der Straßenbahn

mit der Bahn/dem Zug

mit dem Bus

# GOING FURTHER

**Here is some language you may hear at the station.**

| | |
|---|---|
| Achtung auf Gleis 8. Der Zug von München fährt gleich ein. | The train from Munich is just arriving at platform 8. |
| Achtung auf Gleis 10. Der Zug nach Köln fährt gleich ab. | The train standing at platform 10 for Cologne is about to leave. |
| Bitte einsteigen und Türen schließen! | Please get aboard and close the doors. |
| Bitte Achtung beim Einsteigen. | Please take care getting aboard. |
| Die Türen schließen automatisch. | The doors close automatically. |
| Der Zug hat 5 Minuten Verspätung. | The train is five minutes late. |

**You need to be able to interpret a timetable, finding out such information as types of train, platform number and which days services do not run, etc. Here is some useful vocabulary.**

| | |
|---|---|
| gültig nur für Züge des Nahverkehrs | valid only for local trains |
| gilt nur Samstag/Sonntag | only valid on Saturdays/Sundays |
| kein Umtausch | not transferable |
| mit Zuschlag | with supplement (an extra charge for the faster trains) |
| Fahrkarten bitte sofort entwerten. | Please stamp your ticket immmediately. |
| der Entwerter | ticket-stamping machine (on trams and buses) |
| verkehrt nur sonntags | only travels on Sundays (found next to an individual train/bus time) |

**You should be able to report a road accident:**

| | |
|---|---|
| ein Verkehrsunfall | a road traffic accident |
| der Radfahrer/LKWfahrer/Autofahrer | the cyclist/lorry driver/car driver |
| zu schnell fahren | to drive too fast |
| zu scharf bremsen | to brake too hard |
| Er war schuld an dem Unfall. | The accident was his fault. |
| Niemand war verletzt. | Nobody was hurt/injured. |

**The single most difficult aspect of reporting an accident is the collision itself, so look at the following examples carefully:**

| | |
|---|---|
| Der Radfahrer ist mit dem Auto zusammengestoßen. | The cyclist collided with the car. (implies they were going towards each other) |
| Der Lastwagen ist auf das Auto aufgefahren. | The lorry ran into the back of the car. |
| Das Auto ist gegen einen Baum gefahren. | The car ran into a tree. (something stationary) |

# HOW THE GRAMMAR WORKS

## PRONOUNS

The pronouns you know well are the subject pronouns, which you have learned as part of your verb tables. They are in the nominative case. The table which follows shows these pronouns in the accusative case (direct object) and dative case (indirect object), plus the corresponding pronouns to use with reflexive verbs (see Chapter 2).

|  |  | Nominative | Accusative | Dative | Reflexive |
|---|---|---|---|---|---|
| **singular** | I | ich | mich | mir | mich/mir |
| | you (familiar) | du | dich | dir | dich/dir |
| | you (formal) | Sie | Sie | Ihnen | sich |
| | he | er | ihn | ihm | sich |
| | she | sie | sie | ihr | sich |
| | it | es | es | ihm | sich |
| | one | man | einen | einem | sich |
| **plural** | we | wir | uns | uns | uns |
| | you (familiar) | ihr | euch | euch | euch |
| | you (formal) | Sie | Sie | Ihnen | sich |
| | they | sie | sie | ihnen | sich |

The pronouns are used in exactly the same way as the nouns they are replacing, including after prepositions:

**Accusative:** *Sie kennen* **mich**
*Ich besuche* **ihn**
*für* **ihn**
*gegen* **sie**
*ohne* **mich**

**Dative:** *Kauf'* **mir** *ein Eis, bitte.*
*Wie geht's* **dir**?
*bei* **uns**
*mit* **Ihnen**
*zu* **dir**

If you need to use the word 'it' after a preposition, you will nearly always need to add the word *da* to the front of the preposition:

*Ich schreibe gern mit meinem neuen Kuli.* → *Ich schreibe gern* **damit**.
*Ich habe nichts gegen die Idee.* → *Ich habe nichts* **dagegen**.

You should learn the rule for the word order of noun and pronoun objects:

**a** Two nouns – Dative first:
*Ich gebe dem Mann das Geld.*

**b** Two pronouns – Accusative first:
*Ich gebe es ihm.*

**c** Pronoun before noun:
*Ich gebe es dem Mann.*
*Ich gebe ihm das Geld.*

## RELATIVE PRONOUNS: WHO, WHOM, WHOSE, AND WHICH

The relative pronoun takes its number and gender from the word it refers back to. Its case is determined by the part it plays in the relative clause.

First, however, you need to be absolutely clear about when to use them. This is not always straightforward, as they are often omitted in English. Look at these two examples. The relative pronoun in each case is in bold:

The girl, **who** is coming into the room, is my cousin.
The car, **which** mum bought, was an estate.

Both these sentences would more likely appear in English as:

The girl coming into the room is my cousin.
The car mum bought is an estate.

**In German, the relative pronoun can never be omitted.**

With a few exceptions, the relative pronouns in German are the same as the definite article:

|  | **Masculine** | **Feminine** | **Neuter** | **Plural** |
|---|---|---|---|---|
| Nom./subject | der | die | das | die |
| Acc./direct obj. | den | die | das | die |
| Genitive | **dessen** | **deren** | **dessen** | **deren** |
| Dative/ind. obj. | dem | der | dem | **denen** |

Relative clauses are subordinate clauses, so the finite verb is the last word in the clause:

| | |
|---|---|
| Der Mann, **der** den Wagen fährt, ist mein Onkel. | – The man (who is) driving the car is my uncle. |
| Der Mann, **den** ich drüben sehe, ist mein Kunstlehrer. | – The man (whom) I see over there is my art teacher. |
| Die Frau, **deren** Auto in der Garage steht, ist unsere Nachbarin. | – The lady whose car is in the garage is our neighbour. |
| Der Junge, **dem** ich das Buch gab, liest gern Romane. | – The boy to whom I gave the book enjoys reading novels. |

# Check yourself

## QUESTIONS

**Q1** *Replace each noun in bold with the correct pronouns.*

a) Ich habe **meinen Vater** heute morgen nicht gesehen.
b) **Der Mann** hat **die Tasche** getragen.
c) Ich habe **meinem Bruder die Karten** gegeben.
d) **Die Dame** schreibt mit **einem neuen Kuli**.
e) **Mutti** ist mit **den beiden Kindern** in die Stadt gefahren.

**Q2** *Use the correct relative pronoun to complete each sentence.*

a) Die Frau, d...... den Wagen gefahren hat, war meine Nachbarin.
b) Der Mann, d...... Auto es war, hat die Polizei angerufen.
c) Die U-Bahn, mit d...... ich gefahren bin, hatte Verspätung.
d) Die Kinder, d...... ich die Bonbons gebe, sind meine Geschwister.
e) Der Junge, d...... ich auf der Party traf, kommt aus meiner Klasse.

**REMEMBER! Cover the answers if you want to.**

## ANSWERS

**A1**
a) Ich habe ihn heute morgen nicht gesehen.
b) Er hat sie getragen.
c) Ich habe sie ihm gegeben.
d) Sie schreibt damit.
e) Sie ist mit ihnen in die Stadt gefahren.

**A2**
a) Die Frau, die den Wagen gefahren hat, war meine Nachbarin.
b) Der Mann, dessen Auto es war, hat die Polizei angerufen.
c) Die U-Bahn, mit der ich gefahren bin, hatte Verspätung.
d) Die Kinder, denen ich die Bonbons gebe, sind meine Geschwister.
e) Der Junge, den ich auf der Party traf, kommt aus meiner Klasse.

## TUTORIAL

**T1**
a) *Masculine accusative*
b) *Masculine nominative; feminine accusative*
c) *Plural accusative; masculine dative – and notice the change in word order!*
d) *Feminine nominative; note that* mit + ihm *changes to* damit *for 'with it' (although* mit ihm *would be needed for 'with him').*
e) *Feminine nominative; plural dative*

**T2**
a) *Feminine nominative*
b) *Masculine genitive*
c) *Feminine dative after* mit
d) *Plural dative*
e) *Masculine accusative*

# EXAM PRACTICE

**1** Find Chapter 9 – Exam Practice Listening on the CD and listen to the German twice (Track 17).

**LISTENING F H**

**Im Verkehrsamt**
Sie sind im Verkehrsamt. Sie haben einen Stadtplan und wollen herausfinden, wie man sich in der Stadt zurechtfindet. Von einem Wegweiserautomaten hören Sie die folgenden Hinweise.
Schreiben Sie den passenden Buchstaben in den richtigen Kästchen.
Sie brauchen nicht alle Kästchen.

(You are in the tourist office. You have a town plan and want to find out how to get to certain important places. From a machine you hear the following directions. Write the correct letter in the appropriate box. You do not need all the boxes.)

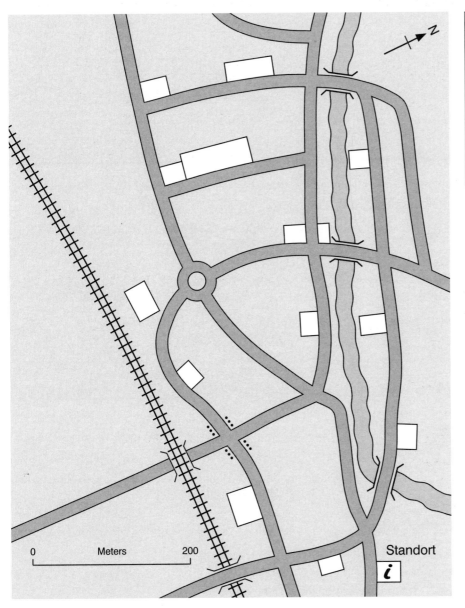

| | |
|---|---|
| Andreaskirche | A |
| Bahnhof | B |
| Einkaufszentrum | E |
| Fernsehturm | F |
| Information | I |
| Kunstmuseum | K |
| Malteserkrankenhaus | M |
| Rathaus | R |
| Stadion | S |
| Theater | T |

*You will find the transcript, with answers and examiner's comments, on page 192.*

F H SPEAKING

**2** First, look at the situation below and think what you might say. Then find Chapter 9 – Exam Practice Speaking on the CD (Track 18) and listen to a candidate doing the role-play with her teacher.

Helfen Sie einem Passanten, der das Kunstmuseum besuchen möchte. Der Passant hat einen Stadtplan und einen Busfahrplan. Es ist 14.50 Uhr.

*You will find the transcript and examiner's comments on page 193.*

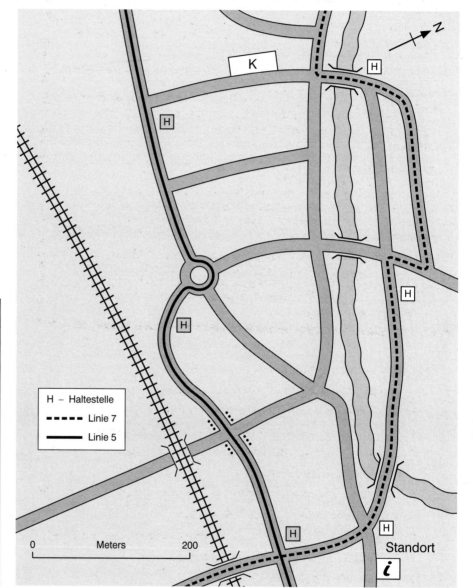

| FAHRPLAN |
| --- |
| Linie 5 |
| 07.00 |
| .15 |
| .30 |
| .45 |
| 08.00 |
| dann alle 15 Minuten bis |
| 22. 30 |
| Linie 7 |
| 06.10 |
| 06.30 |
| 06.50 |
| 07.10 |
| 07.30 |
| dann alle 20 Minuten bis |
| 23.30 |

H – Haltestelle
----- Linie 7
––––– Linie 5

0    Meters    200

Standort
*i*

H WRITING

**3** Write the report in German, then compare your answer with the sample on page 193.

Sie haben einen Verkehrsunfall gesehen. Sie schreiben einen Bericht für die Polizei. Sie sollten folgende Details erwähnen:

- Das Wetter
- Welche Personen und welche Fahrzeuge vom Unfall betroffen wurden
- Die Verletzungen
- Ihre Reaktion auf den Unfall

Schreiben Sie ungefähr 150 Wörter.

*You will find the sample answer and examiner's comments on page 193.*

**4** Read the passage, then answer the questions below.

### Die Reise nach Düsseldorf

Die Schüler haben sich um 9 Uhr am Bahnhof in Reading getroffen, und mußten noch dreißig Minuten auf den Zug warten. Von Paddington sind sie mit der U-Bahn gefahren, was mit ihrem ganzen Gepäck gar nicht so einfach war. Aber als sie endlich in Victoria ankamen, mußten sie sich beeilen, denn der Zug nach Dover stand schon abfahrtbereit.

Die Fähre nach Ostende brauchte über vier Stunden, aber das war ihnen egal, denn an Bord gab es viel zu tun: Spielautomaten, Filme, oder einfach aufs Deck gehen, denn es war für viele von ihnen etwas Neues, mit einem so großen Schiff zu fahren. Das Wetter war herrlich – für selbst Mai ungewöhnlich warm.

Von Ostende aus hatten sie Reservierungen im Zug, aber man brauchte sie eigentlich nicht, denn in den meisten Wagen waren nicht viele Reisende. Sie unterhielten sich mit Kartenspielen und Kreuzworträtseln, und aßen ihre Butterbrote. Die Zeit verging schnell. Sie mußten noch einmal in Köln umsteigen, und eine halbe Stunde später kamen sie schon in Düsseldorf an.

Auf dem Bahnsteig warteten die Partner mit ihren Eltern, und sie grüßten sich alle. Peter freute sich schon darauf, ins Bett gehen zu dürfen, denn die Fahrt war doch ziemlich lang gewesen, aber seine Gastfamilie bestand darauf, ihm noch einiges zu essen anzubieten.

Kreuzen Sie die richtige Kästchen an!

| | richtig | falsch | nicht im Text |
|---|---|---|---|
| 1 Der Zug von Reading fuhr um halb zehn ab. | | | |
| 2 Die Fahrt mit der U-Bahn war schwierig. | | | |
| 3 In Victoria brauchte man gar nicht auf den Zug warten. | | | |
| 4 Die Schüler fanden die Überfahrt ziemlich langweilig. | | | |
| 5 Keiner der Schüler war seekrank. | | | |
| 6 Keiner der Schüler war jemals mit einem so großen Schiff gefahren. | | | |
| 7 Man erwartete sehr warmes Wetter im Mai. | | | |
| 8 Es gab keine direkte Verbindung von Ostende nach Düsseldorf. | | | |
| 9 Der Zug von Ostende war überfüllt. | | | |
| 10 Die Butterbrote schmeckten ihnen gut. | | | |
| 11 In Düsseldorf wollte Peter sofort schlafen gehen. | | | |

*You will find the answers and examiner's comments on on page 194.*

## WHAT YOU NEED TO KNOW

|  |  |
|---|---|
| Ich arbeite als *Verkäufer(in) im Supermarkt. | I work as an assistant in the supermarket. |
| Meine Schwester ist *Staatsbeamtin. | My sister is a civil servant. |
| Meine Mutter arbeitet als *Busfahrerin. | My mother works as a bus driver. |
| Mein Vater hat eine Stelle als *Ingenieur. | My father has a job as an engineer. |
| Meine Mutter ist *Ärztin von Beruf. (by profession) | My mother is a doctor by profession. |

*Remember, you do not need the indefinite article 'ein/eine' before the job.

## BERUFE

| | | | |
|---|---|---|---|
| Angestellte(r) | employee | Apotheker | chemist |
| Bauarbeiter | builder | Bauer | farmer |
| Drogist | chemist | Elektriker | electrician |
| Fahrer | driver | Feuerwehrmann | fireman |
| Krankenpfleger | male nurse | Kaufmann | salesman |
| Schaffner | (bus) conductor | Soldat | soldier |
| Tierarzt | vet | Verkäufer | shop assistant |
| Zahnarzt | dentist | | |

| | | | |
|---|---|---|---|
| Arbeiter | manual worker | | |
| Direktor | director | | |
| Fabrikarbeiter | factory worker | | |
| Geschäftsmann (frau) | business(wo)man | | |
| Matrose | sailor | | |
| Schauspieler | actor | | |
| Zimmermädchen | chamber maid | | |

**Note:** Job names usually form their feminine by adding *-in*.

Arzt

Briefträger

Bäcker

Fleischer/Metzger

Lastwagenfahrer

Mechaniker

Sekretär

Friseur

Taxifahrer

Lehrer

Musiker

Polizist

Koch

Krankenschwester

Kellner

### QUESTIONS/PROMPTS

Was macht deine Mutter/dein Vater?

Hast du einen Job?

Arbeitest du am Wochenende?

Hast du ein Arbeitspraktikum gemacht?

|  |  |
|---|---|
| Meine Schwester/Mein Bruder arbeitet ... | My sister/brother works ... |
| im Betrieb | in a firm/company |
| im Büro | in an office |
| in einer Firma | in a company |
| im Labor | in a laboratory |
| in der Industrie | in industry |
| bei der Bahn | on the railways |
| mit Computern | with computers |
| selbständig | is self-employed |
| Meine Mutter ist ... | My mother is ... |
| arbeitslos | unemployed |
| berufstätig | employed, i.e. my mother works |
| Chef von ... | boss of ... |
| angestellt bei ... | employed at ... |

Ich möchte gern ... werden,
weil das Gehalt/der Lohn/der Stundenlohn so gut ist.
weil ich gern mit Leuten arbeite.
weil ich Routine mag.
weil ich selbständig arbeiten möchte.

weil ich neue Leute kennenlernen möchte.

Ich habe ein Arbeitspraktikum bei einem Tierarzt gemacht.
in einer Werkstatt
in einem Büro
Es hat mir dort sehr gut gefallen, ... }
Ich fand es ganz toll, ...
weil ich gern mit Tieren arbeiten möchte.
weil ich Dinge gern repariere.
weil ich gern am Computer arbeite.

I would like to become a ...,
because the salary/the wage/the hourly rate is so good
because I like working with people.
because I like routine.
because I would like to be self-employed.

because I would like to meet new people.

I did work experience at a vet's.

in a workshop
in an office

I really enjoyed it ...

because I would like to work with animals.
because I like repairing things.
because I like working on a computer.

*Ich trage Zeitungen aus.*

# Check yourself

## QUESTIONS

**Q1** *How would you say in German?*
*(Use different structures for a–c.)*

a) My father is a mechanic.
b) My brother works as a nurse.
c) My uncle works at Waitrose.
d) My cousin (feminine) is a lorry driver.
e) Our neighbour works for herself.

**Q2** *Which is the odd-one-out?*

a) Metzger  Bäcker  Bauer  Friseur
b) Lehrerin  Kindergärtnerin  Schulleiterin  Verkäuferin
c) Mechaniker  Elektriker  Bauarbeiter  Architekt
d) Kinderarzt  Arzt  Tierarzt  Zahnarzt
e) Schauspieler  Fußballspieler  Tänzer  Sänger

**REMEMBER! Cover the answers if you want to.**

## ANSWERS

**A1**
a) Mein Vater ist Mechaniker (von Beruf).
b) Mein Bruder arbeitet als Krankenpfleger.
c) Mein Onkel arbeitet bei Waitrose.
d) Meine Kusine ist Lastwagenfahrerin.
e) Unsere Nachbarin arbeitet selbständig.

**A2**
a) Bauer
b) Verkäuferin
c) Architekt
d) Tierarzt
e) Fußballspieler

## TUTORIAL

**T1** *Make sure you know the jobs of people in your family. Don't leave it until the day of the exam. If you are unsure, or the job is too complicated to describe in a single word, then you must choose between saying what he/she does in general terms (e.g. Er/Sie macht irgendetwas mit Computern.) or saying where he/she works (e.g. Er/Sie arbeitet im Büro/in einer Fabrik/in einem Geschäft.). It would be too embarrassing to say Ich weiß nicht!*

**T2**
a) *The others work in a shop.*
b) *The others work in education.*
c) *The others are manual occupations.*
d) *The others work with people.*
e) *The others work as creative artists.*

## GOING FURTHER

| | |
|---|---|
| Ich gehe/Ich möchte ... gehen, | I am going/I would like to go ... |
| auf die Berufsschule | to further education college |
| auf die Fachhochschule | to (a technical) university |
| auf die Universität | to (an academic) university |
| um Kunst/Mathe/Betriebswirtschaft zu studieren. | (in order) to study art/maths/ business management. |
| um einen Kurs/eine Ausbildung in Elektronik zu machen. | (in order) to do a course on electronics. |
| Ich mache eine Lehre bei .... | I am doing an apprenticeship at .... |
| Ich habe eine Lehrstelle bei .... | I have a traineeship with .... |
| Ich bleibe hier an der Schule/in der Oberstufe. | I'm staying on at school/in the sixth form. |
| Zunächst mache ich meine A-levels in Deutsch, Englisch und Geschichte. | First of all I'm going to do my A-levels in German, English and history. |
| In zwei Jahren weiß ich besser Bescheid, was ich studieren möchte. | I'll know better in two years, what I would like to study. |

## HOW THE GRAMMAR WORKS

### THE FUTURE TENSE

Just as in English, you can use the present tense to suggest future intent:

| | |
|---|---|
| *Ich gehe nächstes Jahr auf die Berufsschule.* | – I am going to college next year. |
| *Ich mache im September eine kaufmännische Ausbildung.* | – I am taking a business course in September. |
| *Ich arbeite ab ersten August in der Bank.* | – I am working in the bank from August 1st. |

However, you should also know how to form the future tense using the present tense of *werden* with an infinitive, in case you are asked a question in that way during your Speaking Test. So, if you are asked:

> *Was wirst du/werden Sie nächstes Jahr machen?*

you could answer:

> *Ich werde nächstes Jahr auf die Berufsschule gehen.*
> *Ich werde im September eine kaufmännische Ausbildung machen.*
> *Ich werde ab ersten August in der Bank arbeiten.*

### USING THE INFINITIVE

You should be able to use the infinitive in the following ways:

**1 After the six modal verbs and *lassen*:**

| | |
|---|---|
| *Darf ich heute abend ins Kino gehen?* | (*dürfen*) |
| May I go to the cinema tonight? | |
| *Ich kann sehr gut schwimmen.* | (*können*) |
| I can swim very well. | |
| *Magst du gern reiten?* | (*mögen*)* |
| Do you like riding? | |
| *Wir müssen unsere Hausaufgaben machen.* | (*müssen*) |
| We must do our homework. | |
| *Ihr sollt bei diesem Wetter nicht in den Park gehen.* | (*sollen*) |
| You shouldn't go to the park in this weather. | |

*Wir wollen im Sommer nach Schottland fahren.*      (*wollen*)
     We want (intend) to go to Scotland this summer.
*Ich lasse mir heute die Haare schneiden.*      (*lassen*)
     I'm having my hair cut today.

*Most commonly, of course, after *Ich möchte* (I would like).

**2 After certain other verbs with *zu*:**
     *Ich hoffe, am Wochenende Fußball zu spielen.*      (*hoffen*)
         I hope to play football at the weekend.
     *Ich brauche es heute nicht zu machen.*      (*brauchen*)
         I don't need to do it today.

**3 After *um ... zu*:**
     *Ich gehe in die Stadt, um einen neuen Schreibblock zu kaufen.*
         I'm going into town to buy a new writing pad.

**4 After *gehen*:**
     *Ich gehe heute in der Stadt einkaufen.*
         I'm going shopping in town today.
     *Wir gehen morgen schwimmen.*
         We're going swimming tomorrow.

## INTERROGATIVES

You should know at least two of the following ways of forming questions:

**1 By inverting (turning round) subject and verb:**
     *Gehst du heute zur Schule?*

**2 By adding *ja?*, *nicht?*, *oder?* or *nicht wahr?* to a statement:**
     *Das ist dein Buch, nicht wahr?*
     *Mutti kommt mit, oder?*

**3 By introducing the question with an interrogative word:**
     *Was machst du?*
     *Wann kommt sie nach Hause?*
     *Wie machen sie das?*
     *Was für Bücher liest du gern?*
     *Wieviele Leute kommen heute abend?*
     *Warum darfst du nicht kommen?*

## NEGATIVES

| | |
|---|---|
| *kein* | no, not one |
| *nichts* | nothing |
| *gar nicht/überhaupt nicht* | not at all |
| *nie/niemals* | never |
| *niemand* | no-one, nobody |
| *nirgends/nirgendwo* | nowhere |

     *Ich habe kein Geld bei mir.* – I have no money on me today.
     *Wir haben ihn nirgends gesehen.* – We haven't seen him anywhere.
     *Ich mag Pizza überhaupt nicht.* – I don't like pizza at all.
     *Wir haben niemanden getroffen.* – We didn't meet anyone.

Note that *jemand* and *niemand* add *-en* in the accusative and dative.

# Check yourself

## QUESTIONS

**Q1** *Translate the following into English.*

a) Mein Bruder studiert Medizin an der Universität.
b) Unser Nachbarssohn macht eine Lehre bei Siemens.
c) Wann mußt du in der Berufschule anfangen?
d) Möchten Sie nicht lieber Tierarzt werden?
e) Wieviel wirst du als Lehrling verdienen?

**Q2** *Complete the questions with the correct form of the modal verb shown in brackets.*

a) Warum ........................ ihr mir nicht helfen? (können)
   Why can't you help me?
b) Um wieviel Uhr ........................ du sie treffen? (müssen)
   What time must you meet them?
c) Wieviel ........................ ich mitnehmen? (dürfen)
   How many/much may I take?
d) Wann ........................ man in Düsseldorf ankommen? (sollen)
   When are we supposed to arrive in Düsseldorf?
e) ........................ ihr nicht mitkommen? (wollen)
   Don't you want to come along?

---

### REMEMBER! Cover the answers if you want to.

---

## ANSWERS

**A1**
a) My brother is studying medicine at university.
b) Our neighbour's son is doing an apprenticeship at Siemens.
c) When do you have to start at college?
d) Wouldn't you prefer to become a vet?
e) How much will you earn as an apprentice?

**A2**
a) könnt
b) mußt
c) darf
d) soll
e) Wollt

## TUTORIAL

**T1**
a) Note that the definite article is needed *before* Universität.
b) Bei is usually translated as 'at' or 'with'.
c) Note that the definite article is needed *before* Berufsschule.
d) Remember how to use lieber, the comparative of gern, to express preference.
e) Remember: the indefinite article is omitted before the name of a job in German.

**T2** Modal auxiliary verbs are extremely common. They are easily learnt from the table in the Grammar section in Chapter 18 (see page 161) and will bring you a great deal of credit in both your Speaking and Writing Tests.

# EXAM PRACTICE

**1** Find Chapter 10 – Exam Practice Listening on the CD and listen to the German twice (Track 19).

LISTENING    H

Im Radio hören Sie eine Quizshow „Was bin ich von Beruf?".

Kreuzen Sie die richtige Kästchen an!

*You will find the transcript and answers, with examiner's comments, on page 194.*

1  Wie findet Herr Löwenzahn seine Arbeit?

immer langweilig ☐

manchmal langweilig ☐

immer interessant ☐

2  Er mag

seine tägliche Routine ☐

keine tägliche Routine ☐

nicht jeden Tag arbeiten ☐

3  In seinem Team

machen alle die gleiche Arbeit ☐

machen alle seine Arbeit ☐

macht keiner seine Arbeit ☐

4  Seine Arbeit ist

meist draußen ☐

oft draußen ☐

meist innen ☐

5  Von Beruf ist Herr Löwenzahn

Praktischer Arzt ☐

Zahnarzt ☐

Tierarzt ☐

6  Er arbeitet lieber

mit Pferden als mit Mäusen ☐

mit Mäusern als mit Pinguinen ☐

mit Pinguinen als mit Ratten ☐

**H SPEAKING**

**2** First look at the situation outlined below and think what you would say. Then find Chapter 10 – Exam Practice Speaking on the CD (Track 20) and listen to how a good candidate might tackle this role-play.

*You will find the transcript and examiner's comments on page 195.*

### Ein Interview

Sie sind in Deutschland und suchen eine Arbeit in einem Supermarkt. Jetzt sind Sie zum Interview eingeladen. Erzählen Sie weiter.

*Wann aufgestanden?*

*Was angezogen?*

*Glücklich?*

*Nervös?*

*Was machen? Mit wem arbeiten?*

*Arbeit gekriegt? Anfang wann?*

*Was gefragt?*

**3** Was bin ich von Beruf?

1. Ich arbeite in einer Werkstatt.

2. Ich schreibe, was jeder lesen kann.

3. Ohne mich kriegt man sehr lange Haare.

4. Ich bringe die guten und auch die schlechten Nachrichten ins Haus.

6. Ich sitze den ganzen Tag an einer Maschine.

5. Ich fahre oder laufe in der Stadt herum.

7. Ich stehe um 3 Uhr auf. Wo ich arbeite, ist es sehr heiß.

8. Jeder möchte von mir etwas bekommen.

Für jede Person schreiben Sie den Buchstaben, der am besten paßt.
Sie brauchen nicht alle Buchstaben.

| | |
|---|---|
| 1 | |
| 2 | |
| 3 | |
| 4 | |
| 5 | |
| 6 | |
| 7 | |
| 8 | |

| | | | |
|---|---|---|---|
| A | Bäcker | G | Ingenieur |
| B | Friseur | H | Mechaniker |
| C | Briefträger | I | Lehrer |
| D | Sekretärin | J | Verkäuferin |
| E | Koch | K | Journalistin |
| F | Elektriker | L | Polizist |

*You will find the answers and examiner's comments on page 195.*

**F** **H** **WRITING**

**4** Sie suchen Arbeit in Deutschland, und schreiben eine Bewerbung an einen Supermarkt.
Schreiben Sie nicht mehr als 100 Wörter.

(You are looking for work in Germany and write an application to a supermarket.
Write no more than 100 words.)

## Sample Student's Answer

### EXAMINER'S COMMENTS

- This is a standard letter of introduction, containing some personal details and anything else which seems appropriate to the job.

- You can mention your hobbies and any work you have done. In effect the letter should be similar to the one you send to your Work Experience employer in Year 10, but you have a limit of only 100 words so you need to be quite brief.

- The letter contains past and present tenses and a reference to the future in bevor ich weiterstudiere.

- The third and fourth paragraphs both contain seit plus present tense, correctly used. This is worthy of credit, because it is not the same usage as in English.

Bristol, den 11. März

Sehr geehrte Herren!

Hiermit möchte ich mich bei Ihnen um eine Stelle in Ihrem Supermarkt bewerben.

Ich heiße David Evans und komme aus Bristol. Ich bin am 14. Januar 1982 geboren und bin also 16 Jahre alt. Ich bin Schulabgänger und möchte ein Jahr in Deutschland verbringen, um meine Deutschkenntnisse zu erweitern, bevor ich weiterstudiere.

Ich arbeite seit zwei Jahren jeden Samstag in einem Supermarkt in einem Einkaufszentrum in Bristol, und ich habe mein Arbeitspraktikum auch dort gemacht.

Ich lerne seit fünf Jahren Deutsch und habe gerade meine GCSE Prüfungen gemacht. Ich lege mein letztes Schulzeugnis, ein Empfehlungsschreiben von meiner Rektorin und auch ein Bild von mir bei.

Hochachtungsvoll,

David Evans

## WHAT YOU NEED TO KNOW

**You should be able to take or leave messages at your place of work.**

| | |
|---|---|
| Hier Schmidt. | This is Mr/Ms Smith speaking. |
| Darf ich ihn/sie sprechen, bitte? | May I speak to him/her, please? |
| Es tut mir leid. | I'm sorry. |
| Frau Bergemann ist im Moment geschäftlich unterwegs. | Mrs Bergemann is out on business at present. |
| Herr Kolbitz ist nicht in Büro/außer Haus. | Mr Kolbitz is not in the office. |
| Kann/Darf ich ihm/ihr etwas ausrichten? | Can/May I take/give him/her a message? |
| Könnten Sie ihm/ihr bitte etwas ausrichten? | Could you please give him/her a message? |
| Ich schreibe ihm/ihr einen Zettel. | I'll write him/her a note. |
| Ich lege ihm/ihr einen Zettel auf den Tisch. | I'll put a note on his/her desk. |
| Ich sage/gebe ihm/ihr Bescheid. | I'll give him/her the message. |
| Er ist jeden Moment wieder da. | He will be back any minute. |
| Sie ist in einer halben Stunde wieder da. | She will be back in half an hour. |

**You should be able to understand simple instructions in the workplace.**

| | |
|---|---|
| Lesen Sie die Betriebsanleitung. | Read instructions for use. |
| einschalten, ausschalten | switch on, switch off |
| der Computer/PC/Laptop | computer/PC/lap-top |
| betriebsbereit | 'ready' |
| drucken/der Drucker (–) | to print/printer |
| das Memory/der Speicher | memory |
| der Netzanschluß (schlüsse) | mains (power) connection |
| der Rechner | calculator |
| die Software | software |
| speichern | to save |
| die Tastatur (en) | keyboard |
| weiter | continue |
| das Zeichen (–) | sign, character |
| der Anrufbeantworter (–) | answering machine |
| das Handy (s) | mobile phone |

**You should be able to make arrangements to be contacted, or have information sent by phone, fax or e-mail.**

| | |
|---|---|
| Ich bin unter dieser Nummer/auf meinem Handy zu erreichen. | I can be contacted on this number/on my mobile. |
| Rufen Sie mich bitte an! | Please call/telephone me. |
| Bitte schicken Sie ein Fax. | Please send a fax. |
| Haben Sie ein Modem? | Have you a modem? |

**You should be able to write a letter and fill out simple forms relating to a job application.**

| | |
|---|---|
| Ich bin am 14. Januar 1982 in Manchester geboren. | I was born in Manchester on the 14th January 1982. |
| Ich lerne Deutsch seit fünf Jahren. | I've been learning German for five years. |
| Ich habe Ihre Anzeige in der Tageszeitung gelesen. | I saw your advertisement in the newspaper. |
| Ich könnte zum 1. September anfangen. | I'm available to start work from 1st September. |
| Könnten Sie mir bitte weitere Details zuschicken? | Please would you send me further information about the job? |

## ICH SUCHE EINE STELLE!

| | |
|---|---|
| Betrifft | concerning (at the top of a letter/fax etc.) |
| das Angebot (e) | offer |
| die Bewerbung | application |
| sich bewerben | apply |
| die Staatsangehörigkeit | nationality |
| der Familienstand | marital status |
| ledig/verheiratet/geschieden | single/married/divorced |
| das Geburtsdatum/geboren am … | date of birth … |
| ich füge bei/ich lege bei | I enclose |
| das Schulzeugnis | school report |
| der Lebenslauf | curriculum vitae (cv) |
| der Empfehlungsbrief (e) | reference |
| Ich interessiere mich für… | I'm interested in … |

# Check yourself

## QUESTIONS

**Q1**   *How would you say in German?*

a) May I speak to Rudi, please?
b) Can you give Mr Braun a message, please?
c) I'll tell her immediately.
d) Would you prefer to send a fax?
e) She'll be back (in the office) around 2.

**Q2**   *Complete the form below*.

| **Bitte in Druckschrift schreiben** |
|---|
| Familienname ................................. |
| Vorname ..................................... |
| geboren am .................................. |
| Familienstand ledig / verheiratet / geschieden (bitte durchstreichen) |
| Staatsangehörigkeit ........................ |
| Adresse |
| Straße ...................................... |
| Ort ......................................... |
| PLZ ......................................... |
| Telefonisch zu erreichen? ja/nein |
| tagsüber .................................... |
| abends ...................................... |

**REMEMBER! Cover the answers if you want to.**

## ANSWERS

**A1**
a) Darf ich bitte Rudi sprechen?
b) Können Sie Herrn Braun etwas ausrichten, bitte?
c) Ich sage ihr sofort Bescheid.
d) Möchten Sie lieber ein Fax schicken?
e) Sie ist so gegen 2 wieder da.

**A2**

| | |
|---|---|
| Familienname | JENNINGS |
| Vorname | MARY |
| geboren am | 6 JUNI 1982 |
| Staatsangehörigkeit | BRITISCH |
| Straße | HONEY END LANE |
| Ort | READING |
| PLZ | RG3 4EL |
| Telefonisch zu erreichen? | ja/~~nein~~ |
| tagsüber | 0118 959011 |
| abends | 0118 9110959 |

## TUTORIAL

**T1**
a) Notice that you do not need to put **mit** Rudi.
b) *Herr adds an -n in all cases but the nominative.*
c) *Bescheid has no obvious translation here.*
d) *Remember how to use* gern, lieber *and* am liebsten *to add the meanings of 'like', 'prefer' and 'like most of all'.*
e) *So gegen gives a good approximation of time.*

**T2**
*The completion of your personal details is easy, but the official language of forms can sometimes be confusing. Although you will encounter this exercise as a writing test, it is much more a test of reading, and you need to have learned the specific vocabulary required on forms such as this one.*

*Note that in Druckschrift schreiben means you should write in capital letters.*

# GOING FURTHER

**You should be able to act as an interpreter at work.**

| | |
|---|---|
| Frau White sagt, daß sie erst morgen kommen kann. | Mrs White says, that she can't come until tomorrow. |
| Sie meint, daß der Wagen nicht in Ordnung ist. | She says that the car is not right. |
| Sie glaubt, daß die Bremsen nicht richtig funktionieren. | She believes that the brakes are not working properly. |
| Sie hofft, daß wir den Wagen morgen reparieren können. | She hopes that we can repair the car tomorrow. |
| Sie fragt, wann sie kommen soll. | She's asking when she should come. |
| Sie fragt, ob wir ihr das Auto zurückbringen können. | She is asking whether we can bring the car back to her. |

**Note:** Don't forget to change the word order after *daß* (see Chapter 6).

# HOW THE GRAMMAR WORKS

## IMPERATIVES

The imperative of a verb tells you to do something or, in many cases, **not** to do it. You need to recognise certain conventions when giving other people orders, or making polite requests.

In a formal situation, use the *Sie* form of the verb as follows:

*Nehmen Sie Platz!* – Take a seat/Sit down.
*Kommen Sie bitte mit!* – Please come with me.
*Bitte unterschreiben Sie hier!* – Please sign here.

Don't be put off by the exclamation mark. It is simply a convention – it doesn't mean that someone is shouting at you.

In informal situations, such as with friends and family, use the familiar form of the imperative. This is adapted from the *du* form of the verb, by taking off the -*st* ending and adding either an -*e* or an apostrophe:

*Komm' mit!* – Come along with me.
*Bringe deine Tasche mit!* – Bring your bag with you.
*Setz' dich!* – Sit down.

If you are talking to more than one friend or member of the family, you use the *ihr* form of the imperative, as follows:

*Kommt mit!* – Come along with me.
*Bringt eure Taschen mit!* – Bring your bags with you.
*Setzt euch!* – Sit down.

You should also recognise the most obvious public notices. In German these simply use the infinitive form:

*Bitte Hände waschen.* – Wash your hands, please. (in a public toilet)
*Nicht hinauslehnen.* – Don't lean out. (of the window on trains)
*Bitte anklopfen.* – Please knock.

# *Check yourself*

## QUESTIONS

**Q1** **Your teacher is talking to you individually. What would she say if she wanted you to:**

a) show her your homework?
b) sit down?

**What would she say to the class if she wanted you to:**

(c) get your books out?
(d) write the date?
(e) carry on?

**Q2** **Your friend, Tom, phones and asks you to pass on the following message to his penfriend's mother. What do you say to her?**

Tom: Tell Frau Marx I can't come home till 8 o'clock. The next bus will arrive at 7.50. Ask her what time the supermarket shuts, and if I should buy anything for her. Tell her I'm very tired.

### REMEMBER! Cover the answers if you want to.

## ANSWERS

**A1**
a) Zeig' mir deine Hausaufgabe!
b) Setz' dich hin!
c) Holt eure Bücher 'raus!
d) Schreibt das Datum!
e) Macht weiter!

**A2** Tom sagt, er kann erst um 8 Uhr nach Hause kommen. Er sagt, daß der nächste Bus um 7.50 Uhr ankommt. Er fragt, wann der Supermarkt schließt, und ob er etwas kaufen soll. Er sagt, daß er sehr müde ist.

## TUTORIAL

**T1** *Now you have practised the regular verbs, check the handful of irregular ones.*

**T2** *This answer uses indirect speech, which in certain tenses can require you to use the subjunctive. This construction is best avoided at this level. Look in the Grammar Summary (page 160) for the few subjunctive uses which you need to recognise.*

# EXAM PRACTICE

**1** Find Chapter 11 – Exam Practice Listening on the CD. Listen to the German twice (Track 21), then answer the questions below.

LISTENING **F H**

Wo sind Sie? Kreuzen Sie die richtige Kästchen an!

**1** a) Am Bahnhof ☐

b) Am Flughafen ☐

c) An einer Bushaltestelle ☐

*You will find the transcript and answers, with examiner's comments, on page 196.*

**2** a) Im Kino ☐

b) In einer Bibliothek ☐

c) In der Praxis ☐

**3** a) Im Sportverein ☐

b) In der Schule ☐

c) In einer Buchhandlung ☐

**4** a) Im Theater ☐

b) Auf dem Campingplatz ☐

c) Auf der Straße ☐

**5** a) Im Supermarkt ☐

b) Im Restaurant ☐

c) Im Warenhaus ☐

[5 marks]

**2** Look at the situation below and think what you might say. Then find Chapter 11 – Exam Practice Speaking on the CD (Track 22) and listen to how a candidate might tackle this role-play.

SPEAKING **F H**

Sie rufen bei einer deutschen Firma an und fragen nach einer Lehrstelle, die in der Zeitung ausgeschrieben ist.
(You telephone a German company and enquire about a traineeship which is advertised in the newspaper.)

*You will find the transcript and examiner's comments on page 196.*

1

2

3

4

5

**H READING**

**3** You read the following humerous notice on the wall in the office where you are working. Your friend does not understand German as well as you, so you tell him some of the funny bits.

## Tips für Anfänger (Die Zehn Gebote!)

**1** Den Chef ist vormittags vor zehn Uhr nicht zu stören!
Zeitunglesen ist wichtiger als die Post öffnen.

**2** Wenn der Chef glücklich ist, müssen wir auch alle glücklich sein.

**3** Geben Sie dem Chef keine schlechte Nachricht in die Hand.
Legen Sie ihm solche Sachen lieber auf den Schreibtisch, bevor Sie um fünf Uhr nach Hause gehen. Er geht immer schon um vier nach Hause.

**4** Vergessen Sie nie den Geburtstag von Ihrem Chef.
Als Geschenk ist immer eine dicke Zigarre zu empfehlen!
Und ein Stück Schokoladenkuchen zur Kaffeestunde.

**5** Noch wichtiger. Vergessen Sie nie den Geburtstag der Ehefrau des Chefs, denn er vergißt ihn immer. Er wird Ihnen ewig dankbar sein. (‚Ewig' dauert übrigens etwa eine Woche!)

**6** Wenn der Chef ‚außer Haus' ist oder ‚geschäftlich zu tun' hat, kann man ihn nicht erreichen. Nur im schlimmsten Notfall, z.B. wenn das Gebäude in Flammen steht, soll man den Golfklub anrufen.

**7** Die Kaffeepause darf grundsätzlich nicht länger als fünfzehn Minuten dauern - wenn der Chef da ist!

**8** Der Chef hat weder Zeit zum Fotokopieren, noch zum FAX-Schicken, noch zur sonstigen technologischen Arbeit.

**9** Der Chef hat über alles zu entscheiden. Auch über unsere Gehälter.

**10** Nicht vergessen: Der Chef hat immer recht.
(Auch wenn es allen anderen so scheint, daß er Unrecht hat!)

Answer the following questions IN ENGLISH.

1 What does the boss apparently like to do first thing every morning?
................................................................................................ [1]

2 How are you supposed to deal with bad news?
................................................................................................ [1]

3 What is even more important than remembering the boss's birthday?
................................................................................................ [1]

4 What does the boss tell his colleagues at work when is playing golf?
................................................................................................ [1]

5 What suggests that the employees do not always work as hard as they should?
................................................................................................ [1]

6 What reason does the boss give for not getting involved with the modern technology of the office?
................................................................................................ [1]

7 Give ONE reason why an employee should not fall out with the boss.
................................................................................................ [1]

*You will find the answers and examiner's comments on page 197.*

**4** Schreiben Sie einen Brief an die Leitung einer Firma, in dem Sie um eine Stelle bitten, in der Sie Deutsch sprechen müssen.

(Write a letter to the management of a company, asking for a job in which you have to speak German.)

**WRITING** **H**

## Sample Student's Answer

Reading, den 14. Juni

Sehr geehrte Herr Krause!

Hiermit möchte ich mich bei Ihnen um eine Stelle in Ihrem Verkaufsbüro bewerben.

Ich heiße Michelle, komme aus Schottland und wohne jetzt in Reading. Ich bin am 14. Januar 1982 geboren und bin also 16 Jahre alt. Ich bin Schulabgängerin und möchte eine Weile in Deutschland arbeiten, um meine Deutschkenntnisse zu erweitern.

Ich möchte später Fremdsprachen an der Universität studieren, wahrscheinlich Deutsch und Japanisch. Ich lerne seit sieben Jahren Französisch und will eine dritte Sprache dazulernen.

Ich arbeite seit zwei Jahren jeden Samstag auf dem Markt in der Stadtmitte. Die Arbeit ist zwar hart, aber ich komme mit den Leuten sehr gut aus, und es macht mir Spaß, etwas anderes zu machen, als für die Schule zu arbeiten.

Ich lerne seit fünf Jahren Deutsch und kann mich gut verständigen, aber ich möchte jetzt in einem modernen Büro arbeiten, wo ich meine Computerkenntnisse gebrauchen kann.

Ich lege mein letztes Schulzeugnis und einen Empfehlungsbrief von meiner Rektorin bei.

Mit bestem Dank im voraus für Ihre Bemühungen.

Michelle Dickinson

### EXAMINER'S COMMENTS

- A letter such as this will inevitably contain a certain amount of pre-learnt material. The trick is to adapt it to fit the requirements of the questions.

- Accuracy in the details about self, school, study and career intentions is essential. While you might be forgiven for making mistakes when attempting a difficult construction, it is the sign of a weak candidate to make errors when covering well-trodden ground such as this.

- Notice in particular the following excellent phrases:
  **Paragraph 2:** Ich möchte ... arbeiten, um ... zu
  **Paragraph 3:** The use of dazulernen, meaning 'in addition to the other two languages'.
  **Paragraph 5:** Ich kann mich gut verständigen, *which is highly appropriate here and makes a good lead-in to the next idea.*
  **Ending:** Mit bestem Dank ... *always strikes a positive note at the end of the letter.*

# CHAPTER 12

# AUSLAND UND TOURISMUS

FOREIGN COUNTRIES AND TOURISM

## WIE SIND SIE GEFAHREN?

mit der Fähre

mit dem Auto/Wagen

mit dem Reisebus

You should be able to talk about a wide range of experiences abroad, saying what you saw and did.

### Wie war die Reise?

| | |
|---|---|
| Wir sind geflogen. | We flew. |
| Der Flug nach Berlin dauerte anderthalb Stunden. | The flight to Berlin took one and a half hours. |
| Wir sind mit der Bahn gefahren. | We travelled by train. |
| Die Fahrt/die Reise dauerte sieben Stunden. | The journey took seven hours. |
| Die Überfahrt war sehr ruhig/stürmisch. | The ferry crossing was very calm/rough. |
| Wir mußten in Brüssel umsteigen. | We had to change trains in Brussels. |
| Wir sind um 7 Uhr morgens abgefahren. | We left at 7 in the morning. |
| Wir sind um 8 Uhr abends angekommen. | We arrived at 8 in the evening. |

### Auf dem Campingplatz

**At the campsite**

| | |
|---|---|
| Wir haben einen Zeltplatz gefunden. | We found a place for the tent/a 'pitch'. |
| die Anmeldung | reception/office |
| die Gebühr (en) | fees/charges |
| Wir haben das Zelt aufgebaut/aufgeschlagen. | We put up the tent. |
| Wir haben das Zelt abgebaut. | We took down the tent. |
| Ich habe die Klappstühle aus dem Auto genommen. | I got the folding chairs out of the car. |
| Ich habe den Klapptisch aufgestellt. | I put up the folding table. |

### In der Jugendherberge

**At the Youth Hostel**

| | |
|---|---|
| der Herbergsvater/ die Herbergsmutter | warden (male and female) |
| Die Herbergseltern waren sehr freundlich. | The wardens were very friendly. |
| Wir haben Schlafsäcke geliehen. | We hired sleeping bags. |
| Der Schlafraum (räume) war im ersten Stock. | The dormitory was on the first floor. |
| Es war verboten, nach 10 Uhr laute Musik zu spielen. | It was forbidden to play loud music after 10 o'clock. |
| Man hat uns erlaubt, den Hausschlüssel mitzunehmen. | We were allowed to take the door key with us. |

### Im Hotel

**At the hotel**

| | |
|---|---|
| Haben Sie ein Zimmer frei? | Do you have a room available? |
| Ich möchte ein Einzelzimmer, bitte. | I'd like a single room. |
| Wir bleiben drei Nächte. | We shall be staying three nights. |
| Um wieviel Uhr gibt es Frühstück/Abendessen? | What time is breakfast/dinner? |
| Wir haben uns gleich angemeldet. | We checked in straight away. |
| Wir hatten zwei Zimmer reserviert. | We had reserved two rooms. |
| Das Hotel war leider voll. | The hotel was unfortunately full. |
| Die Empfangsdame war sehr hilfsbereit. | The receptionist was very helpful. |
| Sie hat uns ein anderes Hotel empfohlen. | She recommended us another hotel. |
| Wir mußten ein Anmeldungsformular ausfüllen. | We had to complete a form at the reception. |
| Unser Aufenthalt in Bonn dauerte fünf Tage. | Our stay in Bonn lasted five days. |

| | |
|---|---|
| Von unserem Fenster haben wir eine herrliche Aussicht über den Rhein gehabt. | From our window we had a superb view over the Rhine. |
| Der Aufenthaltsraum war im Erdgeschoß. | The lounge was on the ground floor. |
| Es gab ab 7 Uhr Frühstück. | Breakfast was served from 7 o'clock onwards. |
| Wir haben Halbpension/Vollpension gehabt. | We had half board/full board. |
| Der Preis war inklusiv. | The price was inclusive. |
| Alle Zimmer hatten fließendes Wasser. | All rooms had running water. |
| Wir haben uns über den Lärm beschwert/beklagt. | We complained about the noise. |

**You should be able to ask for details about a town or region you plan to visit, and give similar details about your own area to a prospective tourist.**

| Im Verkehrsamt | In the tourist office |
|---|---|
| Was gibt es hier in der Nähe zu sehen und zu tun? | What is there to see and do in the area? |
| Was sollte man hier sehen? | What ought we to see here? |
| Haben Sie einen Stadtplan, bitte? | Have you a street map, please? |
| Können Sie ein preiswertes Hotel in der Nähe/Stadt empfehlen? | Can you recommend a reasonable (cheap) hotel in the area/town? |
| Haben Sie ein Hotelverzeichnis? | Have you a list of hotels, please? |
| Kann man irgendwo Fahrräder leihen? | Can you hire bikes somewhere? |
| Kann man eine Stadtrundfahrt/einen Stadtrundgang machen? | Can we do a guided tour of the town? (in a bus or on foot) |
| Ich hätte/möchte gern einen Busfahrplan? | I would like a bus timetable please. |
| Wir möchten gern das Schloß besichtigen. | We would like to visit the castle/palace. |
| Wie kommt man am besten dahin? | What is the best way to get there? |

**IM HOTEL**

ein Einzelzimmer

ein Doppelzimmer

mit Dusche

mit Bad

**QUESTIONS/PROMPTS**

Wo warst du in den Ferien?

Was hast du in den Ferien gemacht?

Hast du Ausflüge gemacht?

# *Check yourself*

## QUESTIONS

**Q1** *Complete the following passage.*

Wir s........ letzt..... Sommer mit der B........
nach Düsseldorf gef................ . Die Reise
da............... zehn St............... .

Mein Freund und ich ha........
Schl.................. reserv................, weil wir
über Nacht gef............. s........ . Wir
m............. in Lille um............... . Wir s........
gegen Mittag in Düsseldorf
an....................... .

**Q3** *Put these sentences into the correct order to make a sensible account.*

Wir haben gegen sieben Uhr in der Pizzeria zu Abend gegessen.
Wir sind auf unsere Zimmer gegangen.
Ich bin ins Verkehrsamt gegangen.
Ich habe geduscht und mich umgezogen.
Wir sind zum Hotel gefahren und haben in der Tiefgarage geparkt.
Wir sind um vier Uhr nachmittags in Bonn angekommen.
Wir haben uns gleich angemeldet.
Man hat uns ein preiswertes Hotel empfohlen.

## ANSWERS

**A1**
Wir sind letzten Sommer mit der Bahn nach Düsseldorf gefahren. Die Reise dauerte zehn Stunden.

Mein Freund und ich haben Schlafplätze reserviert, weil wir über Nacht gefahren sind. Wir mußten in Lille umsteigen. Wir sind gegen Mittag in Düsseldorf angekommen.

**A2**
Wir sind um vier Uhr nachmittags in Bonn angekommen.
Ich bin ins Verkehrsamt gegangen.
Man hat uns ein preiswertes Hotel empfohlen.
Wir sind zum Hotel gefahren und haben in der Tiefgarage geparkt.
Wir haben uns gleich angemeldet.
Wir sind auf unsere Zimmer gegangen.
Ich habe geduscht und mich umgezogen.
Wir haben gegen sieben Uhr in der Pizzeria zu Abend gegessen.

## TUTORIAL

**T1**
*You should have been able to work out that you were travelling by rail, not by bus, because of the words* mit der...*, which needed to be followed by a feminine* Bahn *not a masculine* Bus*. You should not have been tempted to put* geflogen *for the same reason.*
*The use of the modal* mußten *relieves the monotony of the perfect tense construction in every sentence. You might try introducing* wir konnten (nicht) *or* wir wollten *into parts of your journey description.*

**T2**
*Learning a simple account like this, with very few adverbs or adjectives, is just the sort of preparation which can be very useful for your Higher Level writing. From here, you can progress rapidly to double the word count by adding subordinate clauses and phrases about time, weather and mood.*

## GOING FURTHER

**You should be able to discuss a part of a German-speaking country you know.**

| | |
|---|---|
| Düsseldorf ist eine reizende Stadt. | Düsseldorf is an attractive city. |
| Die Altstadt ist weltberühmt. | The old part of town is world famous. |
| Die Stadt hat eine große Messe und liegt am Rhein. | The town has a large trade fair and lies on the Rhine. |
| Vom Rheinturm hat man eine traumhafte Aussicht in alle Richtungen. | From the Rhine tower you have a magnificent view in all directions. |
| Es gibt das zauberhafte Schloß Benrath. | There is the wonderful Benrath Palace. |

**You should be able to compare features of the foreign country with your own area and to express opinions about what you saw and did.**

| | |
|---|---|
| Düsseldorf ist weitaus größer als Newtown. | Düsseldorf is considerably larger than Newtown. |
| viel schöner als | much more beautiful than |
| nachts lebendiger als | more lively at night than |
| ganz anders als | quite different from. |
| Düsseldorf hat mehr große Kaufhäuser als Newtown. | Düsseldorf has more large department stores than Newtown. |
| ein besseres Verkehrsnetz | a better public transport network |
| mehr und größere Museen | more and bigger museums |
| Ich fand die Altstadt ganz toll. | I found the old part of town great. |
| etwas komisch | somewhat strange |
| ganz lustig | quite funny |
| erstaunlich | astonishing |
| ein bißchen deprimierend | a little depressing |

| Die Sehenswürdigkeiten waren ... | The sights were ... |
|---|---|
| ... höchst interessant | ... extremely interesting |
| ... teurer als ich ewartet hatte | ... more expensive than I had expected |
| ... noch freundlicher als ich gehofft hatte | ... even more welcoming than I had hoped |

# HOW THE GRAMMAR WORKS

## VERB TENSES

### The imperfect tense

The imperfect tense is used:

- to report events in the past in newspaper and magazine articles
- to record the prevailing weather
- to report people's mood and feelings.

*Es war gestern sehr stürmisch und es regnete fast den ganzen Tag.*

You need to **recognise** the imperfect more often than you need to use it.

The endings of weak (regular) and strong (irregular) verbs are as follows:

| | | | | Weak<br>*machen* – to make | Strong<br>*fahren* – to travel |
|---|---|---|---|---|---|
| Singular | 1st | I | ich | mach**te** | fuhr |
| | 2nd | you (familiar) | du | mach**test** | fuhr**st** |
| | 2nd | you (formal) | Sie | mach**ten** | fuhr**en** |
| | 3rd | he/she/it | er/sie/es | mach**te** | fuhr |
| Plural | 1st | we | wir | mach**ten** | fuhr**en** |
| | 2nd | you (familiar) | ihr | mach**tet** | fuhr**t** |
| | 2nd | you (formal) | Sie | mach**ten** | fuhr |
| | 3rd | they | sie | mach**ten** | fuhr**en** |

However, it is very unlikely that you will ever need the 'you' forms of the imperfect. The remaining endings are extremely easy to remember:

| | Weak | Strong |
|---|---|---|
| Singular | **-te** | **–** |
| Plural | **-ten** | **-en** |

### The perfect tense

You need to be thoroughly confident in your use of the perfect tense to describe events in the past such as:

- what you did last night, or last weekend
- where you went with the school on a trip
- where you went, what you saw and did on holiday.

The perfect tense of all verbs is formed by using the auxiliary verb *haben* or *sein* with the past participle of the verb concerned:

*Ich habe gestern Tennis gespielt.*
*Wir sind oft schwimmen gegangen.*

You need to know the past participles of at least 50 strong (irregular) verbs from memory. It is well worth while learning these in groups of patterns such as those suggested in the Grammar Summary.

Regular weak verbs form their past participle using the *ge -t* rule:

*lernen → gelernt*     *machen → gemacht*

When the stem of the verb ends in *-d* or *-t*, the past participle ends in *-et*:

*arbeiten → gearbeitet*     *landen → gelandet*

Certain groups of verbs have different ways of forming past participles:

- All separable verbs add *ge* between the prefix and the rest of the verb:

| **Weak separable** | **Strong separable** |
| --- | --- |
| *ein-schalten → eingeschaltet* | *an-kommen → angekommen* |

- Inseparable verbs do not have the *ge* in their past participle, but simply end with *-t* or *-en* according to whether they are weak or strong. These verbs have the prefixes *be-, emp-, ent-, er-, ge-, miß-, ver-* and *zer-*:

| **Weak inseparable** | **Strong inseparable** |
| --- | --- |
| *bezahlen → bezahlt* | *empfangen → empfangen* |
| *erzählen → erzählt* | *entscheiden → entschieden* |
| *verpassen → verpaßt* | *gefallen → gefallen* |
| *zerstören → zerstört* | *mißverstehen → mißverstanden* |

- Weak verbs ending in *-ieren* need no *ge* to form their past participle:

*kapieren → kapiert*     *reparieren → repariert*

### The pluperfect tense

You need to recognise the pluperfect tense and be able to use one or two examples of it in a narrative, for example in describing what you **had** done, or what had happened **before** the event you are now describing.

The pluperfect is formed by adding the imperfect of the auxiliary, *haben* or *sein*, to the past participle of the verb concerned:

*Ich hatte gemacht.*
*Ich war angekommen.*

The pluperfect is frequently used after the conjunctions *bevor, nachdem, weil, als, sobald*, etc. Remember that you then need to change the word order:

*Wir hatten schon um 6 Uhr gegessen, bevor wir ins Kino gegangen sind.*
*Weil das Wetter so schön war, waren wir schon schwimmen gegangen.*

# *Check yourself*

## QUESTIONS

**Q1** *Put the following verbs under the correct heading in the table below. Then write the past participle of each one.*

| | | | |
| --- | --- | --- | --- |
| vorbereiten | ................................... | empfehlen | ................................... |
| anfangen | ................................... | aufräumen | ................................... |
| überraschen | ................................... | verkaufen | ................................... |
| einschlafen | ................................... | vorschlagen | ................................... |
| aufstehen | ................................... | erzählen | ................................... |

| Weak | | Strong | |
| --- | --- | --- | --- |
| **Separable** | **Inseparable** | **Separable** | **Inseparable** |
| | | | |
| | | | |
| | | | |
| | | | |

## QUESTIONS

**Q2** *Complete each of the following sentences using the correct version of the phrases in brackets.*

a) Ich war froh, daß ich ...
   (mein Portemonnaie finden)
b) Mutti schien sehr böse, weil wir ...
   (den Weg verlieren)
c) Wir waren zufrieden, als wir ...
   (die Arbeit zu Ende schreiben)
d) Sie waren alle überrascht, nachdem
   meine Oma ...
   (die Geschichte erzählen)

---

**REMEMBER! Cover the answers if you want to.**

---

## ANSWERS

**A1**

| | |
|---|---|
| vorbereiten | **vorbereitet** |
| empfehlen | **empfohlen** |
| anfangen | **angefangen** |
| aufräumen | **aufgeräumt** |
| überraschen | **überrascht** |
| verkaufen | **verkauft** |
| einschlafen | **eingeschlafen** |
| vorschlagen | **vorgeschlagen** |
| aufstehen | **aufgestanden** |
| erzählen | **erzählt** |

| Weak | | Strong | |
|---|---|---|---|
| **Separable** | **Inseparable** | **Separable** | **Inseparable** |
| vorbereiten | überraschen | anfangen | empfehlen |
| aufräumen | verkaufen | einschlafen | |
| | erzählen | aufstehen | |
| | | vorschlagen | |

**A2**

a) Ich war froh, daß ich mein Portemonnaie gefunden hatte.
b) Mutti schien sehr böse, weil wir den Weg verloren hatten.
c) Wir waren zufrieden, als wir die Arbeit zu Ende geschrieben hatten.
d) Sie waren alle überrascht, nachdem meine Oma die Geschichte erzählt hatte.

## TUTORIAL

**T1** *Of the weak verbs:*

- vorbereiten *needs no ge because of the inseparable prefix be-. This is tricky because the vor- is separable.*
- überraschen *and* verkaufen *similarly needs no ge-.*

*Of the strong verbs, only* empfehlen *does not have a ge- because of its inseparable prefix.*

**T2** *Each of the main clauses in these sentences is in the imperfect tense because it describes someone's mood or feelings. This is a very good way to introduce the pluperfect in your narrative.*

**95**

# EXAM PRACTICE

**H LISTENING**

*You will find the transcript and answers, with examiner's comments, on page 197.*

**1** Find Chapter 12 – Exam Practice Listening on the CD and listen to the German twice (Track 23). Then write the following sentences in the correct order.

Schreiben Sie die folgenden Sätze in der richtigen Reihenfolge.

Ich habe meine Postkarten eingeworfen.

Ich habe meine Postkarten geschrieben.

Wir sind essen gegangen.

Ich habe eine Fahrkarte gelöst.

Ich habe den Fernsehturm bestiegen.

Ich habe am Samstag eine Zeitung am Kiosk gekauft.

Ich habe das Kunstmuseum besucht

Wir haben unten am Rhein gegrillt.

1 ................................................................................

2 ................................................................................

3 ................................................................................

4 ................................................................................

5 ................................................................................

6 ................................................................................

7 ................................................................................

8 ................................................................................

**F H SPEAKING**

*You will find the transcript and examiner's comments on page 198.*

**2** Look at the situation outlined below and work out what you might say. Then find Chapter 12 – Exam Practice Speaking on the CD (Track 24) and listen to how a candidate might tackle this topic.

Erzählen Sie, wo Sie in den letzten Ferien in Urlaub gefahren sind. Beschreiben Sie, was Sie dort gesehen und gemacht haben.

(Say where you went on holiday during the last vacation. Describe what you did and saw there.)

**3** Read the letter, then answer the questions below.

Lesen Sie den Brief.

---

„Hotel Astoria"

den 16. Mai

Sehr geehrter Mr. Thomas,

Vielen Dank für Ihr Schreiben vom 5. Mai. Wir heißen Sie natürlich sehr herzlich willkommen, wenn Sie im August mit Ihrer Familie zu uns ins Hotel kommen. Ich habe zwei Doppelzimmer für Sie reserviert, und beide haben eine ausgezeichnete Aussicht. Da das Hotel so hoch liegt, kann man sehr weit ins Gebirge sehen.

Es gibt sehr viel Sehenswertes in der Gegend, wenn Sie mit dem eigenen Auto unterwegs sind, denn für Touristen sind die öffentlichen Verkehrsmittel, d.h. die Busse, nicht so besonders gut.

Wenn Sie sich für Motorsport interessieren, werden Sie sicherlich den Nürburgring besuchen wollen, die älteste Autorennstrecke der Welt und nicht weit von hier entfernt. Man kann auch mit dem eigenen Auto auf der Rennstrecke fahren - das könnte Ihren beiden Jungen vielleicht gefallen.

Falls Sie und Ihre Frau mehr an der Kultur der Eifel interessiert sind, gibt es das Kloster Maria Laach. Die Kirche dort ist wegen ihrer Architektur sehr berühmt.

Nicht weit von hier ist auch das Ahrtal mit seinen tollen Weinen. An einem heißen Nachmittag lohnt sich eine Besichtigung eines der vielen Weinkeller, denn dort ist es immer schön kühl, und eine Weinprobe ist immer eine lustige Sache. Allerdings würde ich Ihnen empfehlen, an dem Tag doch den Linienbus zu nehmen, damit Sie nicht Auto fahren müssen.

Ich lege Ihnen einige Prospekte bei, die sehr viel mehr Informationen über unsere Gegend bieten. Wir freuen uns sehr auf Ihren Besuch im kommenden Sommer.

Hochachtungsvoll,

*Berthold Weißkopf*

Berthold u. Maria Weißkopf

*You will find the answers and examiner's comments on page 199.*

|   | richtig | nicht im Text | falsch |
|---|---------|---------------|--------|
| 1 Das Hotel liegt in einer Hügellandschaft. |   |   |   |
| 2 Es gibt wenig Sehenswertes in der Eifel. |   |   |   |
| 3 Es empfiehlt sich normalerweise, mit dem Bus zu fahren. |   |   |   |
| 4 Herr Thomas ist ein alter Rennfahrer. |   |   |   |
| 5 Eine Kellerbesichtigung kann sehr lustig werden. |   |   |   |
| 6 Man muß mit dem Linienbus zum Weinkeller fahren. |   |   |   |

**4** Read the letter below, then try to write a similar one based upon it.

Schreiben Sie einen Brief an das Verkehrsamt, in dem Sie um Auskunft bitten.

(Write a letter to the tourist office asking for information.)

## Sample Student's Answer

- Although this sort of letter will always contain the same kind of information and questions, it is the **flow** of this example which makes it worthy of merit.

- In the first four paragraphs, each request for information is preceded by a reason, which gives the letter coherence.

- Instead of a repetition of the same question, the letter uses several different devices:
  - The general ich möchte Sie um Auskunft bitten.
  - Können Sie uns … empfehlen?
  - Haben Sie so etwas?
  - Sie haben sicherlich ein Programm, nicht wahr?
  - Könnten Sie uns … zuschicken?
  **Note:** This last form is the most polite, using the imperfect subjunctive instead of the present tense.

- The natural use of subordinate clauses with wenn, falls and damit shows that the candidate can manage the word order effectively and is worthy of the highest grade.

*By now, you should have a good idea what to write in such formal letters, but it would be a good idea to write down the first idea in each sentence or clause so that when you come to revise you can re-draw the skeleton of the letter very quickly in your mind. Practise saying the whole sentence out loud after seeing only the first few words. This is another way of keeping it fixed in your mind.*

---

Leeds den 26. Mai

Sehr geehrte Herren!

Ich habe vor, im Sommer mit meiner Familie nach Goslar zu fahren. Wir wollen etwa zehn Tage in der Gegend verbringen, und ich möchte Sie um Auskunft bitten.

Wir haben noch keine Unterkunft reserviert, und möchten Sie daher bitten, uns ein Hotelverzeichnis zu schicken. Können Sie uns ein preiswertes Hotel in der Nähe der Stadtmitte empfehlen?

Meine Eltern wandern sehr gern, und suchen eine Wanderkarte. Haben Sie so etwas? Meine Schwester und ich hören gern Jazz und möchten in ein Konzert gehen, wenn eins in der Zeit stattfindet. Sie haben sicherlich ein Programm, nicht wahr?

Falls das Wetter nicht so gut ist, brauchen wir auch eine Liste von den Museen, usw., die man auch bei schlechtem Wetter besuchen kann.

Könnten Sie uns bitte diese Informationen zuschicken, damit wir unseren Urlaub weiter vorbereiten können?

Wir bedanken uns im voraus für Ihre Bemühungen

Hochachtungsvoll,

Lynsey Rivers

All GCSE syllabuses include a section to do with world events and issues. You may meet these in the Reading and Listening Tests, but you are likely to be more comfortable with other topics when it comes to the Speaking and Writing Tests. It is advisable to steer clear of them in the Speaking Test especially, where you could quickly be lost for the necessary vocabulary.

Accordingly, there are fewer exercises in the Check yourself sections, and the Exam Practice questions are shorter, too. However, the words and phrases below will help you understand at least the outline of an issue in the wider world.

## WHAT YOU NEED TO KNOW

**Nachrichten und Aktuelles** — **News and current affairs**

| | |
|---|---|
| die Dritte Welt | the Third World |
| das Entwicklungsland (länder) | developing country |
| die Feier (n) | celebration, festivity |
| das Fest (e) | festival |
| der Frieden | peace |
| der Krieg | war |
| die Katastrophe/katastrophal | catastrophe/catastrophic |
| die Klimaänderung | climate change |
| die Armut | poverty |
| die Hungersnot | famine |
| das Erdbeben | earthquake |
| die Überschwemmung (en) | floods |
| das Hochwasser | floods |
| das Gewitter | storm |
| ums Leben kommen | to die, be fatally injured |

**Grüne Themen** — **Green issues**

| | |
|---|---|
| die Umwelt | environment |
| umweltfreundlich | environmentally friendly |
| bleifreies Benzin | unleaded petrol |
| der Altglascontainer (–) | bottle bank |
| die Altkleidersammlung (en) | collection of old clothes |
| die Wiederverwertung/das Recycling | recycling |
| die Müllverwertung | waste recycling |

**Gesundheitsthemen** — **Health issues**

| | |
|---|---|
| gesund/ungesund | healthy/unhealthy |
| das Rauchen | smoking |
| der Rauschgift (e) | drugs |
| der Alkohol | alcohol |
| der Vegetarier/in | vegetarian |

**Was meinen Sie dazu?** — **What is your opinion?**

| | |
|---|---|
| Ich finde es furchtbar, daß ... | I think it is terrible that ... |
| Ich war sehr überrascht zu hören, daß ... | I was very surprised to hear that ... |
| Wir waren schockiert, als wir die Nachricht(en) hörten. | We were shocked when we heard the news. |
| Ich war froh, als ich hörte, daß ... | I was pleased when I heard that ... |
| Wir sollten etwas machen. | We ought to do something. |
| Man muß mehr machen, um das zu vermeiden. | We must do more to avoid that. |
| Ich halte es für äußerst wichtig, daß .. | I think it is extremely important that ... |
| Ich kann es nicht leiden, wenn ... | I can't bear it when ... |

## LAND – PERSON – STAATSANGEHÖRIGKEIT

**England**
Engländer/in
– englisch

**Schottland**
Schotte/in
– schottisch

**Wales**
Waliser/in
– walisisch

**Irland**
Ire/Irin – irisch

**Belgien**
Belgier/in
– belgisch

**Frankreich**
Franzose/ösin
– französisch

**Griechenland**
Grieche/in
– griechisch

**Holland/die
Niederlande**
Holländer/in
– holländisch

**Deutschland**
Deutscher/
Deutsche
– deutsch

**Italien**
Italiener/in
– italienisch

**Österreich**
Österreicher/in
– österreichisch

**Spanien**
Spanier/in
– spanisch

**Amerika/die
Vereinigten
Staaten**
Amerikaner/in
– amerikanisch

**die Schweiz**
Schweizer/in
– schweizerisch

**die Türkei**
Türke/in
– türkisch

# Check yourself

## QUESTIONS

**Q1**  *How would you say in German?*

a)  In my opinion, smoking is unhealthy.
b)  We were all shocked by the news about an earthquake in Turkey.
c)  There seems no end to the famine in Africa.
d)  We must do more to protect the environment.

**REMEMBER! Cover the answers if you want to.**

## ANSWERS

**A1**
a)  Meiner Meinung nach ist das
    Rauchen ungesund.
b)  Wir waren alle sehr schockiert über die
    Nachricht von einem Erdbeben in
    der Türkei.
c)  Der Hungersnot in Afrika scheint es
    kein Ende zu geben.
d)  Wir müssen mehr unternehmen, um
    die Umwelt zu schützen.

## TUTORIAL

**T1**
*a)*  *Meiner Meinung nach is a stylish introduction to
      your opinion, as long as you remember to invert
      subject and verb afterwards.*
*b)*  Schockiert, *or perhaps even* erschüttert, *suggests
      a much stronger emotion than* überrascht.
*c/d)*  *Sadly, these two huge world problems seem
        unlikely to be solved very quickly, and you will
        need to be able to express an opinion about them,
        even if it sounds a little like a cliché.*

# HOW THE GRAMMAR WORKS

## PRONOUNS

### Indefinite pronouns

You should be able to **use** the following indefinite pronouns:

*Jeder kann das machen.* – **Everyone** can do it.
*Ein paar sind ausgefallen.* – **A few** dropped out.
*Einige sind verhungert.* – **Some** starved.
*Andere haben den Weg verloren.* – **Others** lost their way.

You should be able to **recognise** the following indefinite pronouns:

*Jemand hat das vorgeschlagen.* – **Someone** suggested it.
*Ich habe niemanden\* gefunden.* – I found **no-one**.
*Mehrere sind zurückgeblieben.* – **Some** stayed behind.
*Manche wollten nicht mitfahren.* – **Some** did not want to go.
*Man konnte nur wenig machen.* – We could do **only little**.

\* Used here in the accusative.

### Interrogative pronouns

You should be able to use these **interrogative pronouns:**

*Wer hat das behauptet?* – **Who** said that?
*Wen haben Sie dort gesehen?* – **Who/Whom** did you see there?
*Wessen ist das?* – **Whose** is it?
*Welcher kommt zuerst?* – **Which** comes first?

### Demonstrative pronouns

You should be able to use these **demonstrative pronouns:**

*Ich mag diesen nicht.* – I don't like **the latter (this one)**. (Accusative)
*Jener ist viel besser.* – **The former (that one)** is much better. (Nominative)

## Check yourself

### QUESTIONS

**Q1** **How would you say in German?**

a) Some are happy about it, others are not content.
b) A few have left, but nobody saw them.
c) There is only little one can do.
d) Everyone should do something, but nobody wants to.
e) Which arrived today, this one or that one?

### REMEMBER! Cover the answers if you want to.

### ANSWERS

**A1**
a) Manche freuen sich darüber, andere sind nicht zufrieden.
b) Einige sind weggegangen, aber niemand hat sie gesehen.
c) Es gibt nur wenig, was man machen kann.
d) Jeder soll etwas machen, aber niemand hat Lust dazu.
e) Welcher ist heute angekommen, dieser oder jener?

### TUTORIAL

**T1** *These pronouns must be committed to memory. They are all common and, most importantly, they are just the sort of small words which can change the entire meaning of a passage, when you meet them in a comprehension test.*

# EXAM PRACTICE

**H LISTENING**

*You will find the transcript and answers, with examiner's comments, on page 199.*

**1** Find Chapter 13 – Exam Practice Listening on the CD. Listen to the German twice (Track 25), then answer the questions.

 Answer the following questions **in English**.

1 What disaster has befallen the people of Chile?
2 Which area of the country is affected?
3 What plans have been announced for the President of the USA?
4 What is the state of the flooding in Bangladesh?

**H SPEAKING**

*You will find the transcript and examiner's comments, on page 200.*

**2** **Presentation of a topic: „Die Umwelt"**

 Find Chapter 13 – Exam Practice Speaking on the CD (Track 26) and listen to how a candidate might tackle this topic.

You need to be able to talk at some length about a topic of your choice. Although the choice can be very wide according to the syllabus, it is worth bearing in mind that the examiner needs to be able to join in the topic, too. Something too obscure, such as an unusual interest or an obscure event, will make it difficult for the examiner.

**H WRITING**

**3** *Because of the nature of this topic there are few opportunities to set extended writing tasks which involve this area alone. You might insert a few sentences into a letter to a pen-friend, or perhaps write an account of something your school is doing as part of an environmental project. You can see an example of what you might write in Question 4.*

*Here are a few suggestions to include in a letter to a pen-friend:*

Meine Eltern haben gerade ein neues Auto gekauft, weil sie „etwas für die Umwelt machen" wollten. Sie haben unseren großen Kombiwagen verkauft, der so viel Benzin verbrauchte, und haben jetzt ein „Ka", das neue Kleinauto von Ford, das offensichtlich ganz wenig Sprit braucht.

Ich finde es allerdings ein bißchen doof, denn es ist kaum Platz für uns alle vier drin, und meine Mutter fährt jetzt jede Woche zum Supermarkt anstatt einmal im Monat mit dem größeren Wagen, in dem alles hineinpaßte. Naja, „grün ist schön", so meinen meine Eltern.

Mein Vater bleibt fit, indem er jeden Tag mit dem Rad zur Arbeit fährt. Höchstens wenn es stark regnet, fährt er mit dem Bus.

*With a little thought you can transform an ordinary letter into one with an environmental theme – if you need to. The chances are that you won't, but try this letter for yourself. Think of the common threads of the 'green' arguments and see how they apply to your own situation at home or school.*

**4** Read the following report, then answer the questions below.

# „Umwelt-Woche"

Wir haben gerade unsere „Umwelt-Woche" gehabt, und es war ziemlich interessant.

Jeder Jahrgang mußte etwas anderes machen, und unsere neunte Klasse hat eine große Reinigungsaktion in der Umgebung um die Schule durchgeführt. Es gibt in der Nähe der Schule nämlich einige Stellen, wo sich viel Abfall anhäuft, oder noch schlimmer, wo die Leute einfach ihren Müll abladen

Wir haben ziemlich viele Einkaufswagen gefunden, die die Supermärkte von uns „zurückgekauft" haben, (sie haben der Schule eine Spende gemacht), und wir haben am Ende der Woche einen großen Haufen von Abfallsäcken auf den Schulhof gebracht. Es hat hier ziemlich schlimm gestunken, und wir waren froh, als die Leute von der Müllabfuhr das ganze weggenommen haben.

Eine andere Gruppe hat hinter der Schule einen tollen Garten angebaut, wo es vorher ziemlich wild zugewachsen war.

Das scheint mir alles sehr sinnvoll und vernünftig zu sein, und wir haben viel dabei gelernt. Also, warum müssen wir jetzt schon wieder in den Unterricht gehen?

Answer the following questions **in English**.

1 Name three of the activities in which pupils have been taking part. [3]

2 Why was the writer pleased to see the refuse collectors at the school? [1]

3 Why is the writer less pleased that the week has ended? [1]

*You will find the answers and examiner's comments on page 200.*

# CHAPTER 14

# LISTENING AND RESPONDING

## INTRODUCTION

It is difficult to separate the four skills involved in learning and using a language. Your grasp of vocabulary and basic language structures play a vital role in helping you to understand spoken German, but there are also specific difficulties associated with listening which can be addressed separately. This chapter will help you to identify ways in which you can improve your comprehension of spoken German.

### Problem 1

Your concentration on the two hearings of the recording is vital. You can't ask for it to be played again (unlike in the Reading Test where you can look at the passages as much as you like within the time allowed). Most of us think we have good powers of hearing, but real listening is the application of our hearing to a specific utterance or announcement, etc. Unlike the background noise of a television in the room, or the conversation with a group of friends in the playground, the Listening Test makes demands on you that you have to practise.

### Solution 1

Commit yourself to the practice of concentrating on something recorded from the radio for a minute or two (nothing too long) and writing down the gist of what you hear and as much detail as you can. Listen to your recording again and see how accurately you have listened.

### Problem 2

You may be distracted by a neighbour coughing or someone knocking a pencil on the floor or, worse still, by some loud noise outside the classroom such as a low-flying aircraft. On a warm summer's day your concentration may simply drift and you will end up in a day-dream.

### Solution 2

Make sure you have enough practice of actual listening exams or similar materials, and for a length of time which will give you an idea of what the real exam will be like. You need to be wide awake and fresh for the test, so the usual message is: 'Get enough rest (or sleep) beforehand'. If you are tired from the night before or from the considerable exertion of sport, you will not be in a fit state to listen for a long period.

### Problem 3

Although there are not many regional variations in vocabulary to trouble you at GCSE, German spoken with an Austrian, Bavarian, Berlin or Swiss accent will sound different and may take a little getting used to. You may also not be used to listening to both male and female voices speaking German.

### Solution 3

Your teacher can help by pointing out such regional differences when they occur in your lessons. Other German speakers such as friends, parents or a language assistant will also be of help. Of greatest assistance, however, is satellite television to which many people have access nowadays, even if they do not have their own. Turning on a German TV channel and immersing yourself in a 'game show' or listening to the weather forecast is a very valuable aid to understanding. If you are able to watch like this, it is even better if you can do so at a regular time each week, so that you have the best chance of seeing the same programme.

### Problem 4

Understanding a speaker you can't see is a skill you need to practise. You have none of the clues of gesture or facial expression which aid normal understanding.

### Solution 4

You can try it in class by closing your eyes when the teacher is talking to the whole class – but you might warn the teacher first about what you are doing!

### Problem 5

Unlike in Problem 2, the interference between you and the message you are trying to hear may be a deliberately recorded sound effect such a train, or a bell.

### Solution 5

Don't be alarmed. These sound effects are supposed to help you, to put what you hear in some sort of context, so think about them as well as the verbal message. It should help you.

### Problem 6

You can't use a dictionary to any great extent in the Test, so don't come to rely on it. If your exam board does allow the use of a dictionary at all, it will not be during the main listening part of the Test, only before and after.

### Solution 6

A dictionary will be most useful to you, if allowed, to check words on the question paper and perhaps at the end to check any words you were unsure about. Any further use of a dictionary will almost certainly be counter-productive.

## GENERAL STRATEGIES

### Use the question to help you

In multiple choice questions about simple facts, you know that one answer is correct, so you can go through the answers in your mind before you hear the recording. For example, if the question is:

*Eine Fahrkarte kostet*: DM 4,50   DM 5,40   DM 15,40   DM 15,45?

you can focus on these numbers and disregard everything else.

Even if the factual information is slightly more complex, the same still applies, for example:

*Eine einfache Fahrkarte nach Bonn–Bad Godesberg kostet*:
DM 4,50   DM 5,40   DM 15,40   DM 15,45?

Now you are listening for a particular type of ticket to a specified destination.

If the question wants you to focus on an emotion or attitude, think about the words and expressions associated with those emotions, for example:

*Maria treibt gern Sport.*     RICHTIG   FALSCH?

You should listen out for phrases like *mag gern, interessiert sich für, hat Spaß, findet ... gut/schön*. You are unlikely to hear the exact words of the question in the recording.

### Use the context to help you

*Am Rande des Waldes war ein Teich, in dem Georg immer gern angelte.*
Even without knowing that *ein Teich* means 'a pond', you should be able to work out that it is a stretch of water, because the *angelte* makes it so obvious.

### Use your common sense

If you are at a petrol station, you are more likely to hear someone say:

*Fünfzig Liter Bleifrei, bitte.*

than:

*Fünfzig Kilo Kartoffeln, bitte.*

Similarly you should have some idea from your knowledge of German food that a *Bratwurst mit Pommes Frites* is more likely to cost DM 4,50 than DM 45,00.

# Check yourself 1

Find Chapter 14 – Check yourself 1, Listening on the CD (Track 27). Listen to each section, then answer the questions. Listen for a second time if necessary.

## QUESTIONS

**Q1** *Pick out the detail.*

a) Wann?
b) Um wieviel Uhr?
c) An welchem Tag?
d) Wo?
e) Wieviel?

**Q2** *Pick out the attitude. (Richtig oder Falsch?)*

a) Ahlke mag gern schwimmen.
b) Georg kocht gern.
c) Der Urlaub hat Margret gut gefallen.
d) Rainer mag Tiere nicht.
e) Sabine ist müde.

### REMEMBER! Cover the answers if you want to.

## ANSWERS

**A1**
a) heute abend
b) um halb neun/um 8.30 Uhr
c) am 24. März
d) vor dem Bahnhof
e) DM27.00

**A2**
a) Falsch
b) Richtig
c) Richtig
d) Falsch
e) Richtig

*You will find a transcript of the recording on page 201.*

## TUTORIAL

**T1**
a) *The question could mean an exact time, a time of day, a day or a date. This phrase is common enough. (Do you know at least two other times of day?)*
b) *This question wants an exact time but you do not hear the* Uhr *which normally signals the time. Did you remember the trap of* halb?
c) *You should have learned to deal with numbers beyond 20 by saying them to yourself in English in the same way – one-and-twenty, two-and-twenty, three-and-twenty, etc.* März *is the least obvious of the months from the way it sounds, and may be more frequently used in exams for that reason.*
d) *Don't be distracted by the time. Remember that you will generally hear the time before the place.*
e) *The word* Mark *makes the price easy to spot, but the difficulty with numbers remains, as in c) above.*

**T2**
a) *You might think that she likes swimming because she goes regularly, but* langweilig *tells you otherwise.*
b) *Das gefällt mir or es gefällt mir is always a sign of liking or pleasure, and one you should try to use in your Speaking Test.*
c) *Two clues here:* toll *at the end of the first sentence, and* gut amüsiert *at the end of the second.* Wir haben uns gut amüsiert *is usually translated as 'we had a good time'.*
d) *Ich möchte gern is a clear indication that he likes animals, but don't be distracted by* das geht nicht, *which tells you he can't have a dog.*
e) *You will know* fertig *in class as 'finished', or more generally as 'ready', but it has a common colloquial meaning of 'tired out'. Sometimes you will see* fix und fertig *meaning 'all in'.*

## SPECIFIC POINTS TO PRACTISE

### Numbers

You will already be aware of the importance of numbers at Foundation Level – in times, prices and so on – but even at Higher Level there are questions in which an understanding of numbers is crucial.

Tutorial T1 in Check yourself 1 has already advised you to practise counting numbers in English from twenty upwards with the units before the tens, in order to 'tune in' to the German way of counting.

This becomes increasingly important when listening to telephone numbers, which are usually said as pairs of numbers:
> 285893: *achtundzwanzig, achtundfünfzig, dreiundneunzig*
If there is an odd number it is usually left until last:
> 3572590: *fünfunddreißig, zweiundsiebzig, neunundfünfzig, null*

Remind yourself of the ordinal numbers by reciting them aloud, especially the first few – *erste, zweite, dritte, vierte*.

Watch out for the halves: *eineinhalb, zweieinhalb*, etc! *Anderthalb* can also be used for one and a half.

Be careful with the colloquial expressions of time around the half hour:
> 2.30 – *halb drei*
> 2.20 – *zehn vor halb drei*
> 2.25 – *fünf vor halb drei*
> 2.35 – *fünf nach halb drei*
> 2.40 – *zehn nach halb drei*

### Vowels and consonants

German speakers avoid confusion between similar sounds by making them clearly different from one another. For example, if someone wants to make it clear over the phone that they are talking about June and not July, they will say *Juno*. Or they might say *Julei* instead of *Juli*. Similarly, *zwei* and *drei* are differentiated by using *zwo* instead of *zwei* as necessary.

Most of us tend to visualise the words we hear in our 'mind's eye', rather like the autocue that a newsreader uses. German is largely written as you would expect. There are no hidden sounds and everything is pronounced. Just one or two sounds might confuse this pattern, such as the 'b' at the end of words like *halb*, or the 'd' which sounds like a 't' at the end of H*und*. Similarly, the 's' of S*ee* might make you think the word you hear is *Zeh*, or that *so* is in fact *Zoo*.

Other vowels to listen for are:
**ä** – which can sound like an 'e'. Can you differentiate between *Rädern* and *reden*?
**ü** – in *Tür*. Can you hear the difference between *Tour, Tür* and *Tier*? Or between *für* und *vier*? The context in which the words are heard will definitely help you.

### Negatives

N*icht* is an obvious sound to listen out for, but you can be caught out by *nicht wahr*, when the sentence is, in fact, positive:
> *Das Wetter ist schön, nicht wahr?*
The intonation of the question ending should help you to understand this sentence.

Far more prevalent, and a constant cause of problems, is the *kein/klein* trap:
> *Ich habe einen kleinen Garten./Ich habe keinen Garten.*
Even if you miss the sound of the 'l' in *kleinen*, you should still hear the article before *klein*, which you will not hear in front of *kein*, because it already means 'not a' or 'no'.

### Word separation

Without seeing the gaps between words, as you can when you read, it can be difficult to distinguish the beginnings and ends of words. This can increase the difficulty of a language already well known for its long compound nouns.

Practise listening to a relatively easy piece of German from early in your course book and try to write down what you hear from the recording. You should be able to pick out plenty of shorter words and probably fill in some of the longer ones. If you can borrow the cassette with a transcript of the recording, you will be able to check your spelling as well. Even without this, it is still good practice.

# *Check yourself 2*

Find Chapter 14 – Check yourself 2, Listening on the CD (Track 28).
Listen to each section, then answer the questions. Listen for a second time if necessary.

## QUESTIONS

**Q1** **Write the telephone numbers.**

a)
b)

**Write the 'Lotto' numbers.**

c)

**Write the dates of birth.**

d)
e)

**Q2** **Answer the questions in English.**

a) What is his job?
b) Where does he work?
c) Where did he hurt himself?
d) What did he ask?
e) Do they want to go, or not?

---

### REMEMBER! Cover the answers if you want to.

---

## ANSWERS

**A1**
a) 33 56 88
b) 45 67 29
c) 1, 7, 15, 27, 29, 40 + 31
d) 01.03.82
e) 25.07.83

**A2**
a) He works with the animals in the zoo.
b) In a very pretty building by the lake.
c) On the big toe.
d) He asked whether I had any small change.
e) Yes, they do.

*You will find the transcript of the recording on page 201.*

## TUTORIAL

**T1**
a) The double figures such as thirty-three should prove no problem, so write them down and give yourself time to say 'six-and-fifty' for the middle pair.
b) *Vier* and *fünf* are frequently misheard. Take special care and practise saying them to yourself.
c) A *row* of figures requires special concentration. Keep the pen close to the paper as you probably need to write as you listen.
d/e) Birthdays are usually said quickly because the speaker knows the figures so well. Try it with your own birthday as practice for the Speaking Test. The 19 of the year is frequently omitted, as in English.

**T2**
a) Zoo reinforces the idea of animals. *Türen here* would make little sense.
b) Did you hear the *so*? Would this make you think of Zoo? Did you remember that am See means 'by the lake', not 'by the sea' (*der* See, not *die* See)?
c) Am grossen Zeh *was a deliberate trap after am See in the previous item. Even the question would not help you here. Only the 'ts' sound of Zeh will tell you that he did not hurt himself by the big lake.*
d) Both kein Geld and Kleingeld *make sense.*
e) Doch *is an extra emphasis, which reinforces the wanting. The* nicht? – *an abbreviation of* nicht wahr? – *should be intonated as 'don't we?'.*

# HIGHER LEVEL PERFORMANCE

At Higher Level, you will be expected to be able to do a number of things which are not expected at Foundation Level.

## Understand German spoken at normal speed

At Foundation Level, the German you are likely to hear will be spoken more slowly and deliberately. At Higher Level, you should expect to hear German spoken at near normal speed, appropriate to the situation, and in some cases containing colloquial language or slang.

## Extract information from longer utterances

At Foundation Level, there is little extra language included beyond what you need for the answer. For example, you might be asked about the weather tomorrow from the extract:

>Morgen wird das Wetter wieder schön.

At Higher Level, you are likely to hear a relatively large amount of language from which you have to extract the answer. For example, you might hear:

>Morgen im Süden meist wolkig. Tageshöchsttemperaturen liegen bei 15 Grad. Im Norden wird es wieder schön. Tageshöchsttemperaturen liegen bei 22 Grad.

and be asked about the weather in the north. In both cases the German you need to understand is the same (es wird schön), but at Higher Level you have to sift through more language to get there.

## Pick out the main points from what you hear

For example, you might listen to a discussion on what young people want to do in their free time. One might say:

>Am liebsten möchte ich im See schwimmen gehen.

Another might say:

>Man könnte dort auch segeln oder ein Ruderboot mieten.

While the last might say:

>Unten am Wasser gefällt's mir am besten.

You need to understand that all of them are keen on water sports.

## Identify attitudes and opinions

You will not necessarily always hear key words like langweilig or toll to tell you how people feel. For example, Ich gehe ins Theater, nur wenn meine Eltern bezahlen. might show a reluctance to go to the theatre. Whereas Ich habe für die Theaterkarten schon sehr lange Geld gespart, would show a strong desire to see the performance.

## Make deductions/inferences from what you hear

As an example, if you hear:

>Unterwegs hatte ich eine Reifenpanne und ich mußte eine halbe Stunde am Straßenrand sitzen, bis ich das Rad repariert hatte.

you should be able to deduce that the speaker has been out for a cycle ride.

## Understand the gist of what you hear

If you hear someone say:

>Kein Jugendzentrum, nicht 'mal eine Disco. Ganz wenige Sportmöglichkeiten. In dieser Stadt gibt es zu wenig für unsere Jugend. Kein Wunder, daß sie ab und zu dumme Sachen mit Alkohol machen.

you can deduce that they are talking about problems facing young people today.

## Answer questions using German which you have not heard on the recording

If you had to answer this question about the above utterance:

>Was hält er von den Freizeitsmöglichkeiten in der Stadt?

you would have to answer Er findet die Situation schlecht für junge Leute. If you simply said what was lacking (no disco, no youth club, etc.) you would not score the mark. It is the attitude which is being targeted.

**Understand vocabulary outside the minimum core vocabulary**

All the exam boards specify a minimum core vocabulary for Foundation Level, but there will always be words outside the range of the core which you have not met. You will therefore need to listen beyond the odd words that you don't recognise for the gist of the whole passage. Needless to say, the more vocabulary you **do** know the better, so you need to make a long-term commitment to the regular learning and using of new words.

# *Check yourself 3*

Find Chapter 14 – Check yourself 3, Listening on the CD (Track 29).
Listen to each section, then answer the questions. Listen for a second time if necessary.

## QUESTIONS

**Q1**  **Pick out the detail.**

a)   What is the weather forecast for today in the north?

b)   What are the speakers complaining about?

**Q2**  *Identifying attitudes. Choose the appropriate phrase from this list to describe each speaker.*

Er:  freut sich  findet es schwierig
hat Angst  ist fleißig  ist hilfsbereit.

-------------------------------------------------

**REMEMBER! Cover the answers if you want to.**

## ANSWERS

**A1**  a)   Starting off cool and cloudy, with a chance of rain. Bright and occasionally sunny in the afternoon. Highest temperatures about 17 degrees.

b)   Homework

**A2**  a)   Er freut sich.
b)   Er hat Angst.

*You will find the transcript of the recording on page 201.*

## TUTORIAL

**T1**  *a)   At least with a weather forecast you have a set format and a very limited vocabulary. The difficulty with this one might be that you hear the information right at the beginning and the remainder of the forecast might distract you.*

*b)   Plenty of guiding words here:* schwierig ... für die Schule zu arbeiten; keine Lust; richtig blöd. *You are also helped by the tone, which sounds less than enthusiastic about doing school work at home.*

**T2**  *You may need to check some of the words in the dictionary beforehand.*

*a)   The clues are* Geld gespart *and* Spaß machen.

*b)*   Etwas Furchtbares *and* nicht schlafen *should guide you to the answers.*

# DIFFERENT KINDS OF LISTENING

**Dialogues**

If there is more than one speaker, you need to be clear who is talking. The names are always recorded and may be used by one speaker to another:

– *Wir gehen heute schwimmen. Kommst du mit, Bettina?*
– *Nein, ich habe keine Lust.*

This should make it clear enough that the second speaker is Bettina.

You may be asked to fill in information alongside names in a grid, or to respond *Falsch* or *Richtig* to statements about each named speaker.

## Monologues

Examples include news items, weather forecasts, advertisements, etc.
The question will make it clear who is speaking.

## Announcements

These are usually included at Foundation Level only and include the sort of
things you hear over a loudspeaker in a shop, railway station, airport, etc.
You often need to listen for specific facts like times, prices, platforms, etc.

## Telephone calls and recorded messages

Again, the question will often target points like times and dates, but you may
need to listen out for a change in arrangements.

# DIFFERENT KINDS OF QUESTIONS

## Multiple choice (non-verbal)

This sort of exercise is often called picture matching. There are three main types:
1   In the simplest sort, you may have to pick out a time or a price from the
    recording and match it to one of those on the question paper.
2   You may have to match statements to numbered pictures or symbols, for
    example those representing people's jobs or interests.
3   You may have to decide upon the most appropriate scene from a longer
    recording. For example, is the family at the beach, at the theatre or
    walking in the woods, etc?
In **1** you are listening for a specific detail, whereas in **2** and **3** you need to
pick up the gist of an utterance, probably a longer one. In the case of similar
pictures to choose from, you will need to focus on the detail of the pictures
and decide what differences there are, before you can listen out for them.
It might be a different number of people involved, or different weather,
for example.

## Multiple-choice (verbal)

Again, there are a number of types:
1   One-word answers are fairly straightforward:
        *Georg ist ................ . (glücklich/traurig/böse/müde)*
At Foundation Level you might even hear the missing word required. The more
difficult questions often require more deduction.
2   A phrase may be required instead of a single word. These are less likely to
    be heard exactly as written down:
        *Sie treffen sich ................ . (am Bahnhof/im Café/in der Schule/vor der Schule)*
In this example, the last two choices are very close and you would have to
listen closely to differentiate between 'in' and 'in front of the school'.
3   Sentence answers can take two forms. They might ask you to relate one of
    the choices to a specific person:
        *Was machte Ingrid abends?*
        **A**  *Sie ging einkaufen.*          **C**  *Sie hörte Musik.*
        **B**  *Sie machte Hausaufgaben.*      **D**  *Sie besuchte Freundinnen.*
Or they might ask you to choose a person for each statement, in which case
you will certainly have more people to choose from than there are statements:
        *Schreiben Sie den richtigen Namen.*
        *... ist ein fleißiger Schüler.*          *... fährt gern rad.*
        *... kann sehr gut Volleyball spielen.*   *... sammelt gern Münzen.*
Here, if you are able to use a dictionary, it would be worth checking any words
you don't recognise.

## Answers in German

Again, these may ask for one word, a phrase or a whole sentence.
1   If you are writing one-word answers in a grid-filling exercise, the spelling is
    not usually a problem – unless your mis-spelling happens to create
    another German word. For example, if the correct answer is *eine Tür*, the
    examiner would not be able to accept *eine Tour* or *ein Tier* because the
    answer would mean something different.

2 If you are required to write a phrase, then a one-word answer is unlikely to score the mark. For example, if the question is W*o treffen sich die Freunde*?, the answer B*ahnhof* would not be clear enough to score the mark. You would need to say *am Bahnhof* or *vor dem Bahnhof*, as appropriate.

3 For the highest grades you may be required to write full sentence answers. At the simplest, these are likely to be manipulations of the recording. For example, you might hear someone say *Ich möchte schwimmen gehen*, and for your answer write E*r möchte schwimmen gehen*. However, you might have to create your own sentence in answer to a question like W*as hält Bernd von dem Film*?. Here, your answer might be E*r findet den Film/ihn ziemlich spannend* or *Bernd mochte den Film gar nicht*.

### Answers in English

It is tempting to think that these are going to be easier than anything involving German, but in fact candidates often prove less reliable or less precise when using their own language. These questions are usually reserved for the most difficult passages and test the greatest understanding, particularly in respect of attitudes and emotions. These questions more frequently ask **how?** and **why?** than **what?** or **where?**.

# *Check yourself 4*

Find Chapter 14 – Check yourself 4, Listening on the CD (Track 30). Listen to each section, then answer the questions. Listen for a second time if necessary.

## QUESTIONS

**Q1** **Answer in German.**

a) Frank wird ..................... arbeiten.
b) Er möchte ..................... .
c) Brigitte wird ..................... .
d) Sie möchte nicht ..................... .

**Q2** **Answer in English.**

a) Where does Charlotte want to go?
b) Why?
c) Where does mother prefer to go?
d) What is father's reaction?

---

**REMEMBER! Cover the answers if you want to.**

## ANSWERS

**A1**
a) Frank wird in einer Werkstatt arbeiten.
b) Er möchte ein Motorrad kaufen.
c) Brigitte wird in der Schule bleiben.
d) Sie möchte nicht in der Metzgerei arbeiten.

**A2**
a) To the city
b) There's plenty to see and do.
c) To the countryside
d) He agrees.

*You will find the transcript of the recording on page 202.*

## TUTORIAL

**T1**
a) *Even better*: in der Werkstatt seines Onkels.
b) Ein Motorrad *would be enough in this case*.
c) *Notice that the statement was in the negative, so you can't 'lift' the verb from there.*
d) *This time, the answer has the negative so that you have to use something other than is in the statement.*

**T2**
a) Schön auf dem Campingplatz *could mislead you, but* ich möchte lieber *should be obvious enough*.
b) *The phrase* viel zu sehen und zu tun *is very common in describing town or village life.*
c) Hotel *stands out prominently at the beginning, but the* aber *should lead you to* auf dem Lande.
d) *The answer comes right at the beginning, in this short familiar phrase*: du hast recht.

# EXAM PRACTICE

Find Chapter 14 – Exam Practice Listening on the CD (Track 31). Listen to each item twice, then answer the questions.

**Kreuzen Sie die richtige Kästchen an!**

**1** In der Jugendherberge fragen Sie nach den Eßzeiten. Wann ißt man zu Abend?

    **A** 18.00 – 20.00 Uhr ☐   **C** 18.30 – 19.30 Uhr ☐

    **B** 18.30 – 20.30 Uhr ☐   **D** 19.00 – 20.00 Uhr ☐

**2** Was müssen Sie machen, wenn Sie abends später ausbleiben wollen?

    **A** Einen Schlüssel dalassen. ☐

    **B** Ihre Eltern anrufen. ☐

    **C** Den Herbergseltern einen Schlüssel geben. ☐

    **D** Den Herbergseltern Bescheid sagen. ☐   [1]

**3** Wie ist das Wetter im Süden?

    **A** ☐   **C** ☐

    **B** ☐   **D** ☐   [1]

**4** Wie ist das Wetter im Westen?

    **A** ☐   **C** ☐

    **B** ☐   **D** ☐   [1]

**5** Wie ist das Wetter im Norden?

    **A** ☐   **C** ☐

    **B** ☐   **D** ☐   [1]

**6** Temperaturen im Osten?

    **A** 13-15 Grad ☐   **C** 14-16 Grad ☐

    **B** 13-16 Grad ☐   **D** 14-17 Grad ☐   [1]

**7** Was mag sie am liebsten machen?

    **A** ☐   **C** ☐

    **B** ☐   **D** ☐   [1]

**8** Hören Sie die Anzeige an. Welche Aussagen sind richtig?
Kreuzen Sie **zwei** Kästchen an!

**A** Die Museen sind heute zu. ☐

**B** Alle drei Gruppen besuchen ein Museum oder eine Galerie. ☐

**C** Jeder Besucher kann seine Gruppe wählen. ☐

**D** Einige Leute besuchen einen Vergnügungspark. ☐

**E** Alle Leute essen zusammen zu Mittag. ☐

[2]

**9** Hören Sie das Telefongespräch an und korrigieren Sie den
folgenden Zettel.

[4]

> Lieber Herr Blume,
> Frau Teichmann hat für Sie angerufen.
> Sie kommt erst um 16.00 Uhr.
> Treffpunkt: Vor dem Rathaus

**Hören Sie die Gespräche an. Wählen Sie für Frank und
für Birgit ein passendes Adjektiv.**

**10** Frank ist

**A** egoistisch ☐  **C** traurig ☐

**B** ängstlich ☐  **D** großzügig ☐

[1]

**11** Birgit ist

**A** gut gelaunt ☐  **C** böse ☐

**B** deprimiert ☐  **D** glücklich ☐

[1]

**12** Wo war der Campingplatz?

**A** Am Strand ☐  **C** Nicht weit vom See ☐

**B** Nicht weit vom Wasser ☐  **D** Direkt am See ☐

[1]

**13** Wo waren die Eltern? Schreiben Sie den Satz zu Ende.

Die Eltern waren ........................................ [1]

**14** Warum möchte sie auf die Universität gehen? [1]

**15** Warum möchte sie Fremdsprachen studieren ? [1]

**Answer the following questions in ENGLISH.**

**16** Herr Schwarz is talking about his recent holiday.
a) Name two of the problems at the campsite. [2]
b) What did he decide to do? [1]
c) Why did his decision not work out at first? [1]
d) Why might he have felt pleased in the end? Give **two** details. [2]

[**Total: 25 marks**]

*You will find the transcripts and
answers, with examiner's
comments, on pages 202–204.*

## INTRODUCTION

Unlike in the Listening Test, you have a large degree of control over what you say or choose not to say during the Speaking Test. You have probably been taught to recognise different ways of expressing the same thing in German, but for the purposes of the Speaking Test, it is important that you routinely use the same way of saying, for example, 'Thank you' or 'Excuse me'. It simply makes good sense to reduce the number of things that you need to think about.

In the General Conversation you have a great opportunity to steer the course of the exam and to tell the examiner, your teacher, all the things you have prepared. Of course the examiner needs to probe the depth of your ability, and to find out how you can respond to material which you have not prepared, but you can rest assured that all preparation is worthwhile, and that you will feel more relaxed about the exam as a result of it.

If your Speaking Test includes a presentation, the choice of topic is yours, and it presents you with a good chance to show your preparation.

Here are some of the general problems which candidates encounter in relation to the Speaking Test, and some possible ways to deal with them.

### Problem 1

Most candidates experience a degree of nervousness before the exam. You will probably worry about making a fool of yourself by mispronouncing a word, or by forgetting a simple word or phrase just when you need it. However, it is a real bonus to have a familiar face as the examiner, so make the most of your teacher's experience!

### Solution 1

Nerves are not only to be expected, but are to a certain extent quite helpful in your preparation and will probably stimulate you to do the necessary work beforehand. Your teacher will have talked you through the stages of the exam in the months and weeks preceding the test, and you will certainly have had some practice of exam materials. Always use a tape recorder when practising. Don't just look through a role-play in your bedroom and imagine how you will do it. Turn off the music, press the 'RECORD' button and speak up. Of course it sounds funny at first, but you will soon get used to the sound of your own voice. Try reading a paragraph of a simple text out loud, and get used to the pitch and volume which makes the best recording.

### Problem 2

You are so well prepared that you want to rush through a lot in a short time. Your level of concentration is such that you stare straight past the examiner at the wall behind, creating the impression that you are reading from an invisible auto-cue like a newsreader. It can also lead to a problem if the examiner wants to ask a question out of interest, or to check your understanding of the topic.

### Solution 2

When you make your recordings, speak slowly and clearly, leaving an occasional pause of two or three seconds. These are the pauses which allow the examiner to take in what you are saying and to give you credit for it. Make eye contact with the examiner, so that your facial expression helps with the meaning. Your experienced teacher can read your enthusiasm in your face as well as hearing about your hobbies and interests.

### Problem 3

Too long a gap in your speaking can become a worry for both you and the examiner. Have you forgotten what to say? Have you understood the examiner's question? It could spoil the fluency which you are trying to achieve.

## Solution 3

If you pause while you think of your favourite food or pastime, this is only natural, but try to have an answer ready for most of the obvious questions such as these. They are almost entirely predictable. You may be forgiven for drawing breath while considering something less predictable in the Higher role-play, but you can use a well-timed *ich weiß nicht* to stall for time; at least the examiner knows you are still working on it!

## Problem 4

You finally come up against a difficulty which you can't deal with: either you do not know what the examiner is asking, or you do not know how to answer, perhaps because you are lacking a key word in German.

## Solution 4

In the first case you need to let the examiner know as soon as possible that you are in difficulty. Your eye contact will already have betrayed a lack of comprehension, but for the sake of the person who will later listen to the recording, you need to say what is wrong.

- If the problem is general, then *Ich verstehe nicht* will move the situation along. This is slightly better than *Können Sie das wiederholen?*, because if the examiner repeats the same words exactly, you may be no further forward. The likelihood is that the examiner will see your predicament and re-phrase the question for you.

- If there is one German word that you don't recognise you should say *Ich verstehe das* Wort (German word) *nicht*, or *Was heißt* (German word)? which may also lead to some easier re-phrasing. In either case you will have retrieved the situation, which is to your credit even if you gain no marks for the odd word you don't know.

- If you've forgotten a key word for an answer, simply say *Ich habe das Wort für* (English word) *vergessen*. Your teacher can 'feed' you the word and you can continue without drying up. You may get no credit for that particular sentence, but you do gain credit for coping with the difficulty in as natural a way as possible.

## Problem 5

You may forget what you have rehearsed or the order in which to make your points, resulting in confusion for you or the examiner.

## Solution 5

You may be allowed to make notes on the role-plays, and you should be allowed to take some cue-cards into the exam room to assist your presentation. For the role-plays a note will help you remember what you want to say, and for the presentation the cards help you to maintain your intended order. As a rule, you should limit yourself to single words or short phrases, and not try to write every word you want to say.

## Problem 6

You will only be able to use your dictionary in the preparation area for a limited time.

## Solution 6

Don't look up unnecessary words. Wherever possible choose words where you are certain of gender, plural and pronunciation. For example, on a shopping trip, you can buy *einen Pullover, eine Jacke und ein Paar Schuhe* – don't waste time looking up the words for 'personal stereo with graphic equaliser'!

Try to think through the situation of the Higher role-play and you may be able to predict what the examiner will ask. Incidentally, don't forget to look straight at the examiner when a question is about to be asked, as his/her facial expression will probably help you.

# PRONUNCIATION

## The alphabet

You may have to spell out your name or a place in a role-play or general conversation. Find Chapter 15 – The alphabet, on the CD (Track 32) and listen to the German alphabet. Here is a guide to the pronunciation:

| | | | | | | | |
|---|---|---|---|---|---|---|---|
| **a** | ah | **h** | hah | **o** | oh | **v** | fow |
| **b** | bay | **i** | ee | **p** | pay | **w** | vay |
| **c** | say | **j** | yot | **q** | koo | **x** | icks |
| **d** | day | **k** | kah | **r** | air | **y** | ipsilon |
| **e** | ay | **l** | ell | **s** | ess | **z** | tsed |
| **f** | eff | **m** | emm | **t** | tay | | |
| **g** | gay | **n** | enn | **u** | oo | | |

Notice also the following:

**β** – sounds like 'ss'.
**s** – sounds like an English 'z'.
**z** – is unknown in English, but sounds as if you are saying a 't' before an 's': *Tsimmer*.
If you have to say two of the same letter, simply say *Doppel-ess* for 'ss', etc.

## Vowel sounds

**au** – sounds like 'ow' in cow, or like 'ou' in loud.
The following two sounds are very common but are frequently mixed up:
**ie** – sounds like 'ee' as in reed.
**ei** – sounds like 'i' as in ride.
If in doubt, simply say the second of the two letters in English to remind you which is which.

The following vowels occur with the umlaut or 'sound shift' to modify their sound. The English sound is only very approximate so you may need to ask for further guidance from your teacher, or practise them with your language assistant.
**ä** – is more like the English 'a' as in gate.
**ö** – is like the sound of disgust you might make when you spot something you don't like the look of!
**ü** – is more like the English 'ea' or 'ee' than 'oo', so try saying *Brüder* like 'breeder'.

# *Check yourself 1*

Find Chapter 15 – Check yourself 1, Speaking on the CD (Track 33).
Answer the questions, then compare your answers with the recording.

## QUESTIONS

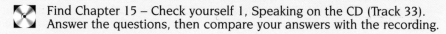

| **Q1** | Spell out the following words. |
|---|---|

a) READING
b) CHARLOTTE
c) VOLKSWAGEN
d) LEICESTER
e) YEOVIL

| **Q2** | Say these words out loud. |
|---|---|

a) zufrieden
b) vielleicht
c) Rückflug
d) Fähre
e) höchst

## ANSWERS

**A1** Listen to the CD. If you spot any errors in your pronunciation, try again.

**A2** Practise these several times, using the pause button after each.

## TUTORIAL

**T1**
a) The vowel sounds EA together often cause difficulty. Practice saying a, e, i, o, u auf Deutsch.
b) Don't forget the Doppel-TAY.
c) Practise the VW sounds FOW-VAY – most Germans drive one!
d) The EI is very confusing as it sounds like the English AE.
e) This contains the difficult ipsilon to start with, and three vowels. Concentrate hard!

**T2**
a) Did you get the ie the right way round straight away?
b) Both difficulties appear in one word.
c) The ü sound followed by the u is difficult to master
d) A common enough word but the tendency is to miss the umlaut, as in ich fahre.
e) Listen carefully. This is not an easy sound for the English ear.

# THE DIFFERENT PARTS OF THE SPEAKING TEST

## ROLE-PLAYS

These test your ability to negotiate a transaction. In simple terms, this means you have to:

- buy something
- ask for directions
- make an arrangement
- use a public service such as a bank, or post office or a combination of these.

The Higher Level role-plays are slightly more complex and often put you in situations where you need to respond to the unexpected, but even this can be prepared. The MEG Higher role-play is a little different, in that it asks you to describe a series of events, such as a day trip, and the situations are often very similar to those in the Higher Level writing.

You may use a dictionary during the preparation time, so remember the guidance given on page 116 in this chapter.

The boards will often use symbols, plus a **?** to show that **you** have to ask a question. You might also meet the following phrases:

Sie beginnen

| | |
|---|---|
| Wählen Sie | Buchstabieren Sie |
| Bestellen Sie | Erklären Sie |
| Beschreiben Sie | Bezahlen Sie |
| Fragen Sie nach ... | Machen Sie einen Vorschlag |
| Sagen Sie | Beantworten Sie |
| Geben Sie | Grüßen Sie |

Ask your teacher to check all the above details for your board.

## Foundation

The tasks will be presented in English, usually with some visuals.

### Preparation

- Look up any individual words that you don't know, but remember, the instructions tell you what the task is. You must **not** translate the instructions into German. For example, if the instruction tells you to ask your friend what he wants to drink, you don't need the German for 'ask' or 'friend'. Simply say *Was möchtest du trinken*?.

- Think through what you will say for each task. You might even be able to say it quietly to yourself as you sit in the preparation area.

- The teacher will start the role-play unless you are told otherwise.

- You should not need to understand what the teacher says in order to fulfil your tasks.

- Make notes if you are allowed to, but don't then read them like a script.

- Don't spend too long on the Foundation; you will need to save your preparation time for the harder tasks.

### In the test

- Be calm – you have done your preparation and you still have the instructions in front of you.

## Foundation/Higher

At this level, there will always be something unpredictable to deal with, so read the instructions through carefully. Again, the scene is set in English, but the tasks are in German.

### Preparation

- Look up any words you need and think through each task.

- Try to guess what the unpredictable element might be. It can often be something as simple as a time, or a spelling, which is required.

### In the test

- Remember your eye contact. Look at the examiner when the unpredictable element is due, and you should understand more easily what is required.

# *Check yourself 2*

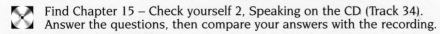 Find Chapter 15 – Check yourself 2, Speaking on the CD (Track 34). Answer the questions, then compare your answers with the recording.

## QUESTIONS

**Q1** *How would you do the following in German?*

a) Ask for a portion of chips.
b) Say it's for three people.
c) Ask if your friend can come.
d) Say excuse me and ask if the seat is free.
e) Find out how much it costs.

**Q2** *Listen to the unpredictable questions on the CD. What do they want to know? How would you reply? You may need to invent the information asked for. The situations are as follows:*

a) You have lost a bag.
b) You have a stomach ache.
c) You have a puncture on your bike.
d) You are booking some seats at the cinema.
e) You are in the tourist information office.

*(Transcript: page 204)*

## ANSWERS

**A1**

a) Ich möchte eine Portion Pommes Frites, bitte.
b) Es ist für drei Personen.
c) Kann mein Freund mitkommen?
d) Entschuldigung. Ist hier frei?
OR:
Entschuldigen Sie, bitte. Ist der Platz frei?
e) Was kostet das?

**A2**

a) What was in it?
b) Since when?
c) How will you get to school tomorrow?
d) Where would you like to sit?
e) What do you need?

## TUTORIAL

**T1**

a) *Even when you are not specifically asked to do so, you should be polite enough to say 'please' and 'thank you'. You could, of course, omit* ich möchte *altogether.*
b) Personen *is more usual than* Leute *in such situations.*
c) *A straightforward direct question, but don't simply use* kommen *in this context. You could, of course, use the feminine* meine Freundin.
d) *Choose one version of each part now, and stick to it. Don't clutter your mind with both.*
e) Wieviel *would be possible but not necessary. Stick to the easiest way at Foundation Level.*

**T2**

a) *Meine Sportsachen (waren drin).*
b) *(Ich habe sie) seit heute morgen.*
c) *(Ich fahre) mit dem Bus.*
d) *(Wir möchten) im Parkett (sitzen), nicht zu weit vorne.*
e) *(Ich möchte) einen Stadtplan, bitte.*

### Higher

Most of these role-plays will contain a problem for you to solve, or something for you to negotiate – they will not be straightforward. The MEG Higher role-play will ask you to describe a series of events in the past tense.

#### Preparation

- You need to think through the situation as set out on the card, and explore some of the avenues which might open up as the conversation develops. Remember, you can't prepare a script in advance. This role-play is really a series of unpredictable questions and ad lib responses on your part.

- For example, if you are returning goods to a shop you will need to think of the reasons why you might do so. Are the goods broken or damaged? Do you want to change the colour/size of clothes? Are you asking politely or complaining bitterly? What tone will you adopt?

#### In the test

- Maintain eye contact and respond appropriately to the examiner.

- Make sure that you are true to the situation on the card and give any information accurately as set down.

### Higher MEG

Remember to use the past tense – perfect for the actions and imperfect (simple past) for the weather and moods.

#### Preparation

- The most important thing is to work out the sequence of pictures and look at the time-scale. It will usually be a day's events, so you can almost certainly use easy vocabulary to describe daily routine like getting up, having breakfast, leaving the house, travelling to school/town, lunch, evening meal, time for bed, etc.

- Try to think of something to say about each picture, remembering to mention how the characters might feel. You are usually offered the choice of telling the story in the 1st person (i.e. you or you and your friend are the main characters), or you can tell it in the 3rd person (saying 'he did this' and 'they did that'). You should feel much more secure in the 1st person.

- The MEG cards always contain helpful vocabulary, individual words and sometimes phrases under each picture. You should use these with care. Don't simply read them out, but make sure you have conjugated the verb. For example, it might say *in die Stadt fahren* under a picture of a bus. Make sure you handle the verb correctly and say *Ich bin mit dem Bus in die Stadt gefahren*.

### In the test

- Keep one eye on the card so that you don't lose the sequence, but make sure you try to interest the examiner in what you are saying. You might even try something humorous, if you feel confident enough. After all, some of the pictures may well lead you to the conclusion that something funny has happened. For example:
  - Georg has put on Udo's trousers after swimming and looks very silly because they don't fit.
  - Margret has found a great skirt to buy but gets to the counter and finds that she has no money.

  A laugh during the test will do you good!

# *Check yourself 3*

Find Chapter 15 – Check yourself 3, Speaking on the CD (Track 35).
Answer the questions, then compare your answers with the recording.

## QUESTIONS

**Q1** **How would you do the following in German?**

a) Ask to see the manager.
b) Ask to exchange the goods.
c) Say you bought them here yesterday.
d) Complain about the state of the shower in your room.
e) Explain why you wish to change your room.

**Q2** **Listen to the unpredictable questions on the CD, and try to answer them.**

a) You are applying for a job as a shop assistant.
b) You are working at a tourist office.
c) You are reporting a theft.
d) You are talking to a friend about holidays.
e) You are buying a present for your father.

(Transcript: page 204)

**REMEMBER! Cover the answers if you want to.**

## ANSWERS

**A1**
a) Ich möchte den Geschäftsleiter sehen, bitte.
b) Ich möchte gern diese Hose (usw) umtauschen, bitte.
c) Ich habe sie gestern hier gekauft.
d) Die Dusche in meinem Zimmer ist ganz dreckig.
e) Ich möchte ein anderes Zimmer haben. In diesem Zimmer funktioniert die Heizung nicht.

## TUTORIAL

**T1**
a/b) *These are both standard introductions to a complaint – don't forget to maintain your polite manner.*

c) *You could mention the price, or the person who served you, etc. These details may be given on the card, or you may have to provide them.*

d/e) *You could, of course, choose a different form of complaint, but these two are quite obvious.*

## ANSWERS

**A2**

a) Ja. Letztes Jahr habe ich im Supermarkt gearbeitet.
b) Es gibt ein tolles Stadtmuseum und ein schönes Schloß.
c) Sie war jung, ziemlich groß und hatte lange blonde Haare.
d) Ich war mit meiner Familie an der Südküste.
e) Mein Vater hat Schuhgröße 45.

## TUTORIAL

**T2**

a) *It is almost obvious from the scene-setting that you will be asked about your experience.*
b) *This is an easy one – you quote straight from the description of your own home town, or you have to make it up.*
c) *Two or three adjectives will be sufficient. It is enough that you have understood and responded appropriately.*
d) *Again, keep it simple. The simple past 'I was' is quite enough here. You need no further details of the holiday.*
e) *You know your own size, so work from that. Any sensible number will do.*

## PRESENTATION AND DISCUSSION

This forms part of the Speaking Test for both MEG and NEAB and may be used as coursework for Edexcel (London). Go on to the next section if you use a different exam board.

You need to speak for 1 minute (MEG) or $1\frac{1}{2}$ minutes (NEAB) on a topic you choose from one of the areas of experience. Then your teacher will ask you some questions about the presentation.

### Choosing your topic

You may choose something you know very well, such as *Meine Schule* or *Meine Familie*, or talk about *Mein Hobby*, *Mein Urlaub* or *Mein Schulaustausch*. Make sure you check the choice of topic with your teacher first and listen to his/her advice, as the choice might restrict the mark you get in the test.

- If you choose a basic topic and talk in simple sentences, you may simply not cover enough ground to raise your mark into the Higher Level range. Simple sentences, simple opinions and present tense will not add up to a good mark. Conversely, if you choose a difficult or obscure topic, you may grind to a halt for lack of vocabulary in German.

- Discuss the presentation with your teacher so that he/she can prepare sensible questions to ask you.

- Introduce the topic in the first sentence for the benefit of the examiner who will listen to the cassette later and who has no prior knowledge of the topic.

### How much detail

Say enough to make the topic interesting, but don't try to impress the examiner with everything you know about the subject in detail. This is not the purpose of the test.

- Avoid lists of more than a few words. On no account should you, for example, try to list all your teachers in school, or all the teams you've played against!

- Try to avoid English words and expressions. It is better to say *Ich höre gern englische Popmusik* than to say *Ich höre gern Oasis*. If you are describing your favourite TV viewing, then stick to a general term like *Sportsendungen*, rather than saying *Match of the Day* or *Grandstand*.

- Make sure you have planned a few sentences in the past and future. This is essential to your scoring well, and even the simplest sentences can do the trick: *Letztes Jahr hat unsere Mannschaft einen Pokal gewonnen* or *Wir werden nächstes Jahr sicherlich besser spielen*.

- Time what you are preparing so that you don't run too far over time or, worse still, don't fill up the allotted time.

## Cue cards

These are vital to stop you forgetting what you want to say and to maintain the order.

- Key words or short phrases are all you need. You are not allowed to bring in a script to read from.

- Don't have too many.

- Number them.

- Don't read from them.

## Delivery

Practise regularly beforehand what you are going to say and make a recording of it so you get used to the sound of your voice.

- You don't need to be word perfect. It usually doesn't sound as good, your voice becomes monotonous and you lose the real communication with the person you should be talking to.

- Don't try to rush. You may trip yourself up or miss vital points. Remember how long you have spent preparing for this one minute.

- If you are allowed to bring in visual aids such as a photograph or an object (no pet reptiles!), this can be a help to you and the examiner, but choose these carefully, and don't simply pick a photo of lot of people and then list who they all are. Try to pick something which can lead to a bit more discussion after you have done your presentation.

## Predicting the questions

- Leave something for the teacher to ask you. You can deliberately leave out saying something obvious like where you stayed on holiday, so that the teacher can make a note of it and come back to the question in the discussion which follows.

- Remind yourself of the German question words *Was? Wann? Was für?*, etc. (see Chapter 10). Go through your presentation and stop frequently and think which question word would be sensible at any point. This is probably what is going through the examiner's mind when you give your presentation.

## GENERAL CONVERSATION

This is the common test of all boards, although there are minor variations in what each one requires. Make sure you understand clearly from your teacher what to do. This is your big chance to show what you can do, and the topics are all familiar to you.

## Tenses

You will not achieve a Grade C unless you can show knowledge of the past, present and future tenses. Your teacher is obliged to make the opportunities available to you and you need to listen out for your 'prompts':

*Was hast du letztes Wochenende gemacht?*
*Wo warst du letzten Sommer in den Ferien?* (for the past tenses)
*Was wirst du im September machen?*
*Was hast du nächstes Jahr vor?* (for the future)

These are obvious introductions which you will probably practise with your teacher beforehand.

### Opinions

Apart from the use of *gern* with simple verb phrases, how will you express what you feel about things? Try some of the following if you want to make an impression:

*Ich glaube, daß ...* – I think that ...
*Ich meine, daß es besser sein könnte.* – I think it could be better.
*Meiner Meinung nach ist das die beste Mannschaft.* – In my opinion they're the best team.
*Ich halte das für dumm.* – I think it's stupid.
*Ich habe es satt.* – I'm fed up with it.

Remember, you need to express opinions for your Grade C.

### Full accounts and descriptions

- Try to link ideas and sentences using conjunctions such as *denn*, *aber*, *dann*.

- Impress the examiner with a relative clause or two, using the relative pronouns, *der*, *die*, *das* (see Chapter 9).

- Think about some more adventurous adjectives and adverbs to add interest to your comments.

- Take every opportunity to expand on a question. Don't 'close down' the possibilities by a *ja/nein* or other brief answer. So, for example, when asked, *Hast du Geschwister?*, instead of just *Ja* or *Ja, zwei Schwestern*, you should continue with some further details: *Die eine heißt Susie und die andere Margaret. Sie sind beide älter als ich und studieren schon auf der Uni.*

### What not to do

- Don't allow pauses to go on too long, or hesitate before every answer.

- Don't make the teacher work hard to get you to talk.

- Don't clam up for fear of making a mistake. You don't have to be word perfect to get the message across.

# Check yourself 4

 Find Chapter 15 – Check yourself 4, Speaking on the CD (Track 36). Answer the questions, then compare your answers with the recording.

## QUESTIONS

**Q1** *Answer these questions (which are also on the CD). Try to give more than just a bare answer.*

a) Hast du Geschwister?
b) Was machst du in deiner Freizeit?
c) Was hast du in den letzten Ferien gemacht?
d) Was machst du im September?
e) Kannst du mir ein bißchen über deine Stadt erzählen?

**Q2** *Answer these questions (which are also on the CD). Make sure you use a second clause in your answer.*

a) Magst du deine Schule?
b) Wie kommst du mit deiner Schwester aus?
c) Was machst du heute abend?
d) Was machst du am Wochenende?
e) Was für Sport treibst du?

**REMEMBER! Cover the answers if you want to.**

## ANSWERS

**A1**

a) Ja, ich habe zwei ältere Brüder, die John und Harry heißen. Der John studiert jetzt Biologie auf der Universität, und der Harry ist schon fertig und arbeitet in Sheffield.

b) Ich gehe gern in die Stadt, weil ich mir sehr gern Kleidung anschaue. Ich kaufe aber dann oft auf dem Markt ein, denn es ist dort viel billiger als in den größeren Geschäften.

c) Ich war letzten Sommer in Frankreich, wo wir zwei Wochen auf einem Campingplatz verbracht haben.

d) Im September werde ich hier bleiben, weil ich Biologie und Physik und Mathe weiterstudieren will.

e) Northampton ist eine relativ große Stadt, aber es gibt nicht sehr viel für die Touristen. Ich wohne gern hier, weil ich viele Freunde in der Nähe habe.

**A2**

a) Ich finde die Schule ganz gut, weil die meisten Lehrer ziemlich engagiert sind. Außerdem gibt es hier viele Klubs und Aktivitäten nach der Schule.

b) Meine Schwester ist schwer in Ordnung, und ich komme mit ihr sehr gut zurecht, außer wenn ich ihre Kleidung trage.

c) Heute abend habe ich viele Hausaufgaben, also kann ich nicht viel fernsehen. Ich werde vielleicht meine Lieblingssendungen aufnehmen.

d) Am Wochenende fahre ich mit meinen Eltern zu unseren Verwandten in Norwich, weil meine Oma Geburtstag hat.

e) Ich spiele ziemlich viel Basketball, und zwar dreimal in der Woche, weil unsere Mannschaft sehr gut in der Liga steht.

## TUTORIAL

**T1**

a) *The relative clause and the extra detail make this an interesting answer.*

b) *This is more adventurous, but quite easy to learn. The* denn *in the second sentence avoids repeating* weil.

c) *This is easy vocabulary linked by a simple conjunction for an effective answer.*

d) *The future using* werden *is followed by the subordinate clause and the modal* will. *All good material to score marks.*

e) *The contrast made by* aber *in the first sentence is straightforward enough. The following sentence includes an opinion and a reason why you like the town.*

**T2**

a) Ganz *and* ziemlich *are better than over-using* sehr. Engagiert *is a much more interesting word than* nett, *and* außerdem *makes a good alternative to* und. *Don't forget that it's followed by the inverted subject/verb construction*

b) Schwer in Ordnung *is rather colloquial, but absolutely right in this context. There is a degree of humour in the next sentence, which is a good reason for making the point.*

c) *This consequence of the amount of homework is well connected by* also, *and the use of the future with* werden *instead of the present is commendable.*

d) *Beginning with the adverb phrase (which forces the inversion after it) is a good style to adopt. The correct use of the dative plural endings in two separate phrases is also something to note.*

e) *This is the appropriate use of* und zwar, *connecting the extra detail to the general phrase* ziemlich viel. *Following this with a reason will further impress your examiner.*

# EXAM PRACTICE

Role-plays vary slightly in presentation from board to board, but you should aim to have the competence to deal with all of them. All visuals and instructions – whether in English or German – will be simple enough to make the intention clear.

Remember to use the dictionary to check only the words you don't understand, and aim to spend no more than 2-3 minutes preparing a Foundation or Foundation/Higher role-play, and 5-6 minutes preparing a Higher role-play. In the case of the Higher, your preparation must include trying to predict what the examiner might ask you.

Then find Chapter 15 – Exam Practice Speaking on the CD (Track 37) and compare the recorded answers with what you have prepared.

**1**  **Im Hotel**  Sie wollen mit Ihrer Familie im Hotel übernachten.

**Situation**  You and your family want to stay overnight in a German hotel.

Your teacher will play the part of the hotel receptionist and will begin the conversation.

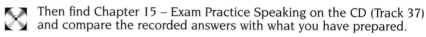

**2**  You and your friend are at a café and want to order. Choose two items for each of you from those in the box. Don't forget to find out where the toilets are, and to start and finish the conversation politely.

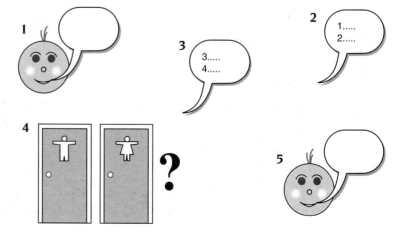

**3** **In der Bank**

Situation   You have run out of money while in Germany and go into a bank to change some of your travellers' cheques. Your teacher will play the part of the bank clerk and will start the conversation.

1   You have travellers' cheques. What do you say?

2   Say what sort of travellers' cheques you have.

3   Answer the question.

4   You have forgotten your passport. What do you say?

5   Ask about the opening times of the bank.

**4** **Am Bahnhof**

You are on holiday in Germany and want to visit your friend in Bonn. You go to the railway station to find out about train times and buy a ticket. Your teacher will play the part of the ticket office clerk and start the conversation.

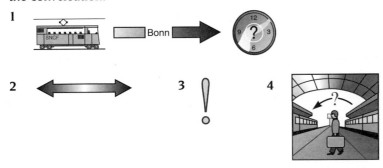

**5** **Situation**   You have bought some trousers at a clothes shop in town, but when you get back to your youth hostel you realise they have a small tear in them. You take them back the following day. The examiner will start the conversation.

**6** **Situation** The notes below give an outline of an exchange visit to Germany you made with your school. Tell the examiner about the journey from your town to Düsseldorf.
Be prepared to respond to any questions or comments from the examiner.

*Wann abgefahren?*  *Wie gefahren?*  *Durchfahrt interessant?*

*Was gemacht?*  *Wann angekommen?*  *Gastfamilie getroffen*  *Was gegessen?*  *Müde?*

## PRESENTATION AND DISCUSSION

Not all candidates are required to do this section, but the material recorded here will give you some further idea of the level required and some ideas of things you might say in the course of general conversation.

Prepare a presentation of about 1½ minutes about your family. Begin your presentation with *Ich werde meine Familie beschreiben.*

 Then find the appropriate point on the CD (Track 38) and listen to the sample presentation. Did you find similar things to say? Did you include a range of tenses and structures? Did you anticipate the questions the teacher was likely to ask?

## GENERAL CONVERSATION

*You will find all the transcripts and examiner's comments on pages 205–210.*

 Find Track 39 on the CD. Listen to the questions which begin this section and answer as fully as you can. The topics covered are School, Home Town, and Free Time and Leisure. Remember to listen carefully to the tense and respond accordingly. Then listen to the sample student's answer and compare it with what you have said.

## INTRODUCTION

Reading is generally thought to be the easiest of the four skills, and it is certainly true that you have more chance to concentrate on the language than when you are listening. However, there are some specific difficulties associated with reading which can be addressed separately. This chapter will help you to identify ways in which you can improve your comprehension of written German.

### Problem 1

The fact that you are allowed a dictionary can unsettle you right from the start, and you should turn to it only after you have thought carefully about why you want to use it. You may look at the passage and feel that you understand so little of it that you wade into the dictionary for the first few words, only to find that you are wasting a huge amount of time and that you are not much the wiser as to the meaning of the whole passage.

### Solution 1

Remember that you have been prepared for a test at this level. The German is intended to be largely within your grasp. First, read the instruction in German (or in some cases in English) before attempting to read the passage. Then read the questions or exercise which form the test. This is a very important guide to the context of passage, and can give you important clues as to the vocabulary you may encounter. Look particularly carefully at the interrogatives at the beginning of questions, if appropriate. Think what you are looking for – an action verb? a noun? a time? a price? Finally, read the passage for the first time, bearing in mind what you already know about the passage. Use your dictionary only if there are any words in the questions you don't understand, or any key words in the passage. Don't waste time looking up any unnecessary words.

### Problem 2

You may be distracted by the style of the print, or any handwriting. Perhaps there are different fonts and sizes of print, or the passage is in newspaper columns.

### Solution 2

Make sure you have enough practice of actual test materials in varying styles. Don't be afraid to pick up a German magazine or newspaper and glance at the advertisements, headlines, or lead paragraphs. Every little helps!

### Problem 3

Speed-reading or 'skimming' can cause you to miss the meaning of words you should know, or you mistake them for another word which appears similar.

### Solution 3

Take your time to read words carefully enough. Check the meaning of a word, if you think it may be the key word needed for the understanding of a phrase or sentence.

### Problem 4

It can be easy to misunderstand the crucial first word of a question.

### Solution 4

Learn these interrogatives NOW!
*Wo?* means 'Where?' not 'Who?'.
*Wer?* means 'Who?' not 'Where?'. This is an unforgivable mistake, even when you are under pressure.

| | |
|---|---|
| *Was?* | What? |
| *Wann?* | When? (general or specific) |
| *Um wieviel Uhr?* | At what time? (specific) |
| *Wie lange?* | How long (for)? |
| *Was für ...?* | What sort of ...? |
| *Wieviel?* | How much?/How many? |
| *Warum?* | Why? |

## GENERAL STRATEGIES

### Use the question to help you

- In multiple choice questions about simple facts, you know that one answer is correct, so you can bear this in mind when reading the passage. For example, if the question is:
  *Eine Rückfahrkarte für einen fünfzehnjährigen kostet:*
  DM 15,00     DM 10,00     DM 7,50     DM 5,00
  you can focus on these facts and disregard everything else.
  **Note:** Exam boards do not want to test your mathematical ability. If you find yourself adding up or dividing by two, you are on the wrong track.

- Similarly, if the question wants you to focus on an emotion or attitude, you can look for words and expressions associated with it, or opposite to it, in the case of a TRUE/FALSE exercise:
  *Maria treibt gern Sport.* RICHTIG *oder* FALSCH?

- Look out for phrases like *mag gern, interessiert sich für, hat Spaß, findet ... gut/schön*, etc. You are unlikely to see the exact words of the question in the text.

- However, some tests use a third category of NICHT IM TEXT in order to make the exercise more difficult. If you really cannot find the evidence to support either RICHTIG or FALSCH, then you may need to tick this third box.

### Use the context to help you

- *Auf dem Markt wollte Peter ein Pfund Kirschen kaufen.*
  Even without knowing that *Kirschen* are cherries, you should be able to work out that it is something which you can buy in kilos at the market because *Markt, Kilo* and *kaufte* are so obvious. Surely you couldn't write 'churches' now!

### Use your common sense

- If you are in a supermarket you are more likely to see a sign which says *Frische Brötchen* than *Ausfahrt freilassen.*

- Similarly, you should have some idea from your knowledge of German food and drink that a *Bratwurst mit Pommes Frites* is something you eat and so could not be the answer to the question *Was hat Georg getrunken?*.

# *Check yourself 1*

## QUESTIONS

**Q1** *Match the answers to the questions.*

**Fragen**

a)  Was kauft sie im Supermarkt?
b)  Wann geht sie nach Hause?
c)  Wieviele Leute waren dort?
d)  Warum war sein Vater böse?
e)  Wer war nicht zu Hause?

**Antworten**

Um halb zehn
Weil Georg so spät nach Hause kam
Lebensmittel
Seine Mutter
Fünfundvierzig

**Q2** **Pick out the attitude.**

**Ahlke** geht am liebsten mit ihrer Freundin ins Hallenbad.
**Georg** macht seine Hausaufgaben in der Küche.
**Margret** ist gerade aus dem Urlaub zurückgekommen.

**Rainer** geht sehr ungern mit dem Hund spazieren.
**Sabine** möchte gern so bald wie möglich ins Bett gehen.

a)   Ahlke mag gern schwimmen.

b)   Georg kocht gern.

c)   Der Urlaub hat Margret gut gefallen.

d)   Rainer mag Tiere nicht.

e)   Sabine ist müde.

| Richtig | Falsch | Nicht im Text |
|---------|--------|---------------|
|         |        |               |
|         |        |               |
|         |        |               |
|         |        |               |
|         |        |               |

**REMEMBER! Cover the answers if you want to.**

## ANSWERS

**A1**
a)   Lebensmittel
b)   Um halb zehn
c)   Fünfundvierzig
d)   Weil Georg so spät nach Hause kam
e)   Seine Mutter

**A2**
a)   Richtig
b)   Nicht im Text
c)   Nicht im Text
d)   Falsch
e)   Richtig

## TUTORIAL

**T1**
a)   Was *must mean a thing or object.*
b)   Wann *needs a general or specific time.*
c)   Wieviele *needs an amount or a number.*
d)   Warum *needs a reason.*
e)   Wer *must have a name, a person or a personal pronoun.*

**T2**
a)   *The superlative* am liebsten *means she must like it.*
b)   *Although* kocht *and* Küche *are associated, there is no evidence of his liking cooking.*
c)   *Again, there is no mention of her feelings about the holiday.*
d)   *Watch out for* ungern. *It means quite definitely **not** liking something!*
e)   *The phrase* so bald wie möglich *gives you sufficient evidence to infer that she is tired.*

# SPECIFIC POINTS TO PRACTISE

## Numbers and time

Watch out for the following expressions:
| | |
|---|---|
| *eineinhalb (or anderthalb)* | one and a half |
| *viereinhalb* | four and a half |
| *eine* Viertelstunde | a quarter of an hour |
| *eine* Dreiviertelstunde | three quarters of an hour |
| *halb zehn* | half past nine (Remember the trap!) |

## Some regular problems for unwary candidates

### See

This word has two genders and two meanings. Because Germany has so little coastline, but the Germans enjoy watersports so much, you can guess it usually means 'lake'. However, there's no substitute for learning it:

**der** See – lake, and **die** See – sea

Phrases such as *am See* show that the noun cannot be feminine and therefore must be 'lake'. Also, don't forget that *das Meer* is more common than *die See*.

131

**Die Küche/der Kuchen**

These two words with food connections can catch you out. If you are unsure, look them up now!

**The *kein/klein* trap**

Enough said? Do you remember the examples from Chapter 14, Listening and responding?

There are other problems involving words which look similar but mean quite different things. A dictionary can help you in such cases, if you think you know which meaning you are looking for.

### Negatives

The negatives *gar nicht/gar kein* and *überhaupt nicht/überhaupt kein* are obvious enough, but watch out for *fast*, which means almost, and can change the whole meaning of the sentence:

> *Er hat den Bus fast verpaßt.*

Did he catch the bus or not? Yes, he did.

Similarly, *nur* can change the whole meaning. *Das kostet nur zwanzig Mark* suggests something is cheap, while *Ich habe nur zehn Mark* suggests that 10 Marks is not enough for your needs.

### Word separation

German is well known for its long compound nouns. Have no fear! Remember the saying: 'Inside every long word there are short words trying to get out!' Look at the end of a long noun to find out what the main noun is. It may be something as simple as *Tisch* or *Wagen*. The words attached to the front of it describe it in some way or other.

### Capital letters

These help you to identify the nouns, but may also mislead you into thinking that a common noun is a place or person. For example, if you see the sentence:

> *Man rief den Arzt an, weil die Frau Hilfe brauchte.*

don't amuse the examiner by talking about *Frau Hilfe*!

# Check yourself 2

## QUESTIONS

**Q1** *Write out the following numbers as figures.*

a) dreiunddreißig
b) hundertfünfundvierzig
c) sechsundsiebzig

*Write out the following prices.*

d) Zwei Mark fünfundneunzig
e) Neunundzwanzig Mark neunundneunzig

**Q3** *Choose the correct word to fit each sentence.*

a) Er hat seinen ... vergessen.
Schloß   schließen   Schüssel   Schlüssel

b) Sie saß im Restaurant und las die ...
Fahrkarte   Landkarte   Speisekarte   Theaterkarte

c) Wir stiegen an der nächsten ... aus.
Station   Haltestelle   Stadion   Bahnhof

d) Sie wartete auf die ...
Post   Pfosten   Posten   Poster

e) Seine Tante lag zwei Wochen im ...
Stadthaus   Hochhaus   Krankenhaus   Rathaus

**REMEMBER! Cover the answers if you want to.**

**ANSWERS**

**A1**
a) 33
b) 145
c) 76
d) DM 2,95
e) DM 29,99

**A2**
a) Schüssel
b) Speisekarte
c) Haltestelle
d) Post
e) Krankenhaus

**TUTORIAL**

**T1**
*If you take your time, none of these need be a problem, but you should be able to do them at speed and without mistake. Anything involving numbers should not need looking up, so be sure you know them thoroughly.*

**T2**
*This exercise forces you to think about the context of the sentence before inserting the missing word. This is exactly what you must do before reaching for the dictionary in the examination. In this case, the words offered as multiple choice are well known, so there is no problem. Check yourself 3 will ask you to think through a similar task and find a word from the dictionary which is correct.*

## HIGHER LEVEL PERFORMANCE

At Higher Level, you will be expected to do a number of things which are not expected at Foundation Level.

### Pick out the main points from a passage

You have read the rubric. When you read the questions, remember that they follow the passage chronologically. More importantly, there will not be masses of material in the passage which is not tested. The examiners might set one or two questions per paragraph, but it unusual for there to be a paragraph which has no question set about it.

Use the paragraph structure of longer passages to help you, and look for key words. Make sure you identify the subject and verb of each sentence, and try to decide which might be key words. If a word appears regularly and you don't know its meaning, it might be worth looking up.

### Identify attitudes and opinions

You will not necessarily always see the key words like *glücklich* or *böse* to tell you how people feel. For example, the sentence:
    *Ich bin gern ins Theater gegangen.*
will tell you that someone enjoyed the experience, whereas:
    *Wenn ich mit meinem Bruder Karten spiele, gibt es immer Ärger!*
might suggest a less pleasant pastime.

### Make deductions/inferences from what you read

If you read:
    *Wir haben ziemlich lange auf die Post gewartet, was sehr ungewöhnlich war.*
you should be able to deduce that the postman is normally punctual.

### Understand the gist of what you read

If you read:
    *Ziemlich viele meiner Klassenkameraden fahren weg, oder machen einen*
    *Campingurlaub irgendwo in der Nähe. Nur ich muß die drei Wochen zu Hause*
    *bleiben. Aber im Winter mache ich einen Skiurlaub.*
you should be able to see that the writer is talking about holidays.

### Answer questions using German which you have not heard on the recording

If you had to answer this question about the previous example:

*Was hält sie davon, daß sie jetzt nicht in Urlaub fährt?*

you would have to answer *Sie ist traurig, daß sie nicht wegfährt. Sie freut sich schon auf ihren Winterurlaub.* If you simply said that she is not going on holiday now, or that she is going in winter, you would not score the mark. It is her feeling about the situation which is being targeted.

### Understand vocabulary outside the minimum core vocabulary

All the exam boards specify a minimum core vocabulary which candidates need in order to deal with the Foundation Level tests, but there will always be words outside the range of this core. The exam setters have many years of experience in the range of vocabulary which can be tested. Needless to say, the more vocabulary you do know the better, so you need to make a long-term commitment to the regular learning and using of new words.

# *Check yourself 3*

## QUESTIONS

**Q1** **Pick out the detail.**

> Herzlich Willkommen bei Bouvier!
> **Der** Buchhändler in Bonn.
>
> Bücher, Spiele, Zeichnen, Malen,
> Geschenkartikel, Zeitungen,
> Zeitschriften, Papier, Taschenbücher,
> Ansichtskarten.
>
> **Im Sonderangebot: Berühmte**
> **Künstler im Postkartenformat**

**What can you buy at the bookshop?**

a) school books
b) drawing materials
c) presents
d) toys
e) postcards

| Richtig | Falsch |
|---------|--------|
|         |        |
|         |        |
|         |        |
|         |        |
|         |        |

**Q2** **Choose a word to complete the sentence. It may be a verb, noun or adjective.**

a) Die Tasche war sehr ........................... zu tragen. (**light**)
b) Er wollte es sofort in den Garten .............................................. .(**plant**)
c) Am Samstagnachmittag gingen sie zum .............................................. .(**match**)
d) Sie kauften ..................................... für ein Kleid. (**material**)
e) Sie wohnt in einer ......................... in dieser Siedlung (**flat**)

## REMEMBER! Cover the answers if you want to.

## ANSWERS

**A1**
a) Falsch
b) Richtig
c) Richtig
d) Falsch
e) Richtig

## TUTORIAL

**T1** *For this exercise there is no* Nicht im Text *column, so the choice is* Richtig *or* Falsch *only. Even in this seemingly easy exercise there are distractors, i.e. words which might mislead you. For example,* Spiele *is not* Spielzeug *(toys), and 'presents' appears as the compound noun* Geschenkartikel. *Did you recognise* Ansichtskarten *as picture postcards?*

**A2**
a) leicht
b) pflanzen
c) Spiel
d) Stoff
e) Wohnung

**T2** *Checking vocabulary in the reading text presents great dangers to the unwary and those who have not practised looking up words and cross-checking them.*
a) *In the dictionary, you will find a long list of nouns including* Licht, Lampe, *etc., a list of adjectives including* leicht, *and some verbs. The key words to understand are* Tasche *and* tragen. *The verb* war *should prevent you from choosing another verb, and steer you towards an adjective. If you check* leicht *in the German-English section of the dictionary you will find reference to weight.*
b) *The first clue is* Garten. Pflanze *exists as a noun, but you should have seen another clue in* wollte, *which needs to be followed by a verb in the infinitive to make sense.*
c) *As obvious as this seems when you see* Spiel, *this is not always the first word given in the dictionary. You are just as likely to come up with the words for 'a good match' (i.e. similar) or a match with which to light a fire.*
d) *The noun you need is likely to come after a list of adjectives and close to the inviting word* Material. Stoff, *however, should have some reference to clothes with it, even before you set out to check it in the German-English.*
e) *Of course you haven't forgotten* die Wohnung! *If you do end up looking for it, you will need to pass a lot of words to do with flat areas, sandflats, etc. It should stand out as a place to live, and you may also find references to* Etagenhaus/Hochhaus *(block of flats).*

# DIFFERENT KINDS OF READING

## Newspaper and magazine articles

These are usually factual and invariably in the past, because the events they describe have already happened. These accounts will be written largely in the imperfect tense, so you need to recognise the verbs quickly. Check the common strong and irregular ones in the verb table in Chapter 18 (page 170).

## Advertisements

Just as in English, there are no rules of grammar for advertisers, so you may find bold imperatives or questions, or simply statements made without a verb:
*Nie so was gesehen? Greifen Sie zu! Kaufen Sie sofort das Neueste von VW!*

## Descriptive passages

These can range from simple accounts about a school trip to tourist brochures which describe the sights of the area you are visiting. Adjectives will play an important part in setting the tone, so think about the mood of the writing as you read. You are unlikely to encounter negative descriptions in a tourist brochure, nor usually in accounts about a holiday, unless things obviously went wrong. If something is good or bad, there is often a clause nearby to tell you why:
*Der Urlaub war fantastisch – zwei Wochen lang ununterbrochene Sonne!*
You may never have encountered *ununterbrochen* but it should be obvious that the sun shone a lot.
*Die Rückfahrt war eine Katastrophe – stundenlang im Auto in der prallheißen Sonne!*

135

What comment does the writer make about the sun this time? Certainly not as pleased to see it as the first writer.

## DIFFERENT KINDS OF QUESTION

### Multiple choice (non-verbal)

This sort of exercise is often called picture matching. These are three forms:
1  In the simplest sort, you may have to pick out a time or a price from the text and match it to one of those on the question paper.
2  You may have to match statements to numbered pictures or symbols, for example those representing people's jobs or interests.
3  You may have to decide upon the most appropriate scene from a longer passage. For example, is the family at the beach, at the theatre, or walking in the woods?

In 1, you are reading for a specific detail, whereas in 2 and 3 you need to pick up the gist of a longer passage. In the case of similar pictures to choose from, you will need to focus on the detail of the pictures and decide what differences there are, before you can search for them in the text. There might be a different number of people involved, for example, or different weather.

### Multiple choice (verbal)

Again, there are different types:
1  At Foundation Level one-word answers are fairly straightforward:
    *Georg ist* ........................... . (*glücklich/traurig/böse/müde*)
    However, the more difficult questions often require more deduction.
2  A phrase may be required instead of a single word. These are less likely to be taken directly from the passage.
    *Sie treffen sich* .................. . (*am Bahnhof/im Café/in der Schule/vor der Schule*)
    In this example, the last two choices are very close and you would have to look closely to differentiate between 'in' and 'in front of' the school.
3  Sentence answers. These might ask you to relate one of the choices to a specific person:
    *Was machte die Mutter am Nachmittag?*
    **A** *Sie ging einkaufen.*          **C** *Sie hörte Musik.*
    **B** *Sie mußte arbeiten.*          **D** *Sie besuchte ihre Mutter.*
    Or they might ask you to choose a person for each statement, in which case you will certainly have more people to choose from than there are statements:
    *Schreiben Sie den richtigen Namen.*
    *… faulenzt sehr gern.*                 *… schwimmt mehrmals in der Woche.*
    *… kann sehr gut Schach spielen.*       *… kauft gern neue Kleidung.*
    If you are able to use a dictionary, it would be worth checking any words in these statements which you do not recognise.

### Answers in German

Some of the above examples are simple ways of making you write German answers. Spellings errors should not occur, because you will simply be copying a word or phrase from the question paper.

If you have to write some original German to express your answer, make it as simple as possible to get the point across. Communication is everything; your German is unlikely to be penalised unless it is unclear what you mean.

### Answers in English

These questions are usually reserved for the most difficult passages, and test the greatest understanding, particularly where they concern attitudes and emotions which you might struggle to describe in German. These questions more frequently ask **how?** and **why?** than **what?** or **where?**.

Answers in English are inherently more dangerous in the Reading Test, because you have longer to study the passage and may want to keep adding to your first thought. The danger of a longer answer is that you may obscure your correct thought with other material which could lose you the mark. Only write more than the minimum if your answer becomes clearer. Always check that your answer does not contain contradictory statements.

# Check yourself 4

## QUESTIONS

**Q1** **Answer the questions in German.**

a) Ilse ist schon seit zwei Jahren mit Sabine befreundet.
Wer ist Sabine?

b) Vater arbeitet nur wochentags im Büro.
Wann sollte er am besten mit den Kindern ans Meer fahren?

c) Heute schläft Papa aus, weil er erst spät gestern abend von seiner Geschäftsreise nach Hause kam.
Wo war sein Vater letzte Woche?

d) Wir haben Mutter von dem Konzert erzählt, als wir nach Hause gekommen sind.
Wo war Mutter während des Abends?

e) Der Wecker hat gar nicht geklingelt, und mein Englischlehrer war ziemlich böse, als ich in die Klasse kam.
Worüber hat sich der Englischlehrer geärgert?

**Q2** **Identify the attitudes. Choose the appropriate phrase from the list to describe each person.**

Tante Maria hört sich 'mal gern abends ein Konzert im Radio an. Klassisches natürlich, denn sie spielt selbst auch sehr gern Geige. Ihr Mann, Gerd, hat eine sehr wertvolle Sammlung alter Münzen, und besucht oft Museen, um sich darüber zu informieren.

Die Kinder dagegen haben keine so ruhigen Freizeitsbeschäftigungen. Hans-Peter spielt Wasserball im Verein, und sein Bruder Franz macht zur Zeit einen Karatekurs an der Abendschule. Nur deren Schwester Eva ist etwas musikalisch und versuchte, Gitarre zu lernen. Dann hatte sie plötzlich keine Lust mehr und hat es aufgegeben.

a) Tante Maria — schwimmt sehr gern.
b) Onkel Gerd — treibt gern Sport.
c) Franz — spielt ein Instrument.
d) Hans-Peter — wollte ein Instrument lernen.
e) Eva — interessiert sich für historische Sachen.

---

**REMEMBER! Cover the answers if you want to.**

---

## ANSWERS

**A1**
a) Sabine ist eine Freundin von Ilse.
b) Am Wochenende.
c) Auf einer Geschäftsreise.
d) Sie ist zu Hause geblieben./Sie war zu Hause.
e) Der Schuler/Die Schulerin kam zu spät in die Klasse.

**A2**
a) Tante Maria spielt ein Instrument.
b) Onkel Gerd interessiert sich für historische Sachen.
c) Franz treibt gern Sport.
d) Hans-Peter schwimmt sehr gern.
e) Eva wollte ein Instrument lernen.

## TUTORIAL

**T1**
a) If you saw the *freund* in *befreundet*, you will have deduced the answer.
b) The statement infers that he can't go during the week, so suggest the obvious.
c) *Geschäftsreise* alone will not score at Higher Level, as it does not communicate the answer.
d) Unless you are told any other information, you must infer that mother stayed at home.
e) Again, you must deduce from the alarm-clock's not working and from the angry teacher, that the pupil arrived late.

**T2** *Several questions should have crossed your mind. There were decisions to make between the two who enjoy sport and the two who enjoy music. Some of the descriptions are more definite than others, for example Onkel Gerd and his collection of ancient coinage, or Hans-Peter and his water-polo. Some are general such as that about Franz, even though he learns karate. Others are misleading, such as Eva and the guitar. She wanted to learn it but gave up, whereas her mother **still** enjoys playing the violin.*

# EXAM PRACTICE

**Questions 1 – 6: Answer each question by ticking one box only.**

**FOUNDATION**

**1** You are in Germany. You need petrol for the car and see the following signs. Which one should you follow?

A Supermarkt ☐      C Gymnasium ☐

B Parkplatz ☐       D Tankstelle ☐

**FOUNDATION**

**2** You want to find the town centre. Which sign do you follow?

A Rathaus ☐        C Stadtmitte ☐

B Bahnhof ☐        D Kunstmuseum ☐

**FOUNDATION**

**3** You want to buy some bread. Which sign do you look for?

A Metzgerei ☐       C Zeitungen ☐

B Schuhgeschäft ☐    D Bäckerei ☐

**FOUNDATION**

**4** You need to visit someone in hospital. Which sign should you follow?

A Verkehrsamt ☐     C Parkanlage ☐

B Krankenhaus ☐     D Stadion ☐

**FOUNDATION**

**5** You pass a job centre and see the following notice in the window.

What job is being offered?

Wir suchen Kellner
(☎) 0122/845678

A ☐    B ☐

C ☐    D ☐

**FOUNDATION**

**6** What job is being offered?

Ihre Chance
Ich suche einen
Elektriker
(☎) 01222/876456

A ☐    B ☐

C ☐    D ☐

**7** Sie gehen essen. Hier ist die Speisekarte.

## ❖ *City Grill* ❖

**Fleischgerichte**

| | | |
|---|---|---|
| Frikadelle | | DM 2,50 |
| Bratwurst | | DM 3, – – |
| Hamburger | | DM 4, – – |
| ½ Hähnchen vom Grill | | DM 6,50 |
| Schnitzel | | DM 7, – – |
| *Mit* | | |
| Nudelsalat | | DM 2, – – |
| Pommes frites | Portion | DM 2,50 |
| Frischer Gurkensalat | | DM 3, – – |

**Getränke**

| | | |
|---|---|---|
| Cola | 0,3 L Dose | DM 1,50 |
| Limo | 0,3 L Dose | DM 1,20 |
| Orangensaft | 0,3 L Dose | DM 2,– – |
| Mineralwasser | 0,3 L Dose | DM 1,50 |
| Tasse Kaffee | | DM 2,50 |
| Tasse Tee | | DM 3,00 |

*Bitte nicht rauchen !*

Richtig oder falsch? Kreuzen Sie die Kästchen an.

| | Richtig | Falsch |
|---|---|---|
| | | |
| | | |
| | | |
| | | |
| | | |

**i)** Eine  kostet DM 2.00.

**ii)** Eine  kostet DM 3,00.

**iii)** Ein  kostet DM 7,00.

**iv)** Eine   kostet DM 1,50.

**v)** Die Speisekarte hat keine warmen Getränke.

**8** Was heißt „Bitte nicht rauchen !"?
Kreuzen Sie das richtige Kästchen an.

A □   C □

B □   D □

**9**  Lesen Sie die Postkarte.

Freitag

Ich sitze hier im Freibad. Ich spiele jeden Tag Fußball mit den Leuten auf dem Campingplatz. Abends spielen wir meistens Tischtennis oder hören Musik.

Übermorgen müssen wir leider schon nach Hause zurück, denn Georg muß wieder arbeiten. Er ist Busfahrer in der Stadt.

Tschüß
Gerd

Kreuzen Sie die richtige Antworten an.
**i)** Wo übernachtet Gerd?

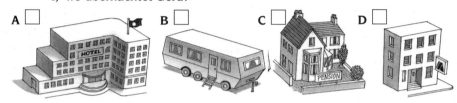

A ☐    B ☐    C ☐    D ☐

**ii)** Wo schreibt Gerd seine Postkarte?

A ☐    B ☐    C ☐    D ☐

**iii)** Was spielt er jeden Tag mit seinen Freunden?
Kreuzen Sie **2** Kästchen an.

A ☐    B ☐    C ☐    D ☐    E ☐    F ☐

**iv)** Wann fährt Gerd nach Hause?

    **A** Am Montag ☐    **B** Am Mittwoch ☐

    **C** Am Freitag ☐    **D** Am Sonntag ☐

**v)** Was ist Georg vom Beruf?

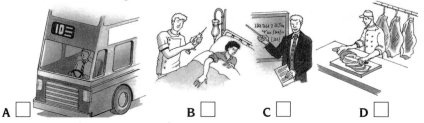

A ☐    B ☐    C ☐    D ☐

**10** Lesen Sie die Anzeigen.

**A Freizeitzentrum**
sucht Jugendliche(n)
zur Aushilfe im Kindergarten

**B Warenhaus** sucht
Jugendliche
zur Ausbildung in der
Musikabteilung

**C Blumen Kohl**
Wir suchen Verkäufer(in)
Anfang September

**D** Haben Sie schon an der
Kasse gearbeitet? Ihr
**Spar Supermarkt**
stellt zum 1. Sept.
neue Mitarbeiter ein.

**E Elektro Statik -**
Ihr Elektrofachgeschäft
Im Citycenter
sucht 2 Auszubildende
für die Werkstatt

**F** Fotografie als Beruf?
Besuchen Sie uns bei
**Foto Brell**
Am Hagedornweg 30

**G Esso** an der Ubierstrasse
braucht Tankwart ab sofort.
Kommen Sie vorbei!

Wo könnten die folgenden Leute arbeiten?

**i)** Angela ist Hobbygärtnerin. ☐

**ii)** Thilo macht gern Aufnahmen. ☐

**iii)** Susi spielt gern mit Kindern. ☐

**iv)** Peter mag Sachen reparieren. ☐

**v)** Linda hört gern Popmusik. ☐

**11**  Ein Brief von Ingrid aus Düsseldorf

Düsseldorf, den 1. Februar

Hallo Frances, Hallo Michael!

Ich habe mich sehr über Eueren Brief gefreut. Vielen Dank für die Fotos von Eurer Familie im Winterurlaub. Das Wetter hier war über die Feiertage nicht so toll wie bei Euch – meist naß, kalt und neblig.

Ich muß bald wählen, was ich in der Oberstufe machen möchte, aber ich weiß noch nicht ganz, was ich für einen Beruf später machen soll. Vielleicht mache ich etwas mit Tieren, aber ich bin in Biologie ziemlich schlecht. Meine Eltern würden das ganz gut finden, glaube ich. Sie meinen, daß viel zu viele junge Leute den ganzen Tag am Computer sitzen. Sie sind mehr für die frische Luft, lange Spaziergänge, usw.

Mein Freund Dirk macht jetzt sein Abitur. Als Hauptfächer macht er Naturwissenschaften, und dazu lernt er Englisch und Mathe. Wenn alles gut geht, möchte er im kommenden Jahr sein Biostudium anfangen. Er freut sich schon darauf. Ich glaube, wir haben beide eine große Liebe für Tiere.

Hoffentlich läuft für Euch beide alles klar in der Schule. Ihr habt wohl auch bald Prüfungen, nicht wahr?

Viele Grüße

Tschüß,

Wählen Sie die Antwort aus, die am besten paßt. Füllen Sie die Lücken aus!

**i)** Frances und Michael sind Ingrids ......................................................
Schulkameraden    Brieffreunde    Nachbaren

**ii)** Frances und Michael waren................................................im Urlaub.
im Sommer    über Weihnachten    zu Ostern

**iii)** Ingrid ........................................ , was sie beruflich machen will.
weiß    ist sicher    hat keine Idee

**iv)** Ingrid ............................................................... .
ist nicht so gut in Bio    ist sehr gut in Bio    findet Bio leicht

**v)** Ingrids Eltern ........................................ Computer.
interessieren sich sehr für    arbeiten gern am    sind gegen

**vi)** Dirk möchte gern ........................................ .
weiterlernen    gleich mit Tieren arbeiten
ein Arbeitspraktikum machen

**12** Lesen Sie den folgenden Artikel.

## WAS WILLST DU BERUFLICH MACHEN?

Mehr als 70 Prozent der Jugendlichen in der Bundesrepublik träumen von einem „richtig tollen Job". So heißt es in einer Umfrage. Sie zeigte auch, wie schnell die Träume sich ändern. Vor gar nicht langer Zeit wollten alle jungen Männer am liebsten als Förster im Freien arbeiten. Heute möchten sie Naturwissenschaftler werden (25%), mit Computern arbeiten (10%) oder als Manager arbeiten (9%). Die jungen Frauen ziehen es vor, als Künstlerin (15%), Managerin in einem Hotel (10%) oder als Fotomodell (7%) ihr Geld zu verdienen.

Eine große Überraschung war es, daß 85% von allen, die einen Beruf haben, mit ihrer Arbeit zufrieden sind! Ihren absoluten Traumberuf haben 12% der Männer und 5% der Frauen - oder so sagen sie.

Und wie möchten die meisten Leute arbeiten? Für viele ist es wichtig, daß sie den sichersten Arbeitgeber haben. Und wer soll das sein? Der Staat, natürlich.

Wann und wie lange Leute arbeiten möchten, steht auch fest: rund die Hälfte der Befragten sind gegen weniger Wochenstunden. Aber 75% wollen Teilzeitarbeit und flexible Arbeitszeiten. Und 90% wünschen sich mehr Urlaub!

Richtig oder falsch? Kreuzen Sie die richtige Kästchen an!

a) Die meisten jungen Leute haben einen Traumberuf.

b) Der beliebteste Traumberuf von Männern bleibt unverändert.

c) Ohne Traumberuf wird man am Arbeitsplatz nicht glücklich.

d) Es gibt mehr Männer mit Traumberuf als Frauen.

e) Die meisten Leute suchen Sicherheit bei der Arbeitsstelle.

f) Die meisten Leute wollen keine feste Arbeitszeiten.

| Richtig | Falsch |
|---------|--------|
|         |        |
|         |        |
|         |        |
|         |        |
|         |        |
|         |        |

**13** Lesen Sie die folgende Broschüre aus dem Verkehrsamt in Bonn.

# Herzlich Willkommen, liebe Besucher!

Genießen Sie einige schöne Ausflüge in der Bonner Gegend.

**Das Siebengebirge (A)** ist das älteste Naturschutzgebiet Europas. Den Gipfel des berühmten Berges **„Drachenfels" (B)**, erreicht man zu Fuß, per Bergbahn oder per Pferd.

Oben auf dem **Petersberg (C)**, steht ein Gasthaus mit einem herrlichen Ausblick, während unten am Rhein das pittoreske Weinstädtchen und Touristenparadies **Königswinter** (D) liegt.

In Rhöndorf können Sie eine Ausstellung über das Leben Konrad Adenauers besuchen. Das ehemalige **Wohnhaus (E)** des ersten Bundeskanzlers ist heute ein Museum.

Auf dem **Michaelsberg (F)** kann man tolle Wanderungen und Ausflüge im Forst machen.

Wie wäre es mit einem Spaziergang im Park des **Schlosses Augustusburg (G)** in Brühl? Auch ältere Leute können diese herrlichen Gärten aus dem Jahr 1725 sehen, ohne weit gehen zu müssen.

Ganz in der Nähe gibt es das Freizeit- und Abenteuerparadies **„Phantasialand" (H)** in Brühl. Dort findet man Unterhaltung und Spaß für Erwachsene genauso wie für Kinder.

Auch nicht weit von Bonn liegt die Stadt **Hennef (J)**, in deren engen Straßen man schöne, mittelalterliche Fachwerkhäuser und auch gemütliche, historische Gaststätten finden kann.

Wir wünschen Ihnen viel Vergnügen.

Ihre

STADT BONN

Finden Sie für jede Person in einer Familie ein passendes Ausflugsziel und schreiben Sie den Buchstaben.

a) Die Eltern wollen eine Weinprobe machen. ☐

b) Die Mutter möchte gern etwas Historisches sehen, aber auch zu Mittag essen gehen. ☐

c) Die kleinen Kinder wollen Spaß haben. ☐

d) Der Opa möchte beim Mittagessen eine schöne Aussicht genießen. ☐

e) Der älterer Bruder studiert die Geschichte der Bundesrepublik. ☐

f) Die Oma kann nicht weit laufen, möchte aber etwas Schönes sehen. ☐

*You will find the answers and examiner's comments on pages 210–211.*

## INTRODUCTION

The final of the four skills is the one which students generally find most difficult. The accuracy required to score well at Higher Level has been rehearsed in the preceding topic-based chapters. However, you also need to be able to express ideas and opinions, and to give detailed accounts.

As in the Speaking Test, however, you have the great advantage of being able to play to your particular strengths, and to choose what you write to a great extent. Even when the topic is specified, along with certain details which you must include in your writing, you are at liberty to express yourself as you wish. This is where you must exercise strong control over the language you use. You have to balance what you would **like** to say but feel unable to cope with structurally, against what you are **able** to say in German, which may be less adventurous. With regular practice of the Higher Level skills shown to you in this book, you should be able to increase what you can write with confidence.

Here are some of the problems specific to writing, with some suggestions as to how you might overcome them.

### Problem 1

Understanding the question.

### Solution 1

Make sure you are familiar with the requirements of the paper set by your exam board. The paper will follow a similar pattern each year, but at Higher Level you need to understand the whole range of questions which could be asked of you, not simply those which were set last year. Remember that you may use your dictionary as necessary, but that it is essential you learn to use it wisely.

### Problem 2

Deciding what you want to write.

### Solution 2

Don't write a piece of English and then try to translate it. This will always cause you major confusion, as you wrestle with the dictionary to put English thoughts into the German language. Instead, allow yourself time to plan, and write your piece once only. This is better than setting off in a rush and making a lot of mistakes and crossings out, hoping that you will have time to make a neater copy before the exam is over. If you are writing a letter which includes five major points, you will need to plan seven paragraphs in order to include the introduction and conclusion. Try to work in German immediately. Write down the phrases you want to include alongside the paragraph number, according to what is required. Adverb phrases of time, manner and place make a good list, along with plenty of familiar words to reassure yourself at this early stage.

### Problem 3

Knowing how much to write.

### Solution 3

Some boards specify the length of what you are to write, in which case you must obviously take note of the guidelines. As a general rule, however, the letter required of you is usually between 80 and 100 words long, whereas the narrative piece is more likely to be between 130 and 150 words long. You shouldn't worry too much about writing up to ten words over the 'limit', but you should realise that you may lose marks for not reaching the required length. This may be because you therefore fail to mention some of the points you should. Alternatively, you may simply not be able to score sufficient marks if your work is too brief.

### Problem 4

How to produce work that is accurate.

### Solution 4

'Check your work' is what all teachers will say to you before you give it in, but if you have made mistakes in the first place, how are you going to recognise them when you re-read your work? Use the following list of specific checks to highlight the most obvious pitfalls.

1   Make sure that *ich* is followed by a verb with an *-e* ending, and that *er* and *sie* and a person's name in the singular are followed by verbs that end in *-t* in the present tense. Verbs following S*ie* (with a small *s* for 'they') will look like the infinitive and end in *-n* or *-en*.

2   Perfect tenses, of which you will have plenty in the Higher Level writing, must have two parts to the verb: the first is a part of *haben* or *sein* and the second is the past participle. A common mistake is to follow the subject with the past participle alone, such as *ich in die Stadt gegangen* or *ich gegangen in die Stadt* instead of *ich bin in die Stadt gegangen*.

3   Remind yourself of ten common verbs which take *sein* and try to use at least five of them in your piece of writing.

4   The adjectival agreement as described in earlier chapters can be quite complicated, but remind yourself of the 'eeeasiest' one of all, and use feminine nouns in the subject and object cases where possible.

### Problem 5

Omitting a specified task and forfeiting the marks attached to it. There must be no mistake here, as marks cannot be awarded for what is missing, no matter how brilliant the rest may be.

### Solution 5

Tick off on the exam paper the necessary items as you complete each one. Make a point of double-checking that you include them in any planning you do.

## USING THE DICTIONARY

As in the Reading Test, you are allowed to use a dictionary during the Writing Test itself. Don't think that it signals the end of all your worries, however, for without a good deal of caution and regular practice, the dictionary could become your worst nightmare. Instead of clarity it could bring you confusion, and instead of order it could bring chaos to your work.

Bear in mind the following important points:

● Use the dictionary as little as possible; it robs you of valuable time.

● Words with a number of meanings can cause you a lot of trouble. For example, if you want to say 'she had a bad accident', how do you know which of the many German adjectives is the correct one for 'bad'? Is it *schlecht, schlimm, schwach, verdorben* or *ungünstig*? The only sure way is to check each of them in the German-English half of the dictionary and find examples which put you on the right track. You might end up asking yourself if you really needed to say this sentence in the first place. Couldn't you have made up another excuse for her not coming to the party?!

● The situation becomes even more complicated if the word can be used as more than one part of speech. For example, the word 'work' can be both noun or verb and the section of German words is a long one. Make sure that you are familiar with the dictionary you are using and that you can recognise the abbreviations it uses for noun, adjective, verb, etc.

# Check yourself 1

## QUESTIONS

**Q1** *Use your dictionary to find a suitable German word for the words underlined below.*

a) Where's my <u>watch</u>?
b) He read the <u>paper</u>.
c) She wants to <u>light</u> the barbecue.
d) He got off at the next <u>stop</u>.
e) We played in the last <u>round</u> of the cup.

**Q2** *Find the mistakes in the German and correct them.*

a) Wir gefahren mit dem Bus zur Schule.
b) Kann du mitkommen ins Kino?
c) Mein Bruder bleiben heute zu Hause.
d) Ich hat eine neues Kassette gekauft.
e) Mein neue Lehrerin is nett.

---

**REMEMBER! Cover the answers if you want to.**

---

## ANSWERS

**A1**
a) Uhr
b) Zeitung
c) anzünden OR anmachen
d) Haltestelle
e) Runde

**A2**
a) Wir sind mit dem Bus zur Schule gefahren.
b) Kannst du mitkommen ins Kino?
c) Mein Bruder bleibt heute zu Hause.
d) Ich habe eine neue Kassette gekauft.
e) Meine neue Lehrerin ist nett.

## TUTORIAL

**T1**
a) *Most of the words you will find are for various verbs meaning 'to watch'.*
b) *If you have just forgotten the word, then you should recognise the correct one quickly.*
c) *Don't be confused by the noun Licht or the adjective leicht. You need a verb.*
d) *You will certainly know Haltestelle, but perhaps it doesn't spring to mind, if you see only 'stop' and not 'bus-stop'. This is where the dictionary really helps to jog your memory.*
e) *Runde or rund, noun or adjective? Again, would you really need such a phrase? Try to avoid that particular detail of your sporting weekend!*

**T2**
a) *This needs sind for the perfect tense.*
b) *The du form needs an -st ending to be correct.*
c) *This had the common mistake of using the infinitive instead of a -t ending.*
d) *Ich habe, of course, and also the feminine ending should be -e on neue.*
e) *Feminine agreement again, and a careless is instead of ist.*

# DIFFERENT KINDS OF QUESTION

Questions vary according to the exam board you use, but they fall into a number of common types:

The first question is usually a list of single words or phrases, and is identified with the F and G grades. This can vary from items you need for travelling, to a list of shopping for a picnic. There is some leeway on spelling and it is advisable not to use more than one or two words which are identical to English, such as *Butter, Anorak, Pullover*, etc.

The second question is usually some sort of message or a postcard, with five tasks to fulfil in 30 - 40 words. The tasks are set either in German or by pictures, or both. You should aim to write in simple sentences. One of the tasks may require the use of a past or future tense. Messages are either left on the phone or by somebody calling by. Learn the two appropriate phrases to begin each of these eventualities:

*Herr Schmidt hat angerufen. Er möchte ....*
*Julia ist heute nachmittag vorbeigekommen. Sie sagt, ....*

The third task – aimed at D and C grades – will probably be a letter, but may be an article, for which you may write up to 100 words. You are sometimes given a written stimulus, for example a letter to which you have to respond. You will need to use a range of past, present and future tenses in answering.

# *Check yourself 2*

## QUESTIONS

**Q1** **Sie schicken eine Postkarte aus dem Urlaub. Schreiben Sie:**

a) wo Sie wohnen
b) was Sie gestern gemacht haben
c) wo Sie heute hinfahren
d) wie das Wetter ist
e) wann Sie wieder zu Hause sind.

**Q2** **Write a full sentence to expand on the idea given.**

a) In den letzten Sommerferien gearbeitet
b) Mein Lieblingshobby
c) Zukunftspläne
d) Einen Tagesausflug
e) Die Hausaufgaben

### REMEMBER! Cover the answers if you want to.

## ANSWERS

**A1** For example:

a) Wir wohnen in einer Pension.
b) Wir sind gestern schwimmen gegangen.
c) Heute fahren wir ans Meer.
d) Das Wetter ist hervorragend.
e) Wir kommen am Wochenende nach Hause.

**A2**
a) Ich habe in den letzten Sommerferien einen tollen Job im Supermarkt gehabt, wo ich ziemlich gut verdient habe.
b) Am Wochenende gehe ich am liebsten mit meinen Eltern segeln, weil ich sehr gern am Wasser bin.
c) Ich werde wahrscheinlich Biologie studieren, weil ich mich sehr für Tiere und die Natur interessiere.
d) Wir sind am Wochenende an die Südküste gefahren, wo wir meine Verwandten in Bournemouth besucht haben.
e) Wir bekommen zwei oder drei Stunden Hausaufgaben pro Tag, was ich zu viel finde.

## TUTORIAL

**T1**
a) *Remember you're on holiday! Don't write the name of your home town or your street name.*
b) *Remember a simple sport in the past tense, or how to say 'we went shopping'.*
c) *The present tense is simple, but an inversion makes a better impression.*
d) *Whatever happens, don't use nett, gut or even schön; they are so over-used. Learn herrlich or sagenhaft – even toll sounds better.*
e) *Use the most obvious phrase. Don't always mimic the question.*

**T2**
a) *You could also have re-used gearbeitet. The subordinate clause allows you to add the detail.*
b/c) *As soon as you express a liking for something, it offers the possibility of giving the reason.*
d) *The subordinate clause again makes it easy to explain the first idea.*
e) *Was relates to the whole concept of having so much homework.*

## HIGHER LEVEL QUESTIONS

The first question at Higher Level is the same as the last question at Foundation. This overlap in the two levels is aimed at candidates working in the area of Grades C and D.

The second question will be a longer narrative, an article, report, or sometimes another letter. The question will be in German and there may be a stimulus in German to help you, or even a set of pictures. The question is aimed at the three highest grades: B, A, and A*. As far as the language goes, accuracy is essential to get into this range of marks, but you are also expected to produce a sensible piece of writing which takes into account the stimulus given.

## DIFFERENT KINDS OF WRITING

### Letters

Always begin with the date, thus: *Norwich, den 27. Mai.*

**Formal** – to a youth hostel, hotel, camp-site, tourist office, etc. Also if you are writing to the parents of your penfriend.
Remember the following points:

- Use *Sie* consistently throughout. Don't forget that the adjective is *Ihr*.
- Begin with *Sehr geehrter Herr Braun, Sehr geehrte Frau Braun*, if you know the name of the person, or *Sehr geehrte Herren*, if you don't.
- Finish with *Hochachtungsvoll* for a simple formal letter, or *Mit freundlichem Gruß*, if you know the person.

**Informal** – to your pen-friend

- Use *Du* and *Dein* throughout the letter, or *Ihr* and *Euch* if you are referring to more than one member of the family. It is convention to write these words with a capital in a letter.
- Begin with *Liebe Ingrid* or *Lieber Klaus*. The use of an exclamation mark is now largely outmoded.
- You can end with *Herzliche Grüße/Schöne Grüße* or similar and then *Dein* or *Deine* before your name.

### Articles

Sometimes you are asked to write an article for a German exchange school's magazine or similar. Once again, you are likely to be set certain tasks to fulfil within the article, or you may be given a written stimulus. You are more likely to stick to one topic within an article, rather than covering several as in a letter. If you can use both 1st person singular and plural – *ich* and *wir* – your writing may become less repetitive.

### Accounts

The longest piece of writing at this level is up to 150 words in length. Daunting as this may seem at first, if tackled methodically you can soon achieve this length. You may even find yourself having to trim back a little when you have finished, if your account runs to more than 160 words.

The account is always set in the past, but if it is possible to include a future tense, perhaps in some direct speech, this is all the better. In an account based on six pictures, you simply need to divide the narrative into six parts and write two to three sentences about each picture. Even if the stimulus is more general, you still need to work out how to break down the narrative into paragraphs of a manageable length. By doing so, you can be certain not to omit a major part of the account.

# Check yourself 3

## QUESTIONS

**Q1** *Complete these tasks in German.*

a) Write one or two sentences to begin a letter booking hotel accommodation for your family. Don't forget to include the dates.

b) At the end of an article about last year's holiday, write two sentences about your future plans.

c) In a letter to the tourist office, write two sentences about what you plan to do in Düsseldorf.

**Q2** *Write one sentence in the past under each of the following headings, then add a further sentence transferring the idea to the future tense.*

a) Die Schule
b) Mein Urlaub
c) Ein Tagesausflug

---

**REMEMBER! Cover the answers if you want to.**

---

## ANSWERS

**A1** For example:

a) Sehr geehrte Herren,
Ich fahre im Juli mit meiner Familie nach Düsseldorf, und zwar vom 4ten bis zum 8ten. Ich möchte zwei Zimmer mit Bad reservieren, wenn Sie noch Platz haben.

b) Ich werde mich bemühen, im kommenden Jahr noch mehr Deutsch zu lernen. Nächstes Jahr werde ich mit meiner Familie nach Düsseldorf kommen.

c) Wir wollen mit Sicherheit das Kunstmuseum besuchen, weil meine Mutter die neue Ausstellung sehen möchte. Ich habe vor, auf den Rheinturm zu gehen, denn die Aussicht soll prächtig sein.

**A2** For example:

a) Ich habe letzten Samstag in der Schulmannschaft Hockey gespielt. Ich werde am kommenden Samstag in der Schulmannschaft Hockey spielen.

b) Ich habe mich sehr gefreut, daß wir das Schloß Hohenzollern besucht haben. Ich freue mich schon darauf, das Schloß Hohenzollern zu besuchen.

c) Wir wollten nach London fahren, um neue Kleider zu kaufen. Wir haben vor, nächstes Wochenende nach London zu fahren, um neue Kleider zu kaufen.

## TUTORIAL

**T1**

a) *This is an absolutely standard letter, and you should be able to complete the rest of it from memory! Don't forget Time, Manner, Place in the first sentence.*

b) *Sich bemühen means 'to try hard' – a little gem well worth learning to impress your examiner.*

c) *Wollen here shows your intention and therefore the future tense by implication. Similarly, Ich habe vor says what you are planning. Notice both intentions are followed by clauses giving reasons.*

**T2**

a) *These are uncomplicated forms of the past and future, but fulfil the basic requirement to use these tenses.*

b) *Sich freuen means 'to be happy'. Sich freuen auf etwas means 'to look forward to', and will give you a variation of the future.*

c) *Remember that you usually use modal verbs in the imperfect not the perfect tense. Vorhaben again helps you to vary the future idea.*

## HIGHER LEVEL PERFORMANCE

- Do remember that you must show your ability to use the past, present and future tenses, and you must be able to express opinions in order to attain a Grade C. Here is a quick reminder of when to use which tense.
  **Perfect** for actions:
  *Ich bin gegangen/Ich habe gekauft*
  **Imperfect** for weather, circumstances, and feelings:
  *Es war herrliches Wetter/wir waren alle müde/ich freute mich, daß …*
  **Imperfect** for modal verbs:
  *Wir wollten/ich mußte/wir sollten/er durfte nicht, usw.*
  Try having a **pluperfect** up your sleeve just to impress the examiner:
  *Es war ein schöner Tag gewesen.*
  *Ich hatte den Film schon gesehen.*
  **Present** – usually for use in the letter not in the narrative. Watch all those common irregular verbs in the 3rd Person:
  *liest/fährt/trifft/sieht, usw.*
  **Future** – with *werden, wollen, vorhaben, planen, hoffen.*

- Don't forget that your work takes on the appearance of the Grade A candidate you want to be, when you express yourself in longer sentences, rather than in the style of your first simple sentences. Use the conjunctions you have learned, in order to achieve double the sentence with little extra effort.

- Remember that coordinating conjunctions (*und, denn* and *aber*) are easier than all the others, which are subordinating and force you to change the word order:
  *Wir mußten lange warten, denn mein Vater hatte seinen Paß vergessen.*
  *Ich bin schnell nach Hause gegangen, weil ich die Tasche holen wollte.*

- *Um … zu* can replace a clause but still has the effect of lengthening your sentence:
  *Ich bin nach Hause gegangen, um die Tasche zu holen.*

- Use the relative clause to add extra detail in a natural way:
  *Mein Bruder hat eine CD gekauft, die im Sonderangebot war.*

- Prepare to express opinions in a variety of ways:
  *Ich fand die Platte nicht besonders gut.*
  *Meiner Meinung nach war die Musik furchtbar.*

- Use adjectives and adjectival phrases:
  *Der Mann mit dem doofen Hut ist mein Onkel.*

- Use adverbs and adverbial phrases:
  *Ich bin erst am späten Nachmittag mit dem Fahrrad in die Schule gekommen.*

- Fill in the background details of weather and circumstance:
  *Ich fand meine Oma zu Hause, weil das Wetter so schlecht war.*

### Making use of any German which is on the question paper

- It is virtually certain that you will not be able to copy a sentence from the question paper and use it in your answer, but there may well be words and even phrases which you can turn to your advantage. Make sure you have understood them correctly – you may need your dictionary here anyway, before you start writing.

- If there are direct questions or instructions, you may simply be able to rephrase for your purposes. For example, if the instruction is:
  *Erzählen Sie, was Sie in den Osterferien gemacht haben.*
  you could base your answer on:
  *In den Osterferien habe ich … gemacht.*

- If the stimulus is an advertisement for a product, service or a job, you may be able to extract specific words which will help. For example, a job advert may contain the words *Ihr Gehalt* or DM 20.- *pro Stunde.*

# Check yourself 4

## QUESTIONS

**Q1** *Make longer, more impressive sentences from these short ones.*

a) Ich bin nach Hause gegangen. Ich habe mein Fahrrad geholt. Ich bin in die Stadt gefahren.
b) Wir sind nach Düsseldorf gefahren. Ich wollte meinen Brieffreund besuchen. Er wohnt in der Nähe der Stadtmitte.
c) Es war tolles Wetter. Wir sind schwimmen gegangen. Wir haben in der Pizzeria gegessen.

**Q2** *Answer each of the following simple questions with an interesting sentence.*

a) Was für eine Stadt ist Newcastle?
b) Was hast du letztes Wochenende gemacht?
c) Was machst du in den Sommerferien?

---

**REMEMBER! Cover the answers if you want to.**

---

## ANSWERS

**A1**
a) Ich bin nach Hause gegangen und habe mein Fahrrad geholt, um in die Stadt zu fahren.
b) Wir sind nach Düsseldorf gefahren, weil ich meinen Brieffreund besuchen wollte, der in der Nähe der Stadtmitte wohnt.
c) Es war so ein tolles Wetter, daß wir in der Pizzeria gegessen haben, nachdem wir schwimmen gegangen waren.

**A2**
a) Ich wohne ganz gern in Newcastle, weil es eine ziemlich lebendige Stadt ist, wo immer sehr viel los ist.
b) Ich wollte ursprünglich nach Oxford fahren, um ein Fußballspiel zu sehen, aber ich hatte doch nicht genug Geld dazu, also mußte ich zu Hause bleiben.
c) Ich habe vor, zuerst im Supermarkt zu arbeiten, um ein bißchen Geld zu verdienen, und erst dann fahre ich mit einem Freund aus meiner Schulklasse nach Spanien.

## TUTORIAL

**T1**
a) *This is a simply constructed but very likely sentence. It is well worth sacrificing the perfect tense in the final part for the more interesting um ... zu.*
b) *Have courage. The subordinate word order is quite straightforward, and it makes a much better sentence.*
c) *The so ... daß and the use of the pluperfect make this much more adventurous.*

**T2**
a) *Much more satisfactory than before – simple language but properly bound together with subordinate clauses.*
b) *Um ... zu expresses your intention, and also helps to establish what happened as a consequence.*
c) *The plan is clearly laid out in this sentence with um ... zu and erst dann to introduce the last idea.*

# EXAM PRACTICE

The following questions offer practice in the type of tasks set by different boards. You need to check the requirements of your particular board with your teacher, especially where you are offered the choice between questions.

**1** Sie wollen mit der Familie einen Picknick machen. Was nehmen Sie mit? (Sie brauchen nicht nur Lebensmittel mitnehmen.)       **FOUNDATION**

**Beispiel:** *Fußball*

1 ............................................................

2 ............................................................

3 ............................................................

4 ............................................................

5 ............................................................

6 ............................................................

7 ............................................................

8 ............................................................

9 ............................................................

10 ............................................................

**2** Ihr Brieffreund kommt Sie bald besuchen. Schreiben Sie, was Sie für die Woche geplant haben.       **FOUNDATION**

**Beispiel:** Samstag: *Zum See fahren*

Sonntag:       ............................................................

Montag:       ............................................................

Dienstag:       ............................................................

Mittwoch:       ............................................................

Donnerstag:       ............................................................

Freitag:       *nach Österreich zurückfahren*

**3** Sie schicken eine Postkarte aus dem Urlaub, in der Sie schreiben:       **FOUNDATION**
    – wo Sie wohnen
    – wie das Wetter ist
    – was Sie gestern gemacht haben
    – was Sie heute vorhaben
    – wann Sie nach Hause kommen.
Sie brauchen keine vollen Sätze zu schreiben.

**4** Sie bleiben bei Ihrem Brieffreund, Georg, in Deutschland. Ein Freund von ihm, Bernd, hat angerufen. Schreiben Sie Georg einen Zettel, in dem Sie sagen:       **FOUNDATION**
    – was Bernd nicht machen kann
    – und warum
    – was er am Wochenende plant
    – wer mitkommen kann
    – wann Georg zurückrufen soll.

**FOUNDATION/HIGHER** **5**  Sie schreiben einen Brief an ein Hotel in der Schweiz und buchen die Unterkunft für Ihren Familienurlaub. Vergessen Sie nicht, sich zu erkundigen, was in der Stadt los ist.
Schreiben Sie 90–100 Wörter.

**FOUNDATION/HIGHER** **6**  Schreiben Sie einen Artikel über Ihre Schule für eine deutsche Schülerzeitschrift. Sie können Folgendes erwähnen:
  – Zahl der Schüler
  – ein typischer Schultag
  – die Lehrer
  – Hausaufgaben
  – Aktivitäten/Sport
Schreiben Sie 90–100 Wörter.

**FOUNDATION/HIGHER** **7**  Sie lesen die folgende Annonce in der Zeitung und schreiben einen kurzen Brief, in dem Sie sich für die Stelle bewerben.

> **Gesucht:** Junge Person
> zur Aushilfe in der Bäckerei.
> 8 Stunden am Tag. DM 11.50/Std.

**HIGHER** **8**  Sie haben einen Verkehrsunfall gesehen. Schreiben Sie einen Bericht für die Polizei. Erklären Sie, was Sie gesehen haben und wie der Unfall passiert ist.
Schreiben Sie 130–150 Wörter.

**9** Beschreiben Sie einen Klassenausflug, den Sie letzte Woche gemacht haben. Schreiben Sie 130-150 Wörter.

(**Note:** You might be offered the following pictures to help you with a framework, or the task may simply be left open. Try covering the pictures straight away and writing the account from your own ideas. Then come back to the exercise again and describe the day out shown in the pictures.)

*You will find all the answers and examiner's comments on pages 211–215.*

## INTRODUCTION

This chapter on grammar is not intended to be exhaustive but to help you achieve a better understanding of some of the language structures mentioned in Chapters 1–13. Where you still have concerns, you should consult your German teacher or one of the many books devoted entirely to the study of the German language. The following guidelines should help you know when to consult this reference and when to avoid the area of difficulty altogether. There are, after all, large areas of the language which you are not expected to understand or use at GCSE level.

### What are you expected to know?

#### Active and receptive use

The words active and receptive are used frequently when talking about vocabulary and language structures. If you know the German for a particular word or phrase, you can use it in the Speaking and Writing Tests – that is active use. If you can't recall the German word or phrase, but recognise it when heard or read, that is called receptive use. Items in this chapter which you need to know for receptive use only in your GCSE, are labelled [**R**].

Where appropriate, you are referred to one of Chapters 1–13, where the particular area of language is covered in more detail. You will, of course, find many examples of language structures pointed out to you in the Check yourself and Exam Practice sections of Chapters 1–17.

## VERBS

The form of the verb in German is determined by the subject, or 'person' doing the verb. The verb is therefore often referred to as being in the 1st, 2nd or 3rd 'person'.

- The **1st** person is used when the person speaking is doing the verb:
  *ich* in the singular
  *wir* in the plural

- The **2nd** person of the verb is the 'you' form:
  *du* for family and friends in the singular
  *ihr* for family and friends in the plural
  *Sie* for polite or formal use, whether singular or plural

- The **3rd** person is used for all other people or things:
  *Georg, Charlotte, er, sie, es* (he/she/it) and *man* (one) are singular.
  *Katherine und Anne, die Leute* and *sie* (they) are plural.

Verb tables are usually written in the following form:

| Singular | Plural |
|---|---|
| ich | wir |
| du | ihr |
| Sie | Sie |
| er/sie/es/man | sie |

**Note:** Because the *Sie* form is used in both singular and plural, it is included in both lists even though the form is identical.

## THE PRESENT TENSE

You use the present tense for:

- what you are doing at the moment:
  *Ich mache meine Hausaufgaben.* – I am doing my homework (right now).

- things which happen all the time:
  *Ich mache meine Hausaufgaben* – I (always) do my homework
  *um 7 Uhr.* at 7 o'clock.
- as an easy way to express what will happen in the future:
  *Ich mache meine Hausaufgaben* – I am doing my homework
  *nach dem Abendessen.* after supper.

One of the worst errors that occurs in written German is when a candidate starts a sentence with a phrase like *ich bin gehen*, when he/she is trying to use the present tense 'I am going'. If you find yourself doing that, think again!

### Formation

See Chapter 2

If an infinitive ends in *-den, -ten, or -nen*, the 2nd and 3rd person singular endings are *-est* and *-et*.
  *du arbeitest; er sendet; sie öffnet; es landet*
The full list of strong and irregular verbs appears on pages 170–171.

## THE FUTURE TENSE

The future tense is used to describe actions in future time – this afternoon, this evening, next week, next year, etc. For example:
  *Ich werde meine Hausaufgaben machen.* – I'm doing my homework.
  – I shall (will) do my homework.

### Formation

See Chapter 10

There is no difference between the strong and weak verbs in the future. Simply use the present tense of the verb *werden* and the infinitive of the verb you want at the end of the sentence.

|        | **werden** |     |        |
|--------|--------|--------|--------|
| ich    | werde  | wir    | werden |
| du     | wirst  | ihr    | werdet |
| Sie    | werden | Sie    | werden |
| er/sie/es | wird | sie    | werden |

  *Ich werde die Jacke kaufen.*
  *Ich werde in die Disco gehen.*

## THE PERFECT TENSE

The perfect tense is used for single, completed past actions and is the most common spoken past tense. There are a number of ways you can translate it into English:
  *Ich habe meine Hausaufgaben gemacht.* – I did my homework.
  – I have done my homework.
  – I have been doing my homework.
  – I was doing my homework.

### Formation

See Chapter 12

The perfect tense is formed using the present tense of *haben* or *sein* (known as the auxiliary verb) with the past participle at the end of the sentence or clause. The various different forms of the past participle are shown in Chapter 12, but you need to look at pages 170–171 for a fuller list of strong and irregular verbs. English has these different forms, too, so don't be surprised that you are supposed to learn them by heart. The usual list quoted for GCSE includes up to 80 verbs, but taken in groups of five or ten at a time, you can soon master the patterns.

Remember, if a verb is irregular, you should know all its 'parts' as written in the list, not just the present or the past participle. You can chant them aloud if it helps:

*schwimmen, schwimmt, schwamm, geschwommen*
*singen, singt, sang, gesungen*
*stehen, steht, stand, gestanden*
or, more fully:
*singen, sie singt, sie sang, sie hat gesungen*
That way, you practise the correct auxiliary for the perfect and pluperfect, too.

The perfect tense of modal verbs (*dürfen, können, mögen, müssen, sollen, wollen*) is formed with the auxiliary *haben* in two different ways, according to whether another verb is dependent on the modal.

The modals all have a past participle formed like a weak verb with *ge – t*, for example *gekonnt*. (None of them has an umlaut.) This is used when there is no other verb involved:
*Hast du die Matheaufgabe gemacht?*
*Nein, ich habe es nicht gekonnt.* – I couldn't (do it).
You will nearly always find an *es* added after the auxiliary.

However, the more frequent form of the perfect uses the **infinitive** of the modal where you would expect to see the past participle:
*Hast du die Matheaufgabe gemacht?*
*Nein, ich habe sie nicht machen können.*

However, above all, you should remember that modal verbs in the past are most frequently seen in the imperfect tense, because they normally relate to circumstances or feelings, rather than single actions.

See Chapter 12

# THE IMPERFECT TENSE

The imperfect tense is used mostly as a reporting style in newspapers and magazine articles for events in the past. You can very often avoid it by using the perfect tense when talking about actions in the past, but you must use it in certain instances:

- for the weather
- for people's moods and feelings
- for the state of things or circumstances

  *Es war sehr kalt und regnerisch* (although you do still hear *es hat den ganzen Tag geregnet*).
  *Ich hatte großen Hunger.*
  *Das Hotel war bequem und gemütlich.*

Remember the simple guide to the key parts of the imperfect tense:

|  | **weak** | **strong** |
|---|---|---|
| **singular** | *-te* | (no ending) |
| **plural** | *-ten* | *-en* |

**[R]** but active at Higher Level

# THE PLUPERFECT TENSE

Just as in English, the pluperfect is used with either the perfect or imperfect tense to show what had happened before something else happened:
*Er hatte schon zu Abend gegessen, bevor er seine Hausaufgaben machte.*

You therefore find the pluperfect especially with the conjunctions *bevor, bis, nachdem* and *sobald*.

See Chapter 12

**Formation**

The auxilary verbs used are the same as for the perfect tense, but this time the imperfect of the auxiliary is used, not the present. The past participle of the verb is formed in the same way as for the perfect tense.

## USE OF SEIN + PAST PARTICIPLE

This is a frequent structure to describe the state of things:

> *Das Fenster war gebrochen.*
> *Der Tisch ist frisch gestrichen (painted).*
> *Ich war überrascht.*

## IMPERSONAL VERBS

These are verbs used in certain fixed expressions, in the 3rd person singular with *es*:

**geben**

> Es *gibt* – There is/are
> Es *gab* – There was/were

(Notice that this form covers both singular and plural.)

**gelingen**

> Es *ist mir gelungen, ... zu* + infinitive:
> Es *ist uns gelungen, Konzertkarten* – We succeeded in getting concert
> *für heute abend zu bekommen.* tickets for this evening.

**stimmen**

> Es *stimmt (nicht).* – That's (not) true./That's (not) right.

**gefallen**

> Es *gefällt mir.* – I like it.
> Es *gefiel ihr nicht.* – She didn't like it.

**weather expressions**

> Es *friert.*
> Es *regnet.*
> Es *schneit.*

## THE CONDITIONAL

This is much more a matter of recognition than of use, although you will, of course, impress the examiner if you can introduce a conditional sentence into your spoken or written work.

If the conditional sentence expresses something which is more or less certain, then you will see the present and future indicative tenses used:

> *Wenn es regnet, wird die Straße naß.*
> *Wenn er kommt, dann gehe ich sofort.*
> *Wenn du Glück hast, kommt er nicht.*

If the condition is less likely to be fulfilled, then you will encounter subjunctives, usually the imperfect tenses of *haben*, *sein* or *werden*, but sometimes the modal verbs in the imperfect subjunctive:

> *Wenn ich viel Geld hätte, würde ich einen Porsche kaufen.*
> *Ich könnte das auch machen, wenn ich müßte.*

Here are some imperfect subjunctive forms which you may well see:

| | | |
|---|---|---|
| **sein** | *ich wäre* | I would be |
| **haben** | *ich hätte* | I would have |
| **werden** | *ich würde* | I would + any infinitive |

MODALS

| | | |
|---|---|---|
| **dürfen** | *ich dürfte* | I would be allowed to |
| **können** | *ich könnte* | I could |
| **mögen** | *ich möchte* | I would like to |
| **müssen** | *ich müßte* | I would have to |
| **sollen** | *ich sollte* | I should, ought to |
| **wollen** | *ich wollte* | I wanted |

See Chapter 11

# THE IMPERATIVE

The imperative is used for giving commands. The three main forms of the imperative match the three 'you' forms of the present tense:

| | | |
|---|---|---|
| *machen* | (*du* form) | *mach'*! (Sometimes this form retains its 'e'.) |
| | (*Sie* form) | *machen Sie!* |
| | (*ihr* form) | *macht!* |

Reflexive verbs keep their object pronouns:
> *Setz' dich!*
> *Bedienen Sie sich!*
> *Benehmt euch!*

In addition the *wir* form of the verb is inverted and is used as a first person imperative, where in English we use 'Let's go!', etc.
> *Gehen wir!*
> *Fahren wir!*
> *Bleiben wir hier!*

**[R]**

# THE PASSIVE

At Higher Level, you need to recognise the passive form in the present, imperfect and perfect tenses. It is formed by using the appropriate tense of *werden* with the past participle:

**Present**
> *Unser Wagen wird heute repariert.* – Our car is being repaired today.

**Imperfect**
> *Unser Wagen wurde gestern repariert.* – Our car was repaired yesterday.

**Perfect**
> *Unser Wagen ist schon repariert worden.* – Our car has been repaired already.

You should be able to use the *man* form in place of the passive at Higher Level:
> *Man schenkt uns oft so 'was.* – We are often given things like that.
> *Man rief ihn gestern abend an.* – He was telephoned last night.
> *Man hat ihnen das geschenkt.* – They were given it.

# THE SUBJUNCTIVE

Your use of this form of the verb need only be very limited.

You should be able to use *möchte* and *könnte* in these common ways:
> *Ich möchte ein Eis.*
> *Möchten Sie/Möchtest du ...?*
> *Ich könnte in die Stadt gehen.*
> *Könnten Sie/Könntest du mitkommen?*

**[R]** You should also be able to **recognise** the imperfect subjunctive of *sein*, *haben* and *werden* in the conditional, as described on page 159.

# THE INFINITIVE

The uses of the infinitive are many, but all are easily understood:

**After modals**
> *Du sollst es lernen.*
> *Ich möchte dahin gehen.*
> *Könntest du mir dein Rad leihen?*

**After *gehen***
> *Ich gehe heute schwimmen.*
> *Sie gingen heute vormittag einkaufen.*
> *Er ist angeln gegangen.*

**After *um ... zu***
> *Ich gehe in die Stadt, um eine Hose zu kaufen.*

**After verbs requiring *zu***
> *Es beginnt zu regnen.*
> *Ich versuche das Problem zu lösen.*

At Higher Level, you should also be able to use *lassen* with an infinitive to imply 'having something done':
> *Ich lasse mir die Haare schneiden.*
> *Meine Mutter läßt das Auto reparieren.*

## INTERROGATIVES

See Chapter 10

You should know how to form questions in the two most frequent ways:

- Subject/verb inversion
  *Kommst du oder kommst du nicht?*

- The addition of *ja* or *nicht* at the end of a statement
  *Wir kaufen diese Platte, ja?*
  *Du kommst mit, nicht?* (shortened form of *nicht wahr?*)

## MODAL VERBS

You have almost certainly been using modals since you first started learning German, in phrases such as:
> *Ich möchte eine Tasse Tee.*
> *Ich kann Schach spielen.*
> *Was willst du machen?*

Here is the present tense of all six modal auxiliary verbs:

|            | **dürfen** | **können** | **mögen** | **müssen** | **sollen** | **wollen** |
|------------|------------|------------|-----------|------------|------------|------------|
| ich        | darf       | kann       | mag       | muß        | soll       | will       |
| du         | darfst     | kannst     | magst     | mußt       | sollst     | willst     |
| Sie        | dürfen     | können     | mögen     | müssen     | sollen     | wollen     |
| er/sie/es/man | darf    | kann       | mag       | muß        | soll       | will       |
| wir        | dürfen     | können     | mögen     | müssen     | sollen     | wollen     |
| ihr        | dürft      | könnt      | mögt      | müßt       | sollt      | wollt      |
| Sie        | dürfen     | können     | mögen     | müssen     | sollen     | wollen     |
| sie        | dürfen     | können     | mögen     | müssen     | sollen     | wollen     |

The modal verb is the 'second idea', just as with all other verbs in the main clause. The verb which is dependent on it goes at the end of the clause or sentence:
> *Ich **soll** meine Hausaufgaben **machen**, aber ich **möchte** lieber **fernsehen**.*

In subordinate clauses, the modal still occupies the the usual verb position:
> *Ich **kann** nicht **fernsehen**, weil ich meine Hausaufgaben **machen muß**.*

In the imperfect and the future, only the modal is affected by the change of tense:
> *Ich wollte nicht ins Kino gehen.*
> *Ich werde meine Hausaufgaben machen müssen.*

In addition to the six modals, the verb *lassen* also acts as an auxiliary as shown in the section on infinitives above:
> *Mein Vater hat das Auto reparieren lassen.*

## SEPARABLE AND INSEPARABLE VERBS

See Chapter 2

### Separable verbs

These verbs have a prefix which is sometimes written at the front of the word, but sometimes breaks off and goes to the end of the clause.

For example: **anfangen**
Present      *Das Konzert **fängt** in zehn Minuten **an**.*
Imperfect    *Das Konzert **fing** um acht Uhr **an**.*
Perfect      *Das Konzert **hat** gerade **angefangen**.*
Future       *Das Konzert **wird** bald **anfangen**.*

With modals:
*Ich wollte gleich **anfangen**.*

When used with verbs followed by *zu*, notice how the *zu* is included within the word:
    *Der Lehrer bat mich anzufangen.*

Many separable verbs have English equivalents in meaning, e.g. to switch on, to go out, to stand up, etc.

### Inseparable verbs

These verbs have a prefix which never breaks off from the main verb. Inseparable prefixes are: *be-, emp-, ent-, er-, ge-, miß-, ver-, zer-*.

The perfect tense is formed without a *ge-* on the past participle:
    *Er hat viele Geburtstagsgeschenke erhalten.*
    *Sie hat ihn mißverstanden.*
    *Das Auto hat die Mauer total zerstört.*

# NOUNS

## GENDER

All German nouns are either masculine, feminine or neuter. It is essential that you adopt the habit of writing down and learning the gender of nouns as you meet them. If you can't remember the gender, you can't use the word effectively in either your speaking or writing. Here are some general rules on gender which may help you.

**Masculine words – *der/ein***
Male people and animals
    *der Manager* – manager
    *der Löwe* – lion
Days, months, seasons
    *der Samstag*
    *der Juli*
    *der Herbst*
Compass points/most types of weather
    *der Süden/im Süden*
    *der Hagel*
    *der Regen*
Nouns ending in:
    -ig      *der Pfennig* – penny
    -ling    *der Lehrling* – apprentice
    -ant     *der Protestant* – protestant (except *das Restaurant*)
    -er      *der Sprecher* – speaker
    -ismus   *der Marxismus* – marxism
    -or      *der Rektor* – headteacher, principal

**Feminine words – *die/eine***
Female people and animals
    *die Tante* – aunt
    *die Löwin* – lioness
Names of numbers
    *die Eins*
    *eine Million*
Nouns ending in:
    -ion     *die Information* – information
    -anz     *die Substanz* – substance

| | |
|---|---|
| *-enz* | *die Lizenz* – licence |
| *-ie* | *die Kopie* – copy |
| *-ik* | *die Republik* – republic |
| *-ur* | *die Figur* – figure |
| *-age* | *die Garage* – garage |
| *-ette* | *die Diskette* – floppy disk |

**Neuter words – *das/ein***
Young people and animals
      *das Kind* – child
      *das Fräulein* – young woman, 'miss'
      *das Mädchen* – girl
      *das Baby* – baby
      *das Lamm* – lamb
Measurements
      *das Meter* – meter
      *das Kilo* – kilogramme
      *das Liter* – litre
Letters of the alphabet
      *ein großes* S – a capital S (*London wird mit großem L geschrieben.*)
Colours
      *das Grün* – green
Languages
      *das Englisch* – English
Words 'borrowed' from other languages
      *das Café* – café
      *das Hotel* – hotel
      *das Mikrofon* – microphone
Nouns ending in:
| | |
|---|---|
| *-um* | *das Wachstum* – growth (except *der Reichtum* [riches] and *der Irrtum* [error]) |
| *-ment* | *das Argument* – argument, reason |
| *-ett* | *das Bukett* – bouquet |
| *-icht* | *das Gewicht* – weight |

## COMPOUND NOUNS

In compound nouns, it is always the last part of the word that determines the gender and plural form of the noun:
      ***der*** *Stunden**plan*** – timetable
      ***die*** *Bushalte**stelle*** – bus–stop
      ***das*** *Schwimm**bad*** – swimming pool

## PLURAL NOUNS

Here are some simple guidelines as to how nouns form their plurals.

**Masculine**
Most form their plural with an *-e*; on some an umlaut is added to the last vowel:
      *Stadtplan* → *Stadtpläne*
If the noun ends in *-el*, *-en* or *-er*, it is usual for it to stay the same in the plural.

**Feminine**
Virtually all form their plural by adding *-n* or *-en*.
Two common exceptions are *Mutter* → *Mütter* and *Tochter* → *Töchter*.

**Neuter**
Most neuter nouns add an *-e* to form their plural.
The other common plural form is an umlaut and *-er*:
      *Blatt* → *Blätter*

## DECLENSION

In the genitive singular of both masculine and neuter nouns, the noun adds an
-s or an -es:

- Words with two syllables or more add -s:
  *das Auto meines Vaters*

- Words with one syllable add -es:
  *der Titel des Buches*

All nouns add -n or -en in the dative plural:
*Sie spricht mit den zwei Kindern.*

**See Chapter 8**

## ADJECTIVES AND ADVERBS

### Formation

You need to be able to use adjectives effectively and correctly. The adjectival
endings are shown in the table in Chapter 8 and should be committed
to memory.

**See Chapter 1**

### Possessive adjectives

| | | | |
|---|---|---|---|
| *mein* | my | *unser* | our |
| *dein* | your | *euer* | your |
| *sein* | his | *Ihr* | your (formal) |
| *ihr* | her | *ihr* | their |
| *sein* | its | | |

The endings of possessive adjectives follow the pattern of the indefinite article.

**See Chapter 3**

### Demonstrative adjectives

| | |
|---|---|
| *dieser* | this/these |
| *jener* | that/those |
| *jeder* | each, every |

*Dieser Wagen ist schneller.*
*Jedes Kind weiß das.*

**See Chapter 7**

### Adverbs

Note these examples of the addition of *hin-* and *her-*:
*Lauf dahin!*
*Kommt hierher!*

**See Chapter 4**

### Comparative and superlative of adjectives and adverbs

Both adjectives and adverbs form their comparatives in a similar way to the
English, with -er and -st or -est. Some of the most common ones also add
an umlaut.
Adjective    *groß → größer → der größte*
Adverb       *schnell → schneller → am schnellsten*

### Quantifiers

These are used to indicate how much the quality expressed by an adjective or
adverb is true.

| | |
|---|---|
| *ein bißchen* | a little |
| *ein wenig* | a little |
| *viel* | much, a lot |
| *zu* | too |
| *sehr* | very |
| *ganz* | quite, really |
| *ziemlich* | quite |

*Du läufst ein wenig schnell für mich.*
*Ich werde ein bißchen langsamer gehen.*
*Er ist ziemlich fleißig.*

# ARTICLES

See Chapter 3

Definite article (the) – *der, die, das*
Indefinite article (a/an) – *ein, eine, ein*
It is important to know these in all cases and genders. Note also the use of the negative article *kein*, which follows the same pattern as *ein*.

# PRONOUNS

## Personal pronouns

See Chapter 9

You should know thse in all persons (including *man*) and in all cases.
>E*r gibt es ihr.*
>*Wir geben es ihnen.*
>B*ring' es mir, bitte!*

## Reflexive pronouns

See Chapter 9

These are the pronouns used with reflexive verbs (see Chapter 2).
>E*r wäscht sich.*
>*Sie kämmt sich das Haar.*

## Relative pronouns

See Chapter 9

The relative pronoun takes its number and gender from the noun it refers back to. Its case depends on its function within the relative clause. Watch out for the position of the verb within the relative clause.
>*Der Mann, der drüben sitzt, ist mein Onkel.*
>*Die Frau, die ich drüben sehe, ist meine Nachbarin.*

## Indefinite pronouns

See Chapter 13

There is nothing essentially difficult about the following vocabulary. Treat it simply as another list of words to learn.

| | | | |
|---|---|---|---|
| *man* | one, (we, you) | *beides* | both |
| *jeder* | each, everybody | *mehrere* | several |
| *ein paar* | a few | *manche* | some |
| *einige* | some | *welcher* | some |
| *andere* | others | *nur wenig* | just a little |

>*Niemand weiß darüber Bescheid.* – Nobody knows anything about it.
>*Jemand muß es wissen.* – Somebody must know (it).

## Interrogative pronouns

See Chapter 13

>**Welcher** *ist das?*
>**Wer** *ist gestorben?*

## Demonstrative pronouns

See Chapter 13

The definite article can also be used to mean 'the one(s)', 'that one' or 'those'.
>**Das** *nehme ich mit.*
>**Den** *mag ich nicht so sehr.*

# NUMBER AND TIME

## Number

### The cardinal numbers

| | | | |
|---|---|---|---|
| 0 | Null | 4 | vier |
| 1 | eins | 5 | fünf |
| 2 | zwei | 6 | sechs |
| 3 | drei | 7 | sieben |

| 8 | acht | 21 | einundzwanzig |
|----|------|----|---------------|
| 9 | neun | 22 | zweiundzwanzig |
| 10 | zehn | 23 | dreiundzwanzig |
| 11 | elf | 24 | vierundzwanzig |
| 12 | zwölf | 25 | fünfundzwanzig |
| 13 | dreizehn | 26 | sechsundzwanzig |
| 14 | vierzehn | 27 | siebenundzwanzig |
| 15 | fünfzehn | 28 | achtundzwanzig |
| 16 | sechzehn | 29 | neunundzwanzig |
| 17 | siebzehn | 30 | dreißig |
| 18 | achtzehn | 31 | einunddreißig |
| 19 | neunzehn | 32 | zweiunddreißig, usw. |
| 20 | zwanzig | | |

| 100 | hundert |
|-----|---------|
| 1000 | tausend |
| 1,000,000 | eine Million |

## Quantity

Notice that you do not need to translate the English 'of':

*achtzig Liter Benzin* – 80 litres of petrol
*vier Kilo Tomaten* – 4 kilos of tomatoes
*drei Meter Seide* – 3 metres of silk

## Dates and Time

You will need to use ordinal numbers for dates:
(der) erste/(der) 1ste
zweite
dritte
vierte
fünfte
sechste
siebte
Then *achte* as far as *neunzehnte* – all adding *-te*.
Then *zwanzigste, einundzwanzigste*, etc. – all adding *-ste*.

*Heute ist der vierundzwanzigste Juni. (der 24ste Juni/der 24. Juni)*
*Vati kommt erst am sechsundzwanzigsten Juli. (am 26sten Juli/am 26. Juli)*

## Seit and *schon*

In German, you use the present tense with *seit* or *schon* to translate the idea of doing something for a length of time:

*Ich lerne Deutsch seit zwei Jahren.* – I have been learning German for
two years.
*Wir sind schon zwei Tage hier.* – We have been here for two days.

Similarly, *seit* or *schon* used with the imperfect tense translates as 'had been ...'.

See Chapter 5

# PREPOSITIONS AND CASES

## Prepositions which take the accusative case

| bis | gegen |
|-----|-------|
| durch | ohne |
| entlang | um |
| für | wider |

*Sie bleibt bis **nächsten** Dienstag.*
*Er lief durch **die** Stadt.*
*Er fuhr **die** Straße entlang*.*
*Ist das für **meinen** Bruder?*
*Wir spielten gegen **die** Mannschaft aus Düsseldorf.*
*Ohne **deinen** Kuli kannst du nichts schreiben.*
*Wir liefen um **das** Schulgebaüde.*

* Note that *entlang* usually follows the noun.

## Prepositions which take the dative case

| | |
|---|---|
| aus | nach |
| außer | seit |
| bei | von |
| gegenüber | zu |
| mit | |

*Sie nimmt das Geld aus **ihrer** Tasche.*
*Niemand weiß es außer **meinem** Vetter.*
*Ich habe bei **meinem** Onkel gewohnt.*
*Das Haus steht gegenüber **dem** Kino.\**
*Sie fährt mit **dem** Zug.*
*Nach **dem** Mittagessen gehen wir nach Hause.*
*Seit **dem** Tod seines Hundes geht er kaum spazieren.*
*Er läuft von **der** Schule zu **der** Haltestelle.*

\* Also: *dem Kino gegenüber*. If *gegenüber* is used with a pronoun, the pronoun must come first: *Er stand mir gegenüber.*

## Prepositions which take either the accusative or dative

These prepositions take either the accusative or dative, depending on whether you wish to show movement or position:

| | |
|---|---|
| an | neben |
| auf | über |
| hinter | unter |
| in | zwischen |

**Accusative**
*Sie fuhren ans (= an **das**) Meer.*
*Die Katze sprang auf **den** Stuhl.*
*Er lief hinter **das** Haus.*

**Dative**
*Sie saßen am (= an **dem**) Strand.*
*Die Katze sitzt auf **dem** Stuhl.*
*Der Wagen stand hinter **dem** Haus.*

## Prepositions which take the genitive case

trotz
während
wegen

*Trotz **des** Regens bleiben wir einen Weile im Garten.*
*Während **des** Tages arbeiten wir zu Hause.*
*Wegen **des** Verkehrs sind wir zu spät angekommen.*

Note that *wegen* is now frequently followed by the dative case: *wegen dem Verkehr, wegen dem Wetter*, etc.

## Contractions of preposition and article

Certain prepositions combine with the definite article as follows:

| | |
|---|---|
| an dem → am | von dem → vom |
| an das → ans | zu dem → zum |
| bei dem → beim | zu der → zur |
| in dem → im | |
| in das → ins | |

*Ich laufe **zur** Haltestelle, fahre **ins** Dorf und kaufe die Wurst **beim** Metzger.*

## Use of *da(r)* with prepositions

If you want to follow a preposition by the word 'it', you use the word *da* in front of the preposition (regardless of the gender of the word to which the pronoun 'it' refers). If the preposition begins with a vowel, add an *r*.

*Ich nehme einen Kuli und schreibe **damit**. (with it)*
*Dort ist dein Stuhl. Setz' dich **darauf**. (on it)*
*Wir haben nur die eine Tasse, aber du darfst **daraus** trinken. (out of it)*

167

## WORD ORDER IN MAIN CLAUSES

In a main clause, the finite verb is always the 'second idea'. (The finite verb is the part of the verb which is governed directly by the subject; it is not the infinitive or the past participle.) That does not mean it is necessarily the second word, as the 'first idea' may be a phrase.

| Subject | Verb | Rest of main clause |
|---|---|---|
| Er | kommt | um zehn Uhr nach Hause. |
| Meine Mutter | fährt | morgen mit ihrer Schwester nach Bonn. |
| Die Dame mit dem Hund | steht | neben meiner Tante. |
| Mein Bruder und ich | wollen | heute nicht einkaufen gehen. |
| Sie | müssen | den neuen Film unbedingt sehen. |
| Ich | hoffe, | morgen die neue CD zu kaufen. |
| Meine Freunde | sind | letzte Woche nach Berlin mitgefahren. |
| Wir | haben | die Hausaufgaben ganz leicht gefunden |

| Adverb/adverb phrase | Verb | Subject, then rest of clause |
|---|---|---|
| Um zehn Uhr | kommt | er nach Hause |
| Morgen | fährt | meine Mutter mit ihrer Schwester nach Bonn. |
| Neben meiner Tante | steht | die Dame mit dem Hund. |
| Heute | wollen | meine Bruder und ich nicht einkaufen gehen. |
| Den neuen Film | müssen | Sie unbedingt sehen. |
| Morgen | hoffe | ich, die neue CD zu kaufen. |
| Letzte Woche | sind | meine Freunde nach Berlin gefahren. |
| Die Hausaufgaben | haben | wir ganz leicht gefunden. |

Watch out for the direct object appearing as the first idea for emphasis. It can sometimes be confusing:

> *Den Knochen hat der Hund schnell gefressen.*

Common sense should dictate whether the dog ate the bone or the bone ate the dog! In this example, the masculine accusative is obvious, but it is not obvious with feminine and neuter nouns:

> *Ihre Tochter hat die Frau sofort mitgenommen.*

You must decide from the context whether this means 'Your daughter took the woman with her straight away' or 'The woman took her daughter with her straight away'. On the other hand, *Das neue Auto fand Fräulein Braun ganz toll* can mean only one thing.

**See Chapter 6** →

## CONJUNCTIONS

### Coordinating conjunctions

The following conjunctions join main clauses but do not affect the word order:

und     denn
aber    sondern
oder

> *Ich bleibe zu Hause **und** mache meine Hausaufgaben.*
> *Ich mache meine Hausaufgaben, **und** meine Mutter hilft mir dabei.*

(Note that you need to use a comma between main clauses when there is a change of subject.)

> *Meine Mutter hilft mir dabei, **denn** ich verstehe nicht alles.*
> *Entweder bleiben wir hier **oder** wir gehen in die Disco.*
> *Ich bleibe abends nicht zu Hause **sondern** besuche meine Freundin.*

### Subordinating conjunctions

The following conjunctions join main and subordinate clauses:

als       ob
bevor    obgleich
bis       obwohl
damit    so daß

| daß | während |
|-----|---------|
| nachdem | wenn |
| weil | |

The finite verb in the subordinate clause always goes to the end of the clause:
*Ich war überrascht, als ich dich heute **sah**.*
If the subordinate clause precedes the main clause, then the subject and verb in the main clause are inverted:
*Als ich dich heute **sah**, **war ich** überrascht.*

Here are some further examples:

| **Main clause** | **Subordinate clause** |
|-----------------|------------------------|
| Ich habe mein Frühstück gegessen, | bevor ich in die Stadt gefahren bin. |
| Ich kaufe mir eine neue Jacke, | wenn ich genug Geld habe. |
| Wir waren in der Stadt, | als wir unseren Vater gesehen haben. |
| Er ist schwimmen gegangen, | obwohl das Wasser so kalt war. |
| Die Musik finde ich ganz toll, | auch wenn du sie nicht gern hörst. |

| **Subordinate clause** | **Main clause** |
|------------------------|-----------------|
| Bevor ich in die Stadt gefahren bin, | habe ich mein Frühstück gegessen. |
| Wenn ich genug Geld habe, | kaufe ich mir eine neue Jacke. |
| Als wir unseren Vater gesehen haben, | waren wir in der Stadt. |
| Obwohl das Wasser so kalt war, | ist er schwimmen gegangen. |
| Auch wenn du sie nicht gern hörst, | finde ich die Musik ganz toll. |

When the subordinate clause precedes the main clause you will see a **verb–comma–verb** pattern in the middle of the sentence. This is a good point to check when re-reading your work.

## VERB TABLES

### WEAK (REGULAR) VERBS

| | | | | | |
|---|---|---|---|---|---|
| abholen | to fetch | gucken | to look | spielen | to play |
| abräumen | to clear away | heiraten | to marry | stecken | to put |
| abspülen | to wash up | hoffen | to hope | stellen | to put |
| anmachen | to switch on | hören | to hear | stimmen | to be correct |
| antworten | to answer | kaufen | to buy | suchen | look for |
| arbeiten | to work | klingeln | to ring a bell | tanzen | to dance |
| aufhören | to stop | klopfen | to knock | teilen | to share |
| aufmachen | to open | kriegen | to get (coll.) | träumen | to dream |
| aufpassen | to pay attention | lachen | to laugh | turnen | to do gymnastics |
| aufwachen | to wake up | legen | to put | üben | to practise |
| ausmachen | to switch off | lernen | to learn | überraschen | to surprise |
| auspacken | to unpack | machen | to make | verdienen | to earn |
| sich beeilen | to hurry | meinen | to think, say | verkaufen | to sell |
| begrüssen | to greet | mieten | to rent, hire | vermieten | to rent out |
| besichtigen | to visit | nähen | to sew | versuchen | to try |
| bestellen | to order | öffnen | to open | vorbereiten | to prepare |
| besuchen | to visit | prüfen | to test, check | wählen | to choose |
| bezahlen | to pay | rauchen | to smoke | warten | to wait |
| brauchen | to need | regnen | to rain | wechseln | to change (money) |
| buchen | to book | reichen | to pass | wecken | to wake |
| danken | to thank | reisen | to travel | wiederholen | to repeat |
| decken | to lay (table) | reparieren | to repair | wohnen | to live |

| | | | | | |
|---|---|---|---|---|---|
| drücken | to press, push | sagen | to say | wünschen | to wish |
| einkaufen | to shop | sammeln | to collect | zahlen | to pay |
| einpacken | to pack up | schauen | to look, watch | zeichnen | to draw |
| fehlen | to be missing | schicken | to send | zeigen | to show |
| fragen | to ask | schmecken | to taste | zuhören | to listen |
| sich freuen | to be pleased | schneien | to snow | | |
| glauben | to believe | segeln | to sail | | |

## STRONG (IRREGULAR) VERBS

| Infinitive | Present (3rd person) | Imperfect (1st & 3rd person) | Perfect (*haben* or *sein*\* + past participle) | Meaning |
|---|---|---|---|---|
| anfangen | fängt an | fing an | angefangen | to begin |
| aufstehen | steht auf | stand auf | aufgestanden\* | to get up |
| beginnen | | begann | begonnen | to begin |
| beißen | | biß | gebissen | to bite |
| bekommen | | bekam | bekommen | to get, receive |
| beschließen | | beschloß | beschlossen | to decide |
| beschreiben | | beschrieb | beschrieben | to describe |
| biegen | | bog | gebogen | to bend |
| bieten | | bot | geboten | to offer |
| bitten | | bat | gebeten | to ask, request |
| bleiben | | blieb | geblieben\* | to stay |
| brechen | bricht | brach | gebrochen | to break |
| brennen | | brannte | gebrannt | to burn |
| bringen | | brachte | gebracht | to bring |
| denken | | dachte | gedacht | to think |
| dürfen | darf | durfte | | to be allowed |
| einladen | lädt ein | lud ein | eingeladen | to invite |
| empfehlen | empfiehlt | empfahl | empfohlen | to recommend |
| erhalten | erhält | erhielt | erhalten | to receive |
| erkennen | | erkannte | erkannt | to recognise |
| essen | ißt | aß | gegessen | to eat |
| fahren | fährt | fuhr | gefahren\* | to travel |
| fallen | fällt | fiel | gefallen\* | to fall |
| fangen | fängt | fing | gefangen | to catch |
| finden | | fand | gefunden | to find |
| fliegen | | flog | geflogen\* | to fly |
| geben | gibt | gab | gegeben | to give |
| gefallen | gefällt | gefiel | gefallen | to please |
| gehen | | ging | gegangen\* | to go |
| geschehen | geschieht | geschah | geschehen\* | to happen |
| gewinnen | | gewann | gewonnen | to win |
| haben | hat | hatte | gehabt | to have |
| halten | hält | hielt | gehalten | to hold |
| helfen | hilft | half | geholfen | to help |
| kennen | | kannte | gekannt | to know |
| kommen | | kam | gekommen\* | to come |
| können | kann | konnte | | to be able to, can |

| | | | | |
|---|---|---|---|---|
| lassen | läßt | ließ | gelassen | to let, leave |
| laufen | läuft | lief | gelaufen* | to run |
| leihen | | lieh | geliehen | to lend |
| lesen | liest | las | gelesen | to read |
| liegen | | lag | gelegen | to lie |
| mögen | mag | mochte | | to like |
| müssen | muß | mußte | | to have to, must |
| nehmen | nimmt | nahm | genommen | to take |
| reißen | | riß | gerissen | to tear |
| reiten | | ritt | geritten* | to ride (horse) |
| riechen | | roch | gerochen | to smell |
| rufen | | rief | gerufen | to call |
| scheinen | | schien | geschienen | to shine |
| schießen | | schoß | geschossen | to shoot |
| schlafen | schläft | schlief | geschlafen | to sleep |
| schlagen | schlägt | schlug | geschlagen | to hit |
| schließen | schließt | schloß | geschlossen | to close |
| schneiden | | schnitt | geschnitten | to cut |
| schreiben | | schrieb | geschrieben | to write |
| schreien | | schrie | geschrieen | to shout, scream |
| schwimmen | | schwamm | geschwommen* | to swim |
| sehen | sieht | sah | gesehen | to see |
| sein | ist | war | gewesen | to be |
| singen | | sang | gesungen | to sing |
| sinken | | sank | gesunken | to sink |
| sitze | | saß | gesessen | to sit |
| sollen | soll | sollte | | should, ought to |
| sprechen | spricht | sprach | gesprochen | to speak |
| springen | | sprang | geprungen* | to jump |
| stehen | | stand | gestanden | to stand |
| stehlen | stiehlt | stahl | gestohlen | to steal |
| sterben | stirbt | starb | gestorben* | to die |
| tragen | trägt | trug | getragen | to wear, carry |
| treten | tritt | trat | getreten* | to tread, step |
| trinken | | trank | getrunken | to drink |
| tun | tut | tat | getan | to do |
| verbringen | | verbrachte | verbracht | to spend |
| vergessen | vergißt | vergaß | vergessen | to forget |
| verlassen | verläßt | verließ | verlassen | to leave (place) |
| verlieren | | verlor | verloren | to lose |
| verschwinden | | verschwand | verschwunden* | to dissappear |
| versprechen | verspricht | versprach | versprochen | to promise |
| verstehen | | verstand | verstanden | to understand |
| waschen | wäscht | wusch | gewaschen | to wash |
| werden | wird | wurde | geworden* | to become |
| werfen | wirft | warf | geworfen | to throw |
| wissen | weiß | wußte | gewußt | to know |
| wollen | will | wollte | gewollt | to want |
| ziehen | zieht | zog | hat gezogen | to pull |

## CHAPTER 1  DIE SCHULE

### Transcript

**1**  Also, was ich in der Schule lerne?

Montag beginnt der Schultag nicht so gut – Englisch ist nicht mein bestes Fach, aber nach der Pause wird es schon besser, denn die Mathelehrerin ist ganz toll. Nach der zweiten Pause habe ich Deutsch, dann Informatik.

Dienstag ist auch nicht so schlecht. Erdkunde haben wir in der zweiten Stunde, das ist meist interessant, aber wir haben Deutsch zweimal an dem Tag, was ich gar nicht so toll finde. Turnen haben wir am Nachmittag, denn die Turnhalle ist sonst immer voll besetzt.

Mittwoch ist immer ganz lustig, denn nach der ersten Pause haben wir eine Doppelstunde Kochen.

Donnerstag haben wir drei Stunden mit unserem Klassenlehrer, Herrn Burger. Er unterrichtet Religion in der ersten, Geschichte in der vierten und Sozialkunde in der fünften Stunde. Glücklicherweise komme ich mit ihm gut aus.

Freitag haben wir eine Doppelstunde Sport. Das gefällt mir gut, weil wir meistens draußen spielen.

Ich finde es sowieso doof, Samstags in die Schule zu gehen, aber wir haben zumindest wieder Erdkunde in der ersten Stunde und eine Doppelstunde Technik, bevor wir nach Hause gehen.

### Answers

| Stunde | Montag | Dienstag | Mittwoch | Donnerstag | Freitag | Samstag |
|--------|--------|----------|----------|------------|---------|---------|
| 1 | Englisch | Deutsch | Mathe | **Religion** | Biologie | **Erdkunde** |
| 2 | Geschichte | **Erdkunde** | Deutsch | Englisch | Deutsch | Englisch |
|   | P | A | U | S | E |  |
| 3 | **Mathe** | Kunst | **Kochen** | Informatik | **Sport** | **Technik** |
| 4 | Musik | Physik | **Kochen** | **Geschichte** | **Sport** | **Technik** |
|   | P | A | U | S | E |  |
| 5 | Deutsch | **Deutsch** | Chemie | Sozialkunde | Englisch |  |
| 6 | **Informatik** | Mathe | Latein | Mathe | Latein |  |
| 7 |  | Turnen |  |  |  |  |
| 8 |  | Turnen |  |  |  |  |

[10 marks]

### Examiner's comments

This looks easy enough to begin with, but some of the answers are slightly disguised. For example, on Monday you hear the word *Mathelehrerin*, and several of the lessons are placed by words or phrases such as *dann*, *nach der Pause*, etc.

On Tuesday you hear E*rdkunde* for lesson 2 but you have to work out that the second gap is D*eutsch*, because Anna emphasises that she has D*eutsch **zweimal** an dem Tag*.

An A Grade candidate should score at least 8 of the 10 marks available for this exercise.

**2** **Teacher:** Also, was haben Sie an einem typischen Schultag gemacht?

**Student:** Ich bin morgens in die Schule gegangen. Der Unterricht hat um acht Uhr begonnen. Es gab zwei Stunden vor der Pause, und die kleine Pause dauerte zehn Minuten.

**Teacher:** Was haben Sie in der Pause gemacht?

**Student:** Wir sind auf den Schulhof gegangen.

**Teacher:** Und dann?

**Student:** Nach der Pause gab es zwei Stunden und dann eine Pause von zwanzig Minuten. Nach der zweiten Pause haben wir wieder zwei Stunden gehabt.

**Teacher:** Was hat Ihnen am besten gefallen?

**Student:** Um Viertel nach eins war die Schule zu Ende. Wir sind nach Hause gegangen und haben zu Mittag gegessen.

## Examiner's comments

This is very short on content and the candidate gives only the briefest outline of the school day. This candidate is likely to achieve at best a C Grade. He misses the opportunities that this very open question offers.

Firstly, you can say what lessons you had and when. This is easy material and should form part of this answer. Secondly, and most important for the Higher Level passes, you should say how you felt about your lessons and teachers. You must be able to express emotions such as pleasure or annoyance, so build up a stock of simple phrases which will add realism and depth to such a narrative.

Here is the same candidate again, but with more to say:

**Teacher:** Also, was haben Sie an einem typischen Schultag gemacht?

**Student:** Ich bin morgens mit meinem Partner in die Schule gegangen. Wir sind mit dem Rad gefahren. Wir waren schon um zehn vor acht da, und der Unterricht hat um acht Uhr begonnen. Wir hatten zwei Stunden vor der Pause, Englisch und Mathematik. Die Englischstunde war ganz lustig, und ich mußte viele Fragen beantworten. Die Mathestunde war schwer, denn ich bin nicht so gut in Mathe. Die kleine Pause dauerte zehn Minuten, und wir haben uns alle auf dem Schulhof getroffen.

**Teacher:** Und dann?

**Student:** Nach der Pause gab es nochmal zwei Stunden, Biologie und Geschichte. In der Biostunde hat die Klasse eine Klausur geschrieben, und ich habe ein Buch gelesen. Geschichte hat mir Spaß gemacht und wir haben dann eine Pause von zwanzig Minuten gehabt.

**Teacher:** Was haben Sie in der Pause gemacht?

**Student:** In der großen Pause haben wir unsere Butterbrote gegessen und ein Milchgetränk vom Hausmeister gekauft. Ich bin auch mit meinem Partner zum Lehrerzimmer gegangen, denn er wollte eine Arbeit abgeben. Nach der zweiten Pause haben wir wieder zwei Stunden gehabt. Dann war es Viertel nach eins und die Schule war zu Ende.

**Teacher:** Was hat Ihnen am besten gefallen?

**Student:** Die deutschen Schüler tragen natürlich keine Uniform, und das hat mir sehr gut gefallen. Wir sind nach Hause gegangen und haben zu Mittag gegessen. Am Nachmittag sind wir schwimmen gegangen, denn es war immer noch sehr sonnig.

With a little extra thought and some simple vocabulary the candidate is now saying much more than the teacher. The responses are much more realistic, and the candidate gives an impressive performance of the sort expected of an A Grade candidate.

Remember, it is you, the candidate, who must take the initiative.

## Answers

**3**  1 falsch; **2** richtig; **3** falsch, **4** richtig; **5** richtig; **6** falsch; **7** richtig;
**8** falsch; **9** falsch; **10** richtig

## Examiner's comments

It is advisable to read the statements through first, before launching into the text. In this way you may identify key words, usually nouns and verbs which you hope to recognise in the text. The answers should be found in the order in which you read the questions. This text is on the long side but the true/false format will save you some time. Most answers themselves are not difficult and you will probably find most at the first reading, but you do have a lot to read. Here are some tips to help you:

**1** *Nach* not *in den Osterferien*.

**2** This is a general comment and should be obvious.

**3** *Für alle zehnten Klassen* is the phrase that tells you it's not for all classes.

**4** You need to know that *ab der neunten Klasse* means 'from Class 9 onwards'.

**5** This is almost the wording of the text.

**6** This is an inference which you must work out from the text. Jürgen is clearly not worried about tests and exams.

**7** *Leider* gives you the clue that Jürgen is not happy about Beate's situation.

**8** *Schulfest* not *Klassenfest*. Did you read it correctly?

**9** Only *abends*.

**10** Again, the word *genug* appears in the text to guide you.

---

**CHAPTER 2**  **MEIN HAUS, MEIN ZIMMER**

## Transcript

**1** **Cornelia:** Also ich? Ich möchte am liebsten eine große Wohnung haben, mit vielen Zimmern. Sie könnte aber ruhig in der Stadt sein, denn ich möchte keinen Garten. Ich mag Hunde sehr gerne, aber in der Stadt ohne Garten ist das nichts. Also, vielleicht kaufe ich mir eine Katze.

**Uwe:** Ich finde es schöner, auf dem Land zu wohnen, auch wenn es manchmal schwierig ist, meine Freunde in der Stadt zu besuchen. Am liebsten würde ich auf einem alten Bauernhof wohnen, wo ich im Haus und im Garten viel Platz für meine Tiere habe. Ich habe nämlich zwei große Hunde, vier Katzen und auch ein paar kleinere Tiere.

**Thomas:** Für mich allein möchte ich eine Luxuswohnung. Nicht unbedingt so groß, aber ganz in der Stadtmitte, wo abends sehr viel los ist. Nicht weit von der Arbeit, und hoffentlich auch nicht weit von einem Park, denn ich gehe sehr gern mit meinem Hund spazieren.

**Eva:** Wenn ich im Lotto das große Geld gewinne, kaufe ich mir ein tolles Haus weit außerhalb der Stadt. Gar kein anderes Haus zu sehen, und mit einem schönen Garten ringsherum, wissen Sie, wo ich mit meinen Hunden laufen und spielen kann.

## Answers

| Name | auf dem Land | in der Stadt | Haus | Wohnung | Garten | Hund | Katze |
|---|---|---|---|---|---|---|---|
| Cornelia | | ✓ | | ✓ | | | ✓ |
| Uwe | ✓ | | ✓ | | ✓ | ✓ | ✓ |
| Thomas | | ✓ | | ✓ | | ✓ | |
| Eva | ✓ | | ✓ | | ✓ | ✓ | |

[15 marks]

## Examiner's comments

This grid may look like a simple exercise, but the language you hear makes it more like Higher Level, for example:

**Cornelia:** Did you hear *keinen* or *kleinen Garten*? There is also a comment about a dog which might distract you.

**Uwe:** He refers to both *Stadt* and *Land*, but which does he prefer?

**Thomas:** Two words you need are slightly disguised in simple compound nouns.

**Eva:** Did you recognise one of the less common prepositions which comes before *Stadt*?

## Transcript

SPEAKING  F  H

**2**

**Teacher:** Also, was machst du morgens, bevor du in die Schule kommst?

**Student:** Ich frühstücke.

**Teacher:** Und dann?

**Student:** Ich packe meine Tasche.

**Teacher:** Um wieviel Uhr verläßt du morgens das Haus?

**Student:** Um acht.

**Teacher:** Wie kommst du in die Schule?

**Student:** Mit dem Auto.

**Teacher:** Wer fährt dich hin?

**Student:** Meine Mutter.

**Teacher:** Kannst du dein Haus beschreiben?

**Student:** Es ist mittelgroß und hat drei Schlafzimmer.

**Teacher:** Und die anderen Zimmer?

**Student:** Wir haben ein Badezimmer, ein Eßzimmer, ein Wohnzimmer und eine Küche.

**Teacher:** Habt ihr auch einen Garten?

**Student:** Ja.

**Teacher:** Wie hilfst du zu Hause?

**Student:** Ich wasche ab.

**Teacher:** Und am Wochenende?

**Student:** Ich mache mein Zimmer sauber.

## Examiner's comments

This is hard work for the teacher and a little disappointing. Although the candidate's German is correct, it is very short on content and has to be dragged out.

The teacher asks some open-ended questions as an opportunity for the student to talk about a familiar subject. When the student makes only short responses, the teacher has to ask more direct questions, which naturally restrict the amount the student can say.

This candidate is likely to achieve at best a Grade C. A Higher Level candidate must be prepared to take the initiative and say at least three sentences on an open-ended question. The addition of some simple adverbs will help, as will some additional words such as *also*.

Now listen to the same candidate taking the initiative, and offering a little more information.

**Teacher:** Also, was machst du morgens, bevor du in die Schule kommst?

**Student:** Normalerweise stehe ich gegen sieben Uhr auf und frühstücke mit meiner Schwester in der Küche. Dann packe ich meine Schultasche und sehe ein bißchen fern. Meine Mutter fährt mich um acht Uhr in die Schule.

**Teacher:** Kannst du dein Haus beschreiben?

**Student:** Wir haben ein mittelgroßes Doppelhaus. Es hat drei Schlafzimmer, eine Küche, ein Bad, ein Wohnzimmer und ein Eßzimmer. Draußen haben wir einen großen Garten. Das finde ich toll. Ich spiele Fußball mit meinen Freunden auf dem Rasen.

**Teacher:** Wie hilfst du zu Hause?

**Student:** Also, ich muß gewöhnlich abwaschen – nach dem Abendessen. Und am Wochenende muß ich das Auto waschen. Ich muß mein Bett machen und mein Zimmer sauberhalten. Naja, und manchmal gehe ich auch einkaufen.

With a little extra thought and some simple vocabulary the candidate is now saying much more than the teacher. The responses are much more realistic, and the candidate gives an impressive performance in German of the sort expected of an A Grade candidate.

**F H READING**

## Answers

**3**
1 Beates neues Haus hat vier Schlafzimmer.
2 Sie teilt ihr Schlafzimmer nicht mehr.
3 Beates Eltern haben eine separate Dusche.
4 Beate macht ihre Hausaufgaben manchmal unten.
5 Beates Eltern freuen sich auf den Garten.

## Examiner's comments

It is advisable to read the questions through first, before launching into the text of the letter. In this way you can identify the key words, usually the nouns and verbs which you hope to recognise in the text. Because this is a multiple choice exercise you can probably see the different possibilities available and watch for them coming up.

Don't forget that in this sort of comprehension exercise the answers should be found in the text in the order in which you read the questions.

In Number 1 you need to identify the number of bedrooms in Beate's house. Although the exam does not set out to test your mathematical skill, you may reasonably be expected to count a small number of items or, in this case, people.

In Number 2 you should recognise from your speaking practice the verb *teilen* in connection with *Schlafzimmer*. You may then remember the phrase *ein eigenes Zimmer* which appears in lines 4–5.

*Dusche* und *Badezimmer* are easy enough in Number 3, but how are they related to the *Eltern* in the passage? Look out for *eine eigene Dusche* in line 9 of the text.

Number 4 presents you with the task of deduction or inference. You should spot that Beate does her *Hausaufgaben ... im Eßzimmer*, but which answer does that lead you to? Clearly not the first or the last alternatives, so check out the second one.

Number 5 asks you to identify what the parents are looking forward to (*sich freuen auf*). You should realise that the answer is in the last paragraph, where the vocabulary is not too difficult. *Garten* is easily spotted, but it does tell you that *Vater mag … Rasenmähen nicht so sehr.*

## CHAPTER 3 ESSEN UND GESUNDHEIT

**Transcript**

LISTENING H

**1**   Herr und Frau Kolbitz und Herr und Frau Radler essen im Restaurant.

| | |
|---|---|
| **Herr Kolbitz:** | Guten Tag, wir haben einen Tisch für vier Personen bestellt. |
| **Kellner:** | Auf welchen Namen, bitte ? |
| **Herr K:** | Kolbitz. Ich habe heute nachmittag angerufen. |
| **Kellner:** | Ach ja. Wenn Sie mir folgen wollen. Ich habe einen Tisch für Sie hier am Fenster reserviert. Nehmen Sie doch bitte Platz. Ich bringe Ihnen gleich die Speisekarte. |
| **Herr K:** | Danke schön. |
| **Kellner:** | Nehmen Sie sich ruhig Zeit. Ich möchte Ihnen das Tagesmenü besonders empfehlen – gleich hier vorne. Es ist ausgezeichnet. Möchten Sie vielleicht schon die Getränke bestellen? |
| **Herr K:** | Ja, bitte. Ich glaube, meine Frau und ich nehmen beide ein Glas Rotwein. Ihren Hauswein, bitte. |
| **Herr Radler:** | Für meine Frau ein Glas Weißwein und für mich ein Mineralwasser. |
| **Kellner:** | Also, hier sind die Getränke. Haben Sie schon gewählt? |
| **Herr K:** | Ja, die beiden Damen möchten das Kotelett mit Dampfkartoffeln und Salat. Ich nehme das Menü, das Sie empfohlen haben. Also, das wäre die Tomatensuppe als Vorspeise, Wiener Schnitzel mit Pommes Frites und ein gemischtes Eis als Nachtisch. Uwe, was möchtest Du denn? |
| **Herr R:** | Ich möchte gern Gulasch mit Reis. Gibt es einen Salat dazu? |
| **Kellner:** | Ja, einen gemischten? |
| **Herr R:** | Ja, schön. Und als Nachspeise nehme ich ein Stück Käsekuchen. |
| **Kellner:** | Mit Sahne? |
| **Herr R:** | Nein, danke. Ohne. |
| **Kellner:** | Was wünschen die Damen als Nachspeise? |
| **Frau K:** | Danke. Wir nehmen keine Nachspeise. Wir achten auf die schlanke Linie. Aber wir möchten beide einen Kaffee nachher. |
| **Kellner:** | Aber gerne. |

**Answers**                                                                                       [20 marks]

| | Vorspeise | Hauptgericht | Nachspeise | Getränke |
|---|---|---|---|---|
| Herr Kolbitz | Tomatensuppe | Wiener Schnitzel, Pommes Frites | Gemischtes Eis | Rotwein |
| Frau Kolbitz | | Kotelett, Salat, Dampfkartoffeln | | Rotwein, Kaffee |
| Herr Radler | | Gulasch, Reis Gemischter Salat | Käsekuchen | Mineralwasser |
| Frau Radler | | Kotelett, Salat, Dampfkartoffeln | | Weißwein, Kaffee |

## Examiner's comments

This item contains plenty of easy food and drink vocabulary, so there should be few problems of spelling but it is made more difficult by the speed of delivery. At this level, you are unlikely to be given credit simply for the word *Suppe* on its own. (Of course, you also have to relate the items to the correct person in the group.)

Not all the orders are given directly. Herr Radler asks about a salad and confirms what the waiter offers him not by repeating it, but by saying *Ja, schön.*

The two women also have a drink with their meal and have a coffee after their main course instead of a dessert. Did you understand the reason given by Frau Kolbitz? *Wir achten auf die schlanke Linie* means that they are watching their waistlines and don't want to be tempted by the sweet course!

F H SPEAKING

## Transcript

**2** **1 Im Restaurant**

**Kellner:** Guten Tag. Bitte schön?
**Sie:** Ich möchte einen Tisch für vier Personen, bitte.
**Kellner:** Hier in der Ecke vielleicht?
**Sie:** Ja, gut. Können wir bitte die Speisekarte haben?
**Kellner:** Also, was wünschen Sie?
**Sie:** Vier Stück Apfelkuchen mit Sahne, bitte.
**Kellner:** Und was möchten Sie trinken?
**Sie:** Zweimal Limonade und zwei Tassen Kaffee.
**Kellner:** Also, bitte sehr. Das macht DM 19.40.
**Sie:** Ist die Bedienung inbegriffen?
**Kellner:** Ja.

**2 Beim Arzt in München**

**Arzt:** Was fehlt Ihnen?
**Sie:** Ich habe Halsschmerzen.
**Arzt:** Seit wann haben Sie Schmerzen?
**Sie:** Seit einer Woche.
**Arzt:** Ich kann Ihnen etwas für die Schmerzen geben.
**Sie:** Wann muß ich es einnehmen?
**Arzt:** Dreimal am Tag nach dem Essen. Wo wohnen Sie hier in München?
**Sie:** In einer Jugendherberge.
(*In einem Hotel/Bei meinem Brieffreund, usw.*)
**Arzt:** Also, hier ist das Rezept.
**Sie:** Wo ist eine Apotheke?

## Examiner's comments

These are fairly straightforward versions of what you could say, achieving the required level of communication without complication.

H READING

## Answers

**4** 1 Herr Nußbaum wollte zu Mittag essen.
2 Herr Nußbaum hatte im voraus einen Tisch reservieren lassen.
3 Am Eßtisch hatte man wenig Platz.
4 Die Beilagen kamen zu spät an den Tisch.
5 Als Nachspeise aßen sie das, was man ihnen empfohlen hat.
6 Herr Nußbaum fand die Bedienung sehr langsam.
7 Herr Nußbaum schrieb am Ende, daß er das Restaurant nie wieder besuchen wollte.

## Examiner's comments

1 The word *Mittagessen* appears right at the beginning of the letter. This should be an easy question to start you off.

2 The use of *lassen* means that he did not reserve the table himself. Herr Nußbaum says in the letter that his secretary booked the table.

3 The phrase *wirklich sehr eng* means that it was 'really very tight', i.e. they had very little room.

4 Clearly the side dishes, *die Beilagen* – usually the vegetables or salads – arrived so late that the meat course which they should have accompanied had gone cold.

5 *Man hat ihnen … empfohlen* appears in the text. The word *Nachspeise* is used in the question instead of *Nachtisch* in the letter.

6 *Langsam*, *nett* and *lustig* are Foundation Level words, but you have to infer Herr Nußbaum's feeling towards the waiter from his words: 'when we eventually', 'waiter was nowhere to be seen' and 'it took a long time'.

7 The phrase *Sie sehen mich nie wieder* should lead you to the correct answer.

In approximate order of difficulty, the questions are: 1, 6, 7, 2, 5, 4, 3. A C Grade candidate might expect to get three or four answers correct, whereas an A Grade candidate should not make more than one error in the seven.

---

## CHAPTER 4   SELBST, FAMILIE UND FREUNDE

### Transcript

SPEAKING   H

**1** **Student:** Also, ich bin letzte Woche mit meinem Austauschpartner, Stefan, zu einem Familientreffen in Ratzeburg gefahren. Es waren viele Leute da, seine Großeltern, zwei Onkel, drei Tanten und viele Vetter und Kusinen.

**Teacher:** Und was haben Sie den ganzen Tag so gemacht?

**Student:** Wir sind so gegen halb elf bei den Großeltern angekommen. Die Mutter von Stefan hat kalte Getränke geholt, und die älteren Leute haben auf der Terrasse geplaudert. Wir haben ein bißchen Fußball gespielt – im Garten.

**Teacher:** Und was haben Sie gegen Mittag gemacht?

**Student:** Zu Mittag hat es ein großes kaltes Essen gegeben und wir haben an einem großen Tisch draußen in der Sonne gesessen. Ich esse gern Salate und es gab verschiedene – Tomatensalat, Nudelsalat, Wurstsalat. Mein kleiner Bruder hat seine Limonade umgekippt, aber es war nicht schlimm, weil wir im Garten waren.

Als Nachtisch gab es Eis. Das hat uns Kindern sehr gut geschmeckt. Nach dem Essen haben wir den Abwasch gemacht. Es war ein herrlicher Tag, also sind wir in den Park spazieren gegangen. Dort gab es einen schönen See, und viele Kinder hatten ihre kleinen Boote mitgebracht.

**Teacher:** Wie lange sind Sie dort geblieben?

**Student:** Ungefähr anderthalb Stunden, dann sind wir zum Café gegangen, denn die Erwachsenen wollten Kaffee trinken und Kuchen essen. Wir fanden das aber nicht so gut und haben große Eisbecher bestellt. Das war toll. Und Oma hat bezahlt!

Wir waren gegen fünf wieder bei den Großeltern, und haben unsere Sachen in den Wagen gepackt. Oma Maria hat mir ein kleines Andenken von Ratzeburg geschenkt. Sie ist wirklich nett.

Wir haben der ganzen Familie „Auf Wiedersehen" gesagt und sind losgefahren. Es ist ein schöner Tag gewesen.

### Examiner's comments

This is the work of a confident candidate, who uses familiar phrases to good effect. It is pleasing to hear the short phrases expressing emotion or feelings used appropriately, e.g. *das hat uns ... geschmeckt*; *das war toll*; *sie ist wirklich nett*.

It is essential to be able to fall back on the set verb patterns at key points in this narrative. You can read more about this technique in Chapter 15, Speaking.

It is impressive to hear how the candidate uses the perfect tense for the actions of the people, but uses the imperfect tense correctly to describe the background scene at various points:

- *Es waren viele Leute da*
- *Es war ein herrlicher Tag*
- *Dort gab es einen schönen See*

This candidate would be assured of a high grade!

### 2  Answers

1 Mutti;  2 Ich;  3 meine Schwester;  4 meine Vetter;  5 mein Onkel;
6 meine Kusine;  7 Tante Ilse;  8 Oma Liddi

### Examiner's comments

In a matching exercise such as this, look for some obvious clues in the descriptions which enable you to pinpoint the correct answer. Amongst these descriptions are two which are not in the 3rd person singular, 'he' or 'she'. From the *bin* and *habe* you should see that one of them is in the 1st person singular and therefore must be connected with the *Ich* in the picture. Another description contains *sind*, *haben* and *beide*, and is therefore plural. The only label it can apply to is *meine Vetter*, who are the twin boy cousins.

Other vocabulary is fairly straightforward but does require you to understand the comparisons being made, such as:

- *größer als ich*
- *so groß wie ihre Mutter*
- *neben ihrer jüngeren Schwester*.

### Transcript

**3** 1 Hallo! Ich heiße Norbert und bin vierzehn Jahre alt. Ich habe einen Bruder, Robert, der zwei Jahre älter ist und eine Schwester, Stefanie. Wir haben einen Hamster und ein Meerschweinchen.

2 Grüß Dich! Ich bin die Edith. Bin erst 13. Ich habe zwei Schwestern. Sie sind beide älter als ich. Mechthild ist 23 und Sigrid ist 21. Die sind beide schon verheiratet. Ich interessiere mich sehr für Popmusik und treibe viel Sport. Ich sammle gern Münzen und habe sehr viele aus England.

3 Margret ist mein Name. Ich bin fünfzehn Jahre alt und habe eine Schwester. Schwimme gern und spiele auch jede Woche Volleyball in der Schule. Das macht mir enorm Spaß. Münzen sammle ich nicht, aber Briefmarken habe ich sehr viele.

4 Ich bin der Martin. Ich bin dreizehn und ich habe keine Geschwister. Ich spiele gern Basketball und fahre auch sehr oft Rad. Mein Hund heißt Sam und ich habe auch zwei Hamster.

## Answers

| | Einzelkind | 1 Br. | 2 Br. | 1 Schw. | 2 Schw. | Haustiere | mag Sport | Briefmarken | Münzen |
|---|---|---|---|---|---|---|---|---|---|
| Norbert | | ✗ | | ✗ | | ✗ | | | |
| Edith | | | | ✗ | | | ✗ | | ✗ |
| Margret | | | ✗ | | | | ✗ | ✗ | |
| Martin | ✗ | | | | | ✗ | ✗ | | |

## Examiner's comments

This is a fairly straightforward task. You may like to listen to the piece again and add details to your answers, such as names of brothers and sisters and types of sport or animals mentioned.

**WRITING    H**

## 4 *Sample Student's Answer*

Worcester, den 15. April

Lieber Johann,

Ich möchte Dir heute etwas über meine Familie erzählen.

Also, wir sind fünf in der Familie: meine Eltern, meine zwei Schwestern, Philippa und Laura, und ich. Meine Schwestern sind Zwillinge und sind zwölf Jahre alt. Sie sind ganz sympathisch und ich verstehe mich meistens gut mit den beiden. Sie gehen zu derselben Schule wie ich und sind in der Klasse 7.

Mein Vater, Bob, ist Ingenieur bei einer großen Firma in der nächsten Stadt und meine Mutter, Jo, ist Kinderärztin in einem Krankenhaus in Hereford. Sie arbeiten beide volltags, also muß ich manchmal nach der Schule auf meine beiden Schwestern aufpassen, bis einer von meinen Eltern nachmittags nach Hause kommt.

Meine Eltern sind ganz in Ordnung und spielen gern mit uns Kindern. Letztes Wochenende sind wir alle zum Park gegangen und haben Volleyball gespielt. Nächsten Sonntag sollen wir ans Meer fahren.

Schreib' bald wieder.

Dein

Daniel

### EXAMINER'S COMMENTS

- This is well balanced. The descriptions of jobs and where parents work is well handled and leads effectively into the reason why the writer has to look after the twins (using an excellent verb: aufpassen ... auf).

- The subordinate clause at the end of the third paragraph is also full and accurate.

- In paragraph 4, the colloquial phrase *ganz in Ordnung* is appropriate in an informal letter of this sort. The paragraph also contains two perfect tenses and a reference to the future with sollen – all necessary to achieve the higher grades.

- Remember that you can make up some of the details if you do not want to write about your own details. Sometimes it can even make it easier for you to score a good mark.

## CHAPTER 5  FREIZEIT UND FERIEN

### Transcript

**1** Ich heiße **Gerd**. In den Sommerferien bin ich fast jeden Tag **geritten**. Nur wenn das Wetter sehr schlecht war, bin ich zu Hause geblieben und habe **Musik gehört** oder **gelesen**.

Ich bin der **Martin**. In den Ferien habe ich wenig Zeit für Sport gehabt, weil ich den ganzen Tag im Supermarkt gearbeitet habe. Abends bin ich dann manchmal mit meiner Freundin entweder **ins Kino** oder **tanzen** gegangen. Das Geld, das ich verdient habe, spare ich für den **Skiurlaub** im Winter.

Hallo! Ich heiße **Jürgen**. Am Wochenende und in den Schulferien muß ich immer arbeiten, denn meine Hobbys sind etwas teuer. Ich habe mein **eigenes Pferd** und bin so oft wie möglich mit ihm unterwegs. Im Winter **fahre** ich gern **Ski**, denn wir wohnen nicht weit weg von Garmisch. **Radfahren** tue ich auch sehr viel, sonst kann ich hier auf dem Land meine Freunde nicht besuchen.

Hallo! Ich heiße **Peter**. Ich bin nicht sehr sportlich. Ich interessiere mich am meisten für **Popmusik**, und ich **lese** auch sehr viel. Wenn ich mit meinen Freunden ausgehe, dann gehen wir meistens in die Stadt, vielleicht mal **ins Kino** oder in die Pizzeria.

Servus! Ich bin der **Norbert**. Hier in der Stadt zu wohnen ist für mich das Ideale. Die **Disco** ist hier an der Ecke, da geh' ich sehr oft hin. Und es gibt auch zwei **Kinos** gleich in der Nähe. Nur am Wochenende nehme ich ganz gern mein **Rennrad** und fahre aufs Land hinaus. Nur bei schönem Wetter natürlich.

### Answers

**1** –;  **2** Martin;  **3** –;  **4** Jürgen;  **5** Norbert;  **6** Gerd;  **7** –;  **8** Peter

### Examiner's comments

The key words to listen out for are in bold in the transcript. Although some of the words appear to be very easy when you read them, they may well be obscured in the course of a longer listening passage.

Remember also that at Higher Level you should be able to draw an inference from a passage without the message being as obvious as in the Foundation Level texts. For example:

- Gerd does not say *ich mag reiten* but says that he had ridden – *geritten* – almost every day of the holidays. Similarly, Jürgen makes no mention of riding but does say that he has his own horse – *eigenes* Pferd.

- Norbert has a racing bike – *ein* Rennrad – and enjoys taking it out into the country at the weekend. He does not specifically say *ich fahre gern* Rad.

Although most of the words are relatively straightforward, you need to retain several items in your mind in order to do the matching exercise. That is what makes this a Higher Level exercise.

### Transcript

**2** **Teacher:** Also, erzähl' mir bitte, was es für Freizeitmöglichkeiten in deiner Stadt gibt.

**Student:** In Reading gibt es ziemlich viel für junge Leute. In jedem Stadtteil gibt es ein großes Sport- und Freizeitzentrum, wo man viel Sport treiben kann. Das finde ich toll, weil ich sehr sportlich bin. Außerdem gibt es zwei Kinos und ein Theater, wo es manchmal Popkonzerte gibt.

**Teacher:** Ist das nicht alles ein bißchen teuer?

**Student:** Eigentlich ja. Aber ich habe einen Samstagsjob, und meine Eltern geben mir auch ein bißchen Taschengeld.

**Teacher:** Was würdest du machen, wenn du viel Geld hättest?

**Student:** Also, ich würde etwas Sportliches machen. Erstens würde ich ein Haus mit einem Schwimmbad kaufen, denn ich schwimme sehr gerne. Zweitens würde ich einen Tenniskurs machen. Ich spiele gern Tennis aber nicht sehr gut. Ich möchte besser spielen können.

**Teacher:** Und was gibt es nicht in deiner Stadt?

**Student:** Es gibt keinen richtigen Jugendklub, wo alle hingehen können. Ich würde einen Klub für meine Freunde bauen – mit guter Musik, und mit Getränken, die man nicht bezahlen muß.

**Teacher:** Danke schön.

## Examiner's comments

The student is well organised to talk about this topic and starts off with some well-prepared statements and opinions. Remember that this can give the examiner a very favourable impression, but you should not necessarily expect to complete reciting all that you have learned. The examiner allows her to carry on for a few moments before directing a few questions at her on the same topic to test her comprehension and responsiveness. Although a weaker candidate might simply have said *Ja* or *Nein*, this candidate sees the opportunity to present a well-learned sentence about pocket money.

Then the examiner asks what she would like to do if she had enough money. Again the candidate sensibly pauses before answering. The formula of *ich würde* (I would) plus the infinitive is enough to answer this question very well indeed.

This is a confident candidate and this extract shows that she would go on to score high marks.

## 3   Answers

READING  F  H

1  Helen – Paula
2  Lorna – Heidi
3  Michelle – Lies
4  Charlotte – Susi
5  Victoria – Margret

## Examiner's comments

This is a task for the C/D level, so you should expect to do very well on it. Having read the questions in English first, you should have highlighted the key items that you are to look for in the text:

1  Helen – likes reading and enjoys all sorts of water sports.
2  Lorna – is very athletic and also listens to a lot of pop music.
3  Michelle – prefers indoor hobbies, enjoys going to plays and films.
4  Charlotte – enjoys cooking. Has ambitions to travel and likes to keep up with fashions.
5  Victoria – her main hobby is horse-riding. She enjoys classical music and plays the piano.

As you underline them, you will probably even recall the German words you might be looking for in order to match the students. Although some of the vocabulary is very easy, you have to contend with the material surrounding both the correct answers and the distractors, that is, the other people whose hobbies are not going to match.

Beware – some of the hobbies appear more than once, e.g. *Musik*, *Kochen* and *Lesen*. Don't simply go for the first word you recognise, but check that everything the person says fits the partner you have chosen.

## CHAPTER 6 FREUNDE UND GESELLIGKEIT

### Transcript

**1** Am Telefon

**Ralf:** Hallo, Bernd. Gehst du mit in den Park? Wir wollen alle Fußball spielen.

**Bernd:** Was! Bei diesem Wetter? Warte zumindest, bis der Regen aufhört. Dann gehe ich mit!

**Ralf:** Willst du heute abend mit ins Kino? Der neue James Bond Film läuft im Gangolf.

**Bernd:** OK. Aber erst nachdem ich meine Hausaufgaben gemacht habe. Sonst kriege ich Krach mit meiner Mutter.

**Ralf:** Und wann kann ich deinen „Gameboy" ausleihen?

**Bernd:** Also jetzt noch nicht, aber bestimmt, bevor wir in Urlaub fahren. Bis dann behalte ich den.

**Ralf:** Und warum fahrt ihr jetzt schon in Urlaub? Wir haben erst im Juli Ferien.

**Bernd:** Mein Vater kann aber dann nicht mitfahren. Er bekommt keinen Urlaub in den Sommermonaten.

**Ralf:** Ach so.

### Answers

1 Bernd will nicht gleich Fußball spielen, weil es (im Moment) regnet.
2 Er will mitgehen, wenn es aufhört zu regnen/wenn der Regen aufhört.
3 Bernd geht ins Kino, nachdem er seine Hausaufgaben macht/nachdem er seine Hausaufgaben gemacht hat.
4 Ralf bekommt den „Gameboy", bevor Bernd in Urlaub fährt/bevor Bernd wegfährt.
5 Bernds Familie macht jetzt Urlaub, damit sein Vater mitfahren kann/damit sein Vater auch Urlaub nehmen kann.

### Examiner's comments

The dialogue is relatively uncomplicated, but you do need to complete the sentences with correct verbs and tenses.

This type of exercise, where your answer is begun for you, steers you towards the right form of answer, but still makes you listen to the passage for the content. Whatever happens, don't simply write out verbs as you hear them. Once you have an idea what the answer is, check that you are using the correct form of the verb.

Sentence 1 needs only a simple *es regnet* to make it correct, but the sentences become progressively more difficult.

The two answers to 2 both require the use of the separable verb *aufhören*, with or without a verb to follow it.

Sentence 4 needs the idea of 'going away' to complete it; these are two straightforward possibilities.

Sentence 5 is more difficult to complete; the answer needs the modal verb *können* in order to make sense, but watch the word order carefully. The modal *kann* is the finite verb and must therefore come at the end of the clause.

### Transcript

**2** Am Telefon

**Student:** Hier Smith. (*Use your own surname.*)

**Teacher:** Hallo Peter. Was machen wir heute? (*The examiner will use your first name.*)

**Student:** Wollen wir ins Kino gehen?

**Teacher:** Was läuft?

**Student:** Im Metropol läuft ein Krimi.

**Teacher:** Ich habe keine Lust dazu. Möchtest du in die Disco gehen?

**Student:** Mit wem willst du gehen?

**Teacher:** Mit Anna und Katherina. Wann und wo treffen wir uns?

**Student:** Treffen wir uns um 8.30 vor der Disco!

**Teacher:** Fein. Tschüß. Bis dann.

## Examiner's comments

This is a task of intermediate difficulty, intended for the C or D candidate. Its difficulty lies in responding to questions which you have not been able to prepare. Remember to look up at the examiner at the appropriate time. The question is always clearer, when you are watching the speaker's face.

You have suggested going to the cinema, so the question from the examiner is a perfectly natural one, not a trick one.

You are told in the rubric that you want to go out with your friend in the evening, so you might think it obvious that you need to arrange a time and place to meet. Again, the question from the examiner should not really come as a surprise to you.

**3** Answers

1 Peter lud die Mädchen ein, Volleyball zu spielen.
2 Suzanne ist nicht so sicher, ob sie spielen will.
3 Peter stellt seine Klassenkameraden vor, nachdem sie spielen.
4 Ingrid und Suzanne sind mit einer Schülergruppe in Düsseldorf.
5 Peter möchte gleich essen gehen.
6 Die zwei Mädchen müssen zuerst um Erlaubnis bitten
7 Die zwei Mädchen müssen zurück in die Jugendherberge, weil sie dann abends ausgehen.
8 Peter will den Mädchen die Sehenswürdigkeiten zeigen.
9 Ingrid findet seine Idee nicht so gut.

## Examiner's comments

The language of the passage is not particularly difficult, but the choice of three possible answers to the questions should make you look very carefully at individual words and phrases.

Some of the possibilities deliberately use words and phrases from the passage. This is not meant to trick you into the wrong answer, but to make sure you have really understood what is going on. For example, *Stadtbummel* in number 5, or *Aufführung* in number 7, might lead you to choose the wrong answer if you do not look at the context of the individual words you recognise. Each of these examples is used in a different way from in the original passage. Conversely, the right answer might be written in language not seen in the passage, for example *um Erlaubnis bitten* (to ask for permission) in number 6.

There are also some inference questions, for example number 9, which require you to have an overall understanding of a longer piece of the passage.

## CHAPTER 7 DIE STADT, DIE UMGEBUNG, DAS WETTER

**Transcript**

**1** Und jetzt die Wettervorhersage **für morgen, Samstag**, den 4. Oktober. Zunächst bleibt das Wetter im gesamten Bundesgebiet wechselhaft, wenn auch etwas wärmer als in den letzten Tagen.

**In der Nacht** zum Samstag meist bewölkt, zeitweise **Regen**. Im Süden kann es zu einzelnen Gewittern kommen. Tiefsttemperaturen liegen bei ein bis zwei Grad Celsius.

Morgen früh meist heiter und sonnig. **Frühtemperaturen vier bis sechs Grad**. Im Laufe des Tages zunehmend wolkig, am Nachmittag **zieht ein atlantisches Tiefdruckgebiet nach Norden**.

**Im Süden teils sonnig**, teils aber auch stark bewölkt und Regenschauer. Tageshöchsttemperaturen liegen bei 12 Grad.

Im Norden wolkig, meist niederschlagsfrei. Tageshöchsttemperaturen liegen bei 10 Grad. In den Nachmittags- und **Abendstunden** gibt es zunehmend Schauer oder **Gewitter**.

Im ganzen Gebiet mäßiger, teils frischer Wind aus dem Südwesten.

### Answers

1 richtig;  2 richtig;  3 falsch;  4 falsch;  5 richtig;  6 falsch;  7 richtig;  8 falsch

### Examiner's comments

Weather forecasts are usually delivered quite quickly, and it is therefore essential that you recognise the key words straight away. This is where listening practice is easily within your grasp. If you don't have access to satellite or cable TV, simply tune in to a German radio station for a few minutes either side of the hour and try to catch a weather forecast. Have the vocabulary list at hand and check off the words as you recognise them. There are a number which are almost only heard in forecasts, so make sure you can spot them.

The key words in this listening passage are in bold in the transcript.

An important point to remember when tackling true/false questions is that you are unlikely to be offered exactly the same words in the task as are in the text. If the examiner wants you to answer *richtig*, the statement will almost certainly be re-worded from the original. Here are some examples from the forecast and statements:

1 The forecast is made on Friday for the following day, Saturday. Friday is not mentioned in the text at all, but you can easily infer it from the context.
2 Similarly here, there is a reversed comparison. 'It's getting warmer' implies that it has been colder in recent days. Therefore, *richtig* is the answer.
5 The statement says that the low pressure system is moving northwards, so it must be true to say that it is coming from the south.
7 The reference to *stürmisch* simply paraphrases the *zunehmende ... Gewitter* in the passage.

The four *falsch* answers are almost exact opposites of what was said in the forecast:

3 Statement – *trocken*; forecast – R*egen*.
4 Statement – E*is auf der Straße*; forecast – *ein bis zwei Grad*.
6 Statement – *keine Sonne*; forecast – *Im Süden teils sonnig*.
8 Statement – *fast keinen Wind*; forecast – *frischer Wind*.

**H SPEAKING**

### Transcript

**2**  **Teacher:** Also, Peter. Erzählen Sie, was Sie an diesem Tag gemacht haben!

**Student:** *(setting the scene)* **Es war in den Osterferien**. Ich habe mit meinen drei Freunden eine Fahrradtour gemacht. **Das Wetter war herrlich**, und wir wollten in die Berge fahren, um das Dorf Humpelheim zu besuchen.

**Wir sind um 8.00 Uhr losgefahren. Das Wetter war herrlich und die Sonne schien. Wir haben unser Picknick im Rucksack mitgenommen**.

Wir sind aus der Stadt herausgefahren, aber nach einer Weile mußten wir zu Fuß gehen, weil die Landstraße ziemlich steil war.

**Teacher:** Haben Sie eine Pause gemacht?

**Student:** Ja. **Um 11 Uhr haben wir haltgemacht, ein bißchen Schokolade gegessen und etwas getrunken.** Von dort aus konnten wir schon das Dorf sehen.

Wir sind zu Mittag im Dorf angekommen und haben vor der Kirche gehalten. Max hat früher in Humpelheim gewohnt, und er hat uns das Dorf gezeigt. **Es war sehr hübsch**, und es gab viele Fachwerkhäuser in den kleinen Straßen.

**Teacher:** Und wo haben Sie denn Ihr Picknick gegessen?

**Student:** Mitten im Dorf ist ein kleiner Fluß, und **wir haben** neben der Brücke **gepicknickt. Wir haben Käsebrote und Wurstbrote gegessen und Orangensaft getrunken.**

**Teacher:** Und danach?

**Student:** **Nach dem Essen** wurde das Wetter schlechter, es wurde ziemlich dunkel, und wir wollten so schnell wie möglich nach Hause. **Leider hat es angefangen zu regnen.**

Der Regen war sehr stark, und keiner von uns hatte einen Anorak.

**Wir sind um 5 Uhr zu Hause angekommen.** Wir waren klitschnaß, und es war uns ziemlich kalt, aber es war nicht so schlimm. Nach einem heißem Bad ging es mir schon besser!

**Teacher:** Danke schön, Peter.

## Examiner's comments

The teacher scarcely needs to help this along. When a candidate is so well prepared, the teacher will need to make only the briefest of comments to create the dialogue.

This candidate has started well by setting the scene and stating what he is going to talk about. Remember, this sort of role-play is an 'old chestnut', i.e. it comes up time and again in various forms. The candidate is clearly prepared to talk about a day out/trip out/sightseeing day, etc. and simply tailors his description to the demands of this question.

The clock in each picture offers you something easy to say, but instead of repeating the time for each of the eight pictures, the candidate has used some different time phrases: *nach einer Weile, zu Mittag* and *nach dem Essen*.

There are many phrases which must be included in any description of a day out, so learn them. They have been highlighted in the transcript. The travelling itself and the eating and drinking phrases must by now be well rehearsed. In the 15–20 minutes preparation time before the exam you can choose what else to say and so steer the conversation away from the difficult elements, while still telling the story in the pictures.

This candidate would score an A for his description of his day out.

**3 Answers**

READING  H

1 falsch; 2 falsch; 3 falsch; 4 richtig; 5 falsch; 6 richtig; 7 falsch; 8 richtig

## Examiner's comments

This is not a dense text to read. You will realise that it is from a tourist brochure and is therefore probably emphasising the positive aspects of the area. This is worth remembering when you read the statements underneath.

Statement 1 is an easy one and will give you confidence. It is the policy of some exam boards to base easy questions on the most difficult passages, in order that even the weaker candidate will find something that he/she can answer with some certainty.

Statement 2: *leckeres Essen* is the clue you need.

Statement 3: The word *Kurkonzerte* implies that people visit Mayrhofen for their health, but there is a disco as well for those who want to dance.

Statement 4: You will find *bekannt* in the text in conjunction with the word *Wintersport*.

Statement 5: Paragraph 3 tells you that *man auch im Hochsommer ... skifahren kann*.

Statement 6: All the four sports mentioned in paragraph 4 are outdoor sports, even swimming (*Freibad* not *Hallenbad*).

Statement 7: The activities for children are mixed. The painting/colouring and model-making are likely to be indoors, but horse-riding and kite-flying must be outdoors.

Statement 8: The holiday is described as healthy (*gesund*) and the *Luft* as *herrlich*, which in itself is a recommendation. You should recognise the word *empfehlen* from role-plays to do with accommodation ('Can you recommend a good hotel?' etc.).

You should score at least 6 out of 8 on this exercise on your way to an A grade.

## H WRITING

### 4 Sample Student's Answer

**EXAMINER'S COMMENTS**

- Remember that successful candidates at Higher Level are able to talk about their feelings about things, and you need to have the phrases at your fingertips when you go into the Writing Test.

- Some of what this candidate feels about his/her town or village is implicit in the description, for example saying that the shops are not particularly good, or that there is not much to do. However, it is always better to give a reason where possible.

- Once again, you might feel constrained by the 150 word limit, so try to get in all the good phrases you can.

---

**Mein Dorf**

Ledbury liegt in Südostengland, nicht weit von der Küste. Ich wohne gerne hier, obgleich es hier nicht viel zu tun gibt. Es ist ganz schön ruhig.

Die Landschaft in der Umgebung ist aber sehr schön, und wir gehen oft am Wochenende im Wald spazieren. Von meinem Fenster aus sieht man einen Bauernhof und viele Tiere – Schafe, Kühe und Pferde.

Nur ein paar junge Leute aus meiner Schule wohnen hier im Dorf. Also, wenn ich meine Freunde besuchen will, muß ich meistens mit dem Bus in die Stadt fahren. Dort kann man auch ins Hallenbad oder ins Kino gehen.

Newbury ist eine Marktstadt. Der Marktplatz selbst ist ganz hübsch und sehenswert, und der Markt findet jeden Donnerstag und Samstag statt. Es gibt aber keine so guten Geschäfte, und wenn man Kleidung kaufen will, fährt man am besten in eine größere Stadt, nach Reading vielleicht, oder am besten nach London.

---

**CHAPTER 8** **EINKAUFEN**

**1** **Mann:** Guten Tag!

**Mädchen:** Grüß Gott!

**Mann:** Wie kann ich Ihnen helfen?

**Mädchen:** Ich habe meine Jacke verloren.

**Mann:** Wissen Sie, wann und wo Sie die Jacke verloren haben?

**Mädchen:** Es war gestern nachmittag, nein, **gestern vormittag im Park**. Ich bin mit meinem Hund spazieren gegangen, und ich habe eine Weile auf einer Bank in der Sonne gesessen. Aber dann mußte ich ganz plötzlich meinem Hund hinterherlaufen. Und als ich ein paar Minuten später zurückgekommen bin, da war die Jacke weg.

**Mann:** Können Sie die Jacke genau beschreiben?

**Mädchen:** Es ist eine ziemlich alte Wildlederjacke, sie ist eigentlich **nicht viel wert**. Sie ist **hellbraun**, aber ziemlich schmutzig. Und es fehlt der obere Knopf.

**Mann:** Und haben Sie außerdem etwas verloren?

**Mädchen:** Leider ja. In der Innentasche waren meine **Hausschlüssel** und ein Portemonnaie mit etwa **zwanzig Mark** drin.

**Mann:** Also, ich glaube, ich kann Ihnen in der einen Sache helfen. Eine solche Jacke ist heute morgen abgegeben worden. Man hat sie auf der Straße in der Nähe vom Park gefunden und gleich hierhergebracht. ... Ist das Ihre Jacke?

**Mädchen:** Ja, Gott sei Dank!

**Mann:** Aber **das Geld und die Schlüssel waren nicht darin**. Es handelt sich in diesem Fall bestimmt um einen Diebstahl. Am besten informieren Sie gleich die Polizei. Und lassen Sie mir auch Ihre Adresse da, falls Ihre Sachen doch auftauchen.

**Mädchen:** Danke für Ihre Hilfe. Ich gehe sofort zur Polizei.

**Mann:** Es tut mir leid, aber Sie müssen noch zwei Mark Gebühr bezahlen.

## Answers

1 Das Mädchen ging ins Fundbüro, um etwas zu finden.
2 Sie hatte die Jacke am Tag davor im Park verloren.
3 Die Jacke war dreckig und nicht mehr neu.
4 In der Tasche der Jacke hatte das Mädchen ihre Schlüssel und etwas Geld.
5 Das Mädchen hat nur eine Sache zurückgekriegt.

## Examiner's comments

This is not the most difficult passage. The words you need to recognise are all in your basic vocabulary. The key words are printed in bold. Although some of the words appear to be very easy when you read them, they may well be obscured in the course of a longer listening passage.

**2** **Teacher:** Also, erzählen Sie mal, was Sie an diesem Tag gemacht haben.

**Student:** Sabine und ich sind frühmorgens mit der Straßenbahn in die Stadt gefahren.

Zuerst sind wir zur Bank gegangen, weil ich etwas Geld wechseln wollte. Der Kurs war sehr günstig, und ich habe fast neunzig Mark bekommen.

Danach sind wir ins Kaufhaus gegangen, weil Sabine eine neue Jeans kaufen wollte. Die Damenbekleidung war im zweiten Stock.

Sabine hat eine Jeans ausgesucht und hat sie anprobiert, aber sie war viel zu lang, und die Verkäuferin konnte keine kürzere finden.

Also, wir sind zum Markt gegangen und haben eine Jeans im Sonderangebot gefunden. Die war ganz toll und auch gar nicht teuer. Sabine war sehr froh, daß sie so viel Geld gespart hatte, und wir sind gleich zum Eiscafé gelaufen. Dort haben wir zwei Kaffee und zwei große Eisbecher bestellt.

Das war ein erfolgreicher Einkaufsbummel!

**Teacher:** Danke schön.

## Examiner's comments

The student is well prepared and it is clear that a number of well-rehearsed phrases have been included. This is not a criticism. Indeed, this is the very sort of preparation which you can do before the oral, and entirely without knowledge of the story you are going to tell. There are more details of this technique in Chapter 15, Speaking.

**F H READING**

**3 Answers**

1 falsch;  2 richtig;  3 richtig;  4 nicht im Text;  5 nicht im Text;  6 richtig;  7 falsch;  8 falsch;  9 richtig

## Examiner's comments

Remember how the questions are spread through the passage and try to identify exactly which phrase or sentence is being targeted.

This is a task for the C/D grades so you should expect to do very well on it – a score of 7 or more should be your aim at this level.

**4** *Sample Student's Answer*

An den Geschäftsführer
,Junge Mode'                            den 14. Januar


Sehr geehrte Herren,


Ich war letzte Woche am Montag bei Ihnen im Geschäft und wollte
eine neue Jeanshose kaufen. Ich mußte leider zehn Minuten warten,
bis die Verkäuferin kam, obwohl die Abteilung fast leer war.


Ich habe ihr erklärt, was ich suchte, aber es dauerte sehr lange, bis
sie mir einige Hosen gebracht hat. Ich habe drei Jeans anprobiert,
und fand die letzte sehr bequem. Obgleich sie zwanzig Mark teurer
als die anderen war, war ich mit dem Kauf sehr zufrieden.


Ich habe die Jeans jetzt ein paar Mal getragen, und habe sie
am Wochenende zum ersten Mal in der Maschine gewaschen. Als
ich sie wieder anziehen wollte, war ich sehr enttäuscht. Die Hose
war um einige Zentimeter kürzer, und auch oben sehr eng geworden.
Sie sieht immer noch toll aus, aber paßt mir gar nicht mehr.


Ich komme also am Samstag noch'mal ins Geschäft, und möchte
diese Hose umtauschen. Ich hoffe, daß Sie mir helfen können.


Ihre


Maria Faßbinder

## EXAMINER'S COMMENTS

- Any background details, such as how you felt or your opinion, will use the imperfect tense, as will the modal verbs:
  ich fand (die Hose) bequem
  ich war zufrieden
  ich war enttäuscht
  ich wollte kaufen

- As soon as you relate the individual events or actions, you will of course use the perfect tense.

*There will be more about use of tenses in Chapters 10 and 12.*

## CHAPTER 9   WIE KOMMT MAN DAHIN?

### Transcript

**1**   **Die Andreaskirche**
Gehen Sie hier geradeaus, über die Kreuzung. An der nächsten Kreuzung biegen Sie nach rechts. Gehen Sie am Rathaus vorbei bis zur nächsten Kreuzung. Die Andreaskirche liegt schräg gegenüber an der Ecke.

**Der Bahnhof**
Gehen Sie an der Kreuzung links und an der nächsten Kreuzung rechts. Gehen Sie geradeaus über die Ampel und der Bahnhof liegt auf der linken Seite nach etwa zweihundert Metern.

**Das Einkaufszentrum**
Gehen Sie hier gleich links und dann an der nächsten Kreuzung rechts. Das Einkaufszentrum liegt auf der linken Seite nach etwa hundert Metern.

**Der Fernsehturm**
Gehen Sie an der Kreuzung rechts, über die Brücke. Der Fernsehturm liegt auf der linken Seite nach etwa zweihundert Metern.

**Das Kunstmuseum**
Gehen Sie über die erste Kreuzung und biegen an der zweiten Kreuzung rechts ab. Sie laufen am Fluß entlang etwa zweihundert Meter, über die nächste Kreuzung und dann noch mal so weit, bis zur zweiten Kreuzung. Dort biegen Sie nach links ab, und das Kunstmuseum ist gleich auf der rechten Seite.

**Das Malteserkrankenhaus**
Gehen Sie hier geradeaus über die erste und die zweite Kreuzung. Sie gehen am Kreisverkehr immer weiter geradeaus und nehmen die erste Straße rechts. Das Malteserkrankenhaus ist das zweite Gebäude auf der linken Seite.

**Das Rathaus**
Sie gehen geradeaus über die erste Kreuzung und biegen an der zweiten Kreuzung nach rechts. Das Rathaus liegt auf der linken Seite nach etwa hundert Metern. Das können Sie gar nicht verfehlen.

**Das Stadion**
Hier an der Kreuzung rechts, und dann gehen Sie immer geradeaus über den Fluß und über die nächste Kreuzung. Das Stadion liegt links direkt am Fluß nach etwa hundert Metern.

**Das Theater**
Das Theater ist gar nicht weit. Hier an der Kreuzung rechts, über den Fluß und Sie sehen das Theatergebäude direkt nach der Brücke auf der rechten Seite.

### Answers

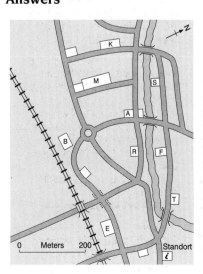

### Examiner's comments

The vocabulary itself is simple enough, but the sections are long and you have a good deal to retain if you do not follow them immediately. The best way to tackle such map questions is to keep your finger or a pointer on the map as the directions are given. The first time you listen you might get halfway to your destination, and in the pause you should look ahead to see what alternatives present themselves.

The phrase *schräg gegenüber* in the first item means 'diagonally opposite', i.e. not directly opposite. Notice that there was the alternative of directly opposite on the map.

D*er Fluß* and *die* B*rücke* provide obvious support in a number of the items, and if it was not obvious enough, the station must be one of the buildings near the railway line.

D*as zweite Gebäude* was used to identify the hospital from the building next door. It is worth remembering that the directions people give often finish with some reference to the building itself, such as *das große Gebäude*, *das rote Gebäude*, or to the building next to it – *neben der Kirche*, etc.

You should score at least 7 out of 9 on this exercise for a Grade C and above.

**Transcript**

**2**

**Teacher:** Also, ich bin fremd hier und suche das Kunstmuseum. Können Sie mir helfen?

**Student:** Ja, ich glaube schon. Also. Wir sind hier. (*Zeigt auf das Informationsbüro.*) Das Kunstmuseum ist hier oben. (*Zeigt auf das K*). Es ist ziemlich weit zu laufen. Sie brauchen bestimmt zwanzig bis fünfundzwanzig Minuten.

**Teacher:** Ach, das ist schwierig, wissen Sie, denn ich habe einen ziemlich schweren Rucksack. Kann ich mit dem Bus fahren?

**Student:** Ja, das geht natürlich auch. Es gibt zwei Buslinien, die Fünf und die Sieben. Schauen Sie mal. Die Sieben hält hier vorne rechts und fährt alle zwanzig Minuten. Der nächste Bus fährt um zehn nach drei.

**Teacher:** Und die Linie Fünf?

**Student:** Die Fünf fährt alle fünfzehn Minuten und der nächste Bus kommt in zehn Minuten. Die Haltestelle ist nicht weit. Hier links, bis zur nächsten Kreuzung. Die Haltestelle ist gleich rechts um die Ecke. Sie haben genug Zeit.

**Teacher:** Herzlichen Dank!

**Student:** Nichts zu danken. Gern geschehen.

**Examiner's comments**

The student has had enough time to study the map and timetable and has worked out the alternatives. The unexpected element was the passer-by's heavy rucksack and his unwillingness to walk, but since the candidate had the bus timetables to consult beforehand, something of this sort was to be expected, and the candidate managed it very well.

**3** *Sample Student's Answer*

Ich war auf dem Weg zur Stadt, als ich den Unfall sah. Das Wetter war herrlich sonnig.

Ich ging am Park vorbei, als ein kleiner Ball vor uns auf die Straße rollte. Eine Sekunde später kam ein schwarzer Hund hinterher und lief über die Straße, um den Ball zu holen. Das Auto, das gerade vorbeifuhr, mußte scharf bremsen, aber der Lastwagenfahrer, der dahinter fuhr, hatte nichts gemerkt, und fuhr auf das Auto hinten auf. Ich war für einen Augenblick ganz erschrocken.

Beide Fahrer hielten dann am Straßenrand an und stiegen aus. Der Hund war natürlich nirgendwo zu sehen. Der Autofahrer erzählte, was passiert war, aber der Lastwagenfahrer wollte es zuerst nicht glauben.

Glücklicherweise war niemand verletzt, aber ein Streifenwagen erschien kurze Zeit später. Die beiden Fahrer schrieben gerade ihre Namen und Adressen auf, als ich plötzlich eine Dame mit dem schwarzen Hund an der Leine sah. Ich zeigte sie sofort dem Polizisten, und er nahm beide zur Polizeiwache mit.

*159 words*

**EXAMINER'S COMMENTS**

- This report is correctly written in the imperfect tense, but it would be acceptable to write it in the perfect tense. If you do find it easier to write in the perfect, don't forget that you still need the imperfect tense for weather, feelings, etc.

- The account contains the following structures which bring it credit:
  – subordinate clauses with correct word order
  – an um … zu construction
  – relative clauses – das Auto, das ...; der Lastwagenfahrer, der ...
  – a pluperfect tense – hatte nichts gemerkt
  – modal verbs correctly followed by infinitives
  – separable verbs correctly used

- The account is a few words too long, but not so long that the candidate risks losing marks. This answer is worthy of an A Grade.

**H READING**

### 4 Answers

1 richtig; 2 richtig; 3 richtig; 4 falsch; 5 nicht im Text; 6 falsch; 7 falsch; 8 richtig; 9 falsch; 10 nicht im Text; 11 richtig

#### Examiner's comments

This is a task for Higher Level, so you should expect to have to look very closely at the text for detail. Having read the bank of true/false statements first, you can get an idea of whereabouts you need to look closely for the answers. There are no difficult items of vocabulary. Even a word like *abfahrtbereit* is made up of two easier words and should not pose a problem.

A score of 7 out of 9 would be appropriate for an A Grade candidate.

### CHAPTER 10  AUSBILDUNG UND BERUF

**H LISTENING**

#### Transcript

### 1  „Was bin ich von Beruf?"

| | |
|---|---|
| **Frage:** | Herr Löwenzahn, finden Sie Ihre Arbeit langweilig? |
| **Antwort:** | **Ganz und gar nicht. Es gibt jeden Tag 'was Neues.** |
| **Frage:** | Haben Sie gar keine tägliche Routine? |
| **Antwort:** | Doch, aber trotzdem ist **jeder Tag anders.** |
| **Frage:** | Arbeiten Sie im Team? |
| **Antwort:** | Eigentlich ja, aber **es kann kein anderer im Team meine Arbeit machen.** |
| **Frage:** | Arbeiten Sie draußen im Freien? |
| **Antwort:** | Ich bin **sehr viel im Freien**, aber **nicht die ganze Zeit.** |
| **Frage:** | Und ich nehme an, Sie mögen diese Arbeit? |
| **Antwort:** | Oh ja. Ich bin mit meinem Beruf sehr zufrieden. |
| **Frage:** | Arbeiten Sie auf dem Lande? Sind Sie Bauer oder Forstarbeiter? |
| **Antwort:** | Nein. Meine Arbeit ist immer in der Großstadt. |
| **Frage:** | Also, in der Großstadt, aber oft draußen. Vielleicht im Park? |
| **Antwort:** | Nein, nicht so ganz. |
| **Frage:** | Im Tierpark? |
| **Antwort:** | Ja. |
| **Frage:** | Ich hab' es. Sie arbeiten im Zoo. |
| **Antwort:** | Ja. |
| **Frage:** | **Sind Sie Tierarzt?** |
| **Antwort:** | **Ja, das bin ich.** Ich bin seit 1995 Tierarzt im Berliner Zoo. Ich arbeite mit den meisten Tierarten, doch nicht mit Vögeln. **Ich arbeite lieber mit den größeren Tieren.** |
| **Moderator:** | Ich danke Ihnen, Herr Löwenzahn. |

#### Answers

1 immer interessant
2 seine tägliche Routine
3 macht keiner seine Arbeit
4 oft draußen
5 Tierarzt
6 mit Pferden als mit Mäusen

#### Examiner's comments

The key words in the listening passage are in bold. Although some of the words appear to be very easy when you read them, they may well be obscured in the course of a longer listening passage.

Remember also that at Higher Level you should be able to draw an inference from a passage without the message being as obvious as in the Foundation Level texts.

**2** **Teacher:** Erzählen Sie, was Sie an diesem Tag gemacht haben.

**Student:** Also, ich bin ziemlich früh aufgestanden – so gegen halb sieben. Ich habe mich geduscht und schick angezogen. Ich habe meine beste Bluse und eine Hose angezogen, keine Jeans.

Nach dem Frühstück bin ich mit dem Bus in die Stadt gefahren, denn das Vorstellungsgespräch war um 9.00 Uhr, und ich wollte pünktlich sein. Ich war schon um Viertel vor neun dort. Ich wollte nicht im Supermarkt warten, also habe ich noch zehn Minuten draußen gestanden.

Der Manager heißt Herr Kaufmann, und er war sehr freundlich. Ich habe gesagt, ich wolle mein Deutsch verbessern. Er hat mich gefragt, was ich in der Schule lerne, und er wollte auch wissen, was ich für Hobbys habe. Ich habe ihn gefragt, was man im Supermarkt verdient und wieviele Stunden pro Tag man arbeiten muß.

Das Vorstellungsgespräch hat zwanzig Minuten gedauert, und er hat gesagt, ich sollte in der folgenden Woche anfangen. Ich habe mich natürlich sehr gefreut.

Herr Kaufmann hat mich dann einigen anderen jungen Leuten vorgestellt. Sie schienen mir sehr sympathisch zu sein.

Ich bin gegen Mittag nach Hause gefahren und habe der Gastfamilie alles erzählt. Sie waren auch sehr froh.

**Teacher:** Danke schön.

### Examiner's comments

This candidate is well prepared, and uses some simple language very effectively. Remember, not everything has to be very complex. It is, after all, a conversation.

The simple time phrases are enhanced slightly – *so gegen halb sieben* instead of *um halb sieben* and *noch zehn Minuten* instead of just *zehn Minuten*.

*Denn* is very useful if you not entirely confident with subordinate clause word order. It allows you to use complex sentences without any change to the main clause word order.

The candidate uses *ich wollte* frequently and correctly, and this confidence is certainly worthy of credit.

*Sich freuen* enables you to avoid *ich war glücklich* all the time. The candidate also uses *froh* rather than the overworked *glücklich*.

The most complex construction used is that of introducing someone to somebody else. The candidate must have learned this carefully and worked it in well. It would certainly make a great impression on the examiner.

This candidate's performance is worthy of a Grade A.

**3** **Answers**

1 H; **2** K; **3** B; **4** C; **5** L; **6** D; **7** A; **8** J

### Examiner's comments

The jobs included in the list are all common enough for there to be little difficulty with the single words. However, the exercise requires a good deal more understanding of the descriptions before you can successfully pair up the letters and the numbers. Watch out for the gender of the job names, which will help you. This task is at the easier end of the C/D level, so you should expect to do very well on it.

Don't commit yourself too soon to any one of the answers without considering the other options. Even at this level, there may be more than one alternative and the rubric will always tell you to choose the one which fits best (*der am besten paßt*).

## CHAPTER 11   AM ARBEITSPLATZ

### Transcript

**1**   1   Bitte einsteigen und Türen schließen. Der Zug fährt gleich ab.
   2   Nehmen Sie bitte Platz! Die Sprechstunde beginnt in fünf Minuten.
   3   Packt eure Sachen wieder weg! Die Stunde ist gleich zu Ende.
   4   Seien Sie jetzt bitte ruhig! Es ist schon elf Uhr. Wir möchten schlafen.
   5   Meine Damen und Herren. Heute im Sonderangebot. Jede Hose nur DM19.50. Greifen Sie zu!

### Answers

1 a;  2 c;  3 b;  4 b;  5 c

### Examiner's comments

These are simple enough to read, but did you recognise the key words delivered at normal speed in these announcements and statements?

1   This is the standard announcement on the station platform before the train leaves.
2   At Higher Level, you should be able to connect the *Sprechstunde* with *Praxis*.
3   All students of the language should recognise this classroom command at the end of the German lesson.
4   This is not an announcement, but a grumpy camper being kept awake by others on the campsite. The emphasis on *wir* and the *schlafen* should point you in the direction of the correct answer.
5   *Sonderangebot* is easy enough. You simply have to spot that a *Hose* is less likely to be on sale in the supermarket than the department store.

An A Grade candidate should score all these five marks without too much difficulty!

### Transcript

**2**   **Student:** Guten Tag. Mein Name ist Jennings. Mit wem spreche ich, bitte?
**Teacher:** Hier spricht Frau Lehmann.
**Student:** Wie schreibt man das, bitte?
**Teacher:** L – E – H – M – A – N – N.
**Student:** Ich rufe wegen der Lehrstelle an. Wie sind die Arbeitszeiten für Lehrlinge?
**Teacher:** Wir beginnen jeden Tag um 7 Uhr und machen um 5 Uhr Feierabend. Am Freitag kann man schon um 2 Uhr Schluß machen.
**Student:** Danke schön. Ich möchte auch wissen, wieviel man als Lehrling bei Ihnen verdient.
**Teacher:** Es ist unterschiedlich, aber am Anfang würden Sie mindestens tausendzweihundert Mark im Monat verdienen.
**Student:** Danke schön. Das hört sich sehr gut an. Kann ich Ihnen meine Telefonnummer geben, falls Sie mich anrufen wollen?
**Teacher:** Gerne.
**Student:** Also, die Vorwahl von England ist 00 44. Dann ist die Vorwahl von Reading 118 und meine Nummer ist 9590911.
**Teacher:** Danke schön. Auf Wiederhören.
**Student:** Also, vielen Dank für Ihre Hilfe. Auf Wiederhören.

## Examiner's comments

The student is well prepared and asks all the appropriate questions. She remembers to say 'thank you' for each of the pieces of information she is given, and the addition of words like *auch*, *dann* and *also* show a degree of confidence, which is expected of candidates dealing with relatively simple language.

At this level, the candidate might also expect to have to respond to an unprepared question, for example about age, school subjects or interests.

## 3  Answers

READING  H

1  Read the newspaper.
2  Put it on the boss's desk after he has gone home.
3  Remembering his wife's birthday (and reminding him).
4  That he is out on business or has a meeting.
5  They probably have longer coffee breaks when the boss is out.
6  He has no time.
7  He decides their wages.

## Examiner's comments

This is a task for Higher Level, so you expect fewer direct answers to spring out at you. There are generally more inference questions at this level.

Having read the questions in English first, you should have picked out the key items in each that you are to look for in the text. These are:

**1:** *Zeitunglesen*
**2:** *schlechte Nachricht; Legen Sie ... auf den Schreibtisch.*
**3:** *Noch wichtiger. Vergessen Sie nie den Geburtstag der Ehefrau des Chefs.*
**4:** *« außer Haus" ist oder « geschäftlich zu tun" hat.*
**5:** *wenn der Chef da ist.*
**6:** *Der Chef hat weder Zeit*
**7:** *entscheiden. Auch über unsere Gehälter.*

You are told in the rubric that the text is humorous. Don't expect to burst out laughing, but be prepared for some sarcasm, irony and light-hearted comments. In this passage, the employees are poking fun at their boss.

## CHAPTER 12  AUSLAND UND TOURISMUS

### Transcript

LISTENING  H

**1**  Ein Mädchen erzählt von ihrem Urlaub.

Am Samstag bin ich in die Altstadt gegangen. Ich wollte am Nachmittag die Kunstausstellung sehen; die sollte großartig sein. Wir hatten schon am Tag vorher den Fernsehturm bestiegen und anschließend unten am Rhein gegrillt.

Also, ich habe meine Karte am Automaten gekauft, da geht's schneller. Ich hatte schon auf dem Weg zur Haltestelle eine Zeitung am Kiosk gekauft, damit ich genug Kleingeld hatte.

Dann bin ich mit der Bahn bis zur Post gefahren, um die Postkarten einzuwerfen, die ich auf dem Fernsehturm geschrieben hatte.

Um 3 Uhr bin in die Kunstausstellung gegangen und habe mich etwa zwei Stunden dort umgesehen.

Nachdem wir aus dem Kunstmuseum gekommen sind, haben wir uns alle vor dem Rathaus getroffen und sind gemeinsam essen gegangen.

### Answers

Ich habe den Fernsehturm bestiegen.
Ich habe meine Postkarten geschrieben.
Wir haben unten am Rhein gegrillt.
Ich habe am Samstag eine Zeitung am Kiosk gekauft.
Ich habe eine Fahrkarte gelöst.
Ich habe meine Postkarten eingeworfen.
Ich habe das Kunstmuseum besucht.
Wir sind essen gegangen.

### Examiner's comments

Remember that at Higher Level you should be able to draw an inference from a passage without the message being as obvious as it is in Foundation Level texts.

Although the piece starts off talking about Saturday's plans, the second sentence introduces the events of the previous day – *am Tag vorher*. The word *anschließend* puts the barbecue after the climbing of the tower.

The pluperfect *ich hatte schon ... gekauft* shows you that this action came before the buying of the ticket.

The relative clause following *die Postkarten* tells you that she wrote the postcards at the TV tower, thus placing this action between the visit to the tower and the barbecue.

The order of the remaining actions is quite straightforward.

**F H SPEAKING**

### Transcript

**2** **Teacher:** Also. Können Sie mir erzählen, wo Sie in den letzten Ferien im Urlaub waren.

**Student:** Sicher. Ich bin mit meiner Familie nach Griechenland geflogen. Es war ganz toll. Wir haben eine Ferienwohnung gemietet, die ganz nah am Meer war.

Die Strände in der Nähe der Wohnung waren ganz fantastisch – viel sauberer als bei uns und auch nicht so voll.

Wir haben mit unseren Nachbarn oft Volleyball gespielt, und wenn es uns zu warm war, sind wir schnell ins Wasser gegangen. Auch das Wasser war klarer als an der englischen Küste.

Das Wetter war auch herrlich. In den zwei Wochen hat es nur einmal in der Nacht geregnet, aber wir haben kaum etwas davon gemerkt.

**Teacher:** Und was haben Sie am Abend so gemacht?

**Student:** Am Abend sind wir immer auswärts essen gegangen, was mir sehr gefallen hat. Und ich habe jeden Abend etwas Neues probiert. Es gibt sehr viele kleinere Gaststätten, und das Essen ist ziemlich preiswert, bestimmt billiger als in England.

Ich war ein bißchen traurig, als wir nach Hause fliegen mußten, aber meine Eltern wollen nächstes Jahr wieder dahin.

**Teacher:** Danke schön.

### Examiner's comments

This is a polished account containing numerous structures which are worthy of merit. The relative clauses, subordinate clauses, the comparative adjectives and the moods expressed, all help to create a high quality piece. There is no doubt that the candidate has developed this as a written passage first and learned it thoroughly. He appears to be very familiar with the prepared material, and it is unlikely that he would be put off by further questions from the examiner. A clear Grade A candidate.

**3** **Answers**

**1** richtig;  **2** falsch;  **3** falsch;  **4** nicht im Text;  **5** richtig;  **6** falsch

**Examiner's comments**

Again, you have the added difficulty of the third column in what is normally a true/false exercise. Remember that you can only tick *richtig* or *falsch* if you see the information in the text to support the answer. Otherwise use *nicht im Text*.

**1** The phrases *das Hotel so hoch liegt* and *ins Gebirge* both tell you about mountains.
**2** This statement is the opposite of what is stated in the second paragraph (*viel Sehenswertes*).
**3** When he says *die öffentlichen Verkehrsmittel, d.h. die Busse, nicht so besonders gut*, Herr Weißkopf is clearly saying that the public transport is not particularly good in the region.
**4** It does not say so in the passage.
**5** This is clearly stated (*eine Weinprobe ist immer eine lustige Sache*).
**6** This is neither stated, nor implied. The inference is only that if you want to enjoy the wine-tasting, it might be better to go by bus (*würde ich Ihnen empfehlen*). There is no compulsion and the *muß* is therefore wrong.

You ought to score at least 5 on this exercise to be aiming at a Grade C.

## CHAPTER 13   DIE WELT

**Transcript**

**1** **Heute Journal**

Hier sind die Kurznachrichten.

Bei einem **Erdbeben** in Chile sind mindestens **achtzig Menschen ums Leben gekommen**. Das Erdbeben traf gestern einige kleinere Städte **im Norden des Landes**.

Der amerikanische Präsident plant, **den Festtag am 4. Juli dieses Jahres in Mainz zu feiern**, so gab das Weiße Haus gestern bekannt. Weitere Details sind noch nicht vorhanden.

Die Gefahr von starken **Überschwemmungen** in Bangladesh **scheint noch kein Ende zu nehmen**. Das Hochwasser hat in einigen Gebieten zwar um einige Zentimeter nachgelassen, aber **es soll noch weitere tropische Gewitter geben**.

**Answers**

**1** There has been an earthquake/Eighty people have been killed.
**2** In the north of the country.
**3** He intends to celebrate the 4th July in Mainz.
**4** The flooding is not yet over/seems set to continue/there are further storms on the way.

**Examiner's comments**

The key words in the passage have been highlighted. 'Journalese' is usually more difficult to understand than other forms of language. Sometimes the message of the television or radio news seems almost hidden by the structures used. Notice, for example, the sentence at the beginning of paragraph 3 which begins with a dative. Fortunately, a simple English rendering would at least begin with the same noun: 'danger'.

Remember also that at Higher Level you should be able to draw an inference from a passage without the message being as obvious as in the Foundation Level texts. The fact that there is more rain forecast (paragraph 3) supports the idea that the danger of flooding is not yet over.

**H SPEAKING**

**Transcript**

**2**

**Teacher:** Was meinen Sie zu dem Thema Umwelt?

**Student:** Ich glaube, man muß viel mehr machen, um die Umwelt zu schützen. Alle Autos müssen bleifrei fahren. Man muß weniger Auto fahren, und immer bessere Verkehrsmittel bauen und benützen. Ich halte es für äußerst wichtig, daß man mehr Sonnenenergie und Windenergie gebraucht und weniger Kohle und Erdöl.

**Teacher:** Und was machen Sie selber für die Umwelt?

**Student:** Ich sammle alles, was man wiederverwerten kann – Altglas, Altpapier und natürlich die Aludosen. Meine Mutter sortiert den Müll und hat Extrabehälter für Papier und Kunststoff. Das scheint mir sehr vernünftig zu sein.

**Teacher:** Danke schön.

**Examiner's comments**

These are the sort of brief comments and statements that one can reasonably expect from a candidate looking for the highest grades. Nothing more technical can be demanded, and this candidate expresses a general opinion, backed up by some concrete suggestions.

Remember that this is only a small part of the Speaking Test, and that the examiner will already have a good idea of the level at which the candidate is performing. These last few minutes of the oral offer the candidate the opportunity to show the examiner something a little special.

**H READING**

**4 Answers**

1 ANY THREE OF:
   clearing/collecting rubbish
   putting rubbish in sacks
   collecting sacks of rubbish in the playground
   retrieving dumped supermarket trolleys
   clearing a wild area/building a garden

2 They took away the rubbish sacks/stinking rubbish.

3 He has to go back to lessons again./He found the environment week made more sense than lessons.

**Examiner's comments**

This is a task for Higher Level, so you should expect to do well on it to earn a high grade. Having read the questions in English first, you will have an idea of the items that you need to look for in the text.

The words to do with cleaning and rubbish – *Reinigung*, *Müll* and *Abfall* – should give you enough to go on for an answer to the first question. The 'garden' answer is much easier to recognise.

The answer to the second question is made easy to spot by the obvious *gestunken* and *weggenommen*.

It is worth repeating that the topic of *Umwelt* does not have to be understood in any technical way in order to answer these questions.

# CHAPTER 14

**LISTENING AND RESPONDING**

## TRANSCRIPTS OF RECORDINGS FOR CHECK YOURSELF EXERCISES

### Check yourself 1

**Q1**
a) Kommst du heute abend mit ins Kino?
b) Die Vorstellung beginnt erst um halb neun.
c) Vati kommt am vierundzwanzigsten März nach Hause.
d) Wir sollen ihn um sieben Uhr vor dem Bahnhof abholen.
e) Eine Rückfahrkarte zweiter Klasse kostet siebenundzwanzig Mark.

**Q2**
a) Also, ich schwimme fast jede Woche mit meiner Familie, aber ich finde es etwas langweilig.
b) Wir haben heute nachmittag Kochen. Das gefällt mir immer.
c) Unser Urlaub in der Schweiz war toll. Wir haben uns dort auf dem Campingplatz sehr gut amüsiert.
d) Ich möchte gern einen Hund haben, aber wir haben nur eine kleine Wohnung, also geht das nicht.
e) Wir haben gestern eine lange Fahrradtour gemacht. Ich war gestern abend ganz schön fertig.

### Check yourself 2

**Q1**
a) Meine Telefonnummer ist dreiundreißig, sechsundfünfzig, achtundachtzig.
b) Meine Telefonnummer ist fünfundvierzig, siebenundsechzig, neunundzwanzig.
c) Die Lottozahlen für heute: eins, sieben, fünfzehn, siebenundzwanzig, neunundzwanzig, vierzig – und die Zusatzzahl einunddreißig.
d) Ich bin am ersten dritten zweiundachtzig geboren.
e) Sie ist am fünfundzwanzigsten siebten dreiundachtzig geboren.

**Q2**
a) Er arbeitet mit den Tieren in einem Zoo.
b) Er arbeitet in einem so schönen Gebäude unten am See.
c) Er hat sich letzte Woche am großen Zeh weh getan.
d) Vater fragte mich, ob ich Kleingeld hätte.
e) Wir wollen doch ins Kino gehen, nicht?

### Check yourself 3

**Q1**
a) Und hier die Wettervorhersage für morgen. Im Norden zuerst kühl und bewölkt mit einzelnen Niederschlägen. Am Nachmittag heiter, teils sonnig. Tageshöchsttemperaturen liegen bei 17 Grad. Im Süden sonnig und warm. Leichter Wind aus östlicher Richtung. Tageshöchsttemperaturen liegen bei 19 Grad.
b) – Ich finde es schwierig, wenn ich nach Hause komme, weiter für die Schule zu arbeiten. Ich habe schon genug gearbeitet. Ich halte es für wichtiger, daß ich mich ausruhe, oder etwas für meine Gesundheit mache. Deshalb möchte ich lieber ins Schwimmbad gehen. Und abends habe ich erst recht keine Lust mehr, meine Schulbücher anzugucken.
– Du hast recht. Manchmal finde ich es richtig blöd. Ich soll noch zwei Matheaufgaben zu Hause schreiben, auch wenn ich die Sache schon perfekt verstanden habe. Nur weil der Lehrer ein paar Noten mehr in sein Buch schreiben möchte.

**Q2** a) Für mich sind die Sommerferien sehr wichtig. Ich habe schon sehr viel Geld für den Segelkurs gespart. Das wird mir schon großen Spaß machen.

b) Aber die Prüfungen sind für mich immer etwas Furchtbares. Man hat dafür gearbeitet, aber man weiß nie so richtig, was kommt. In der Nacht davor werde ich bestimmt nicht schlafen können.

## *Check yourself 4*

**Q1** a) Ich habe Glück gehabt. Mein Onkel hat eine Autowerkstatt, und er hat mir eine Lehrstelle angeboten.

b) Wenn ich dort gut verdiene, werde ich bald mein eigenes Auto haben.

c) Fein, aber ich möchte die Schule nicht so schnell verlassen.

d) Meine Eltern haben eine Metzgerei, aber ich möchte etwas anderes machen.

**Q2** a) Letztes Jahr war's schön auf dem Campingplatz am See, aber ich möchte diesmal lieber in eine Großstadt fahren.

b) Es gibt so viel mehr zu sehen und zu tun, wenn wir nach Paris oder London fahren.

c) Also, ein Hotel ist zwar schön, aber ich mag keine Hektik. Ich möchte lieber eine ruhige Woche irgendwo auf dem Lande verbringen.

d) Du hast recht, Ilse. Ich kann mich auch am besten ausruhen, wenn ich nicht die ganze Zeit im Verkehr stecke.

## ANSWERS TO EXAM PRACTICE AND TRANSCRIPTS OF RECORDINGS

**Transcript**

1 Also, Abendessen gibt es zwischen halb sieben und halb acht hier unten im großen Saal.

2 Wenn Sie abends länger ausbleiben wollen, sagen Sie uns Bescheid, und wir geben Ihnen einen Hausschlüssel.

3 Im Süden leichter bis mäßiger Wind aus dem Südwesten, zeitweise Regen. Temperaturen zwischen 8 und 10 Grad.

4 Im Westen wird es wieder stark bewölkt.

5 Im Norden wieder trocken – heiter und sonnig. Höchsttemperaturen erreichen 14-16 Grad.

6 In östlichen Gebieten leichter Wind aus dem Westen. Sonnig und warm. Temperaturen zwischen 14-16 Grad.

7 Wir wohnen fast an der Küste, wissen Sie, und ich treibe sehr gern Wassersport, besonders segeln.

8 Meine Damen und Herren, Sie haben bei diesem Rundgang durch die Stadt eine tolle Auswahl an Museen und Galerien. Wer sich für die moderne Kunst interessiert, kommt mit mir zusammen in die Gruppe 1, während Gruppe 2 das Heimatmuseum besucht. Falls Sie bei diesem Wetter lieber draußen sind, besucht die Gruppe 3 den botanischen Garten und die Parkanlage der Universität. Wir treffen uns wieder um 12.30 Uhr vor dem alten Rathaus und essen zu Mittag im Ratskeller.

9 Guten Tag! Können Sie bitte Herrn Blum eine Nachricht hinterlassen? Hier spricht Frau Tiegel – T–I–E–G–E–L. Können Sie ihm bitte sagen, daß ich erst um siebzehn Uhr kommen kann? Wir treffen uns wie geplant im Rathaus. Danke schön.

10 **Frank:** Kommst du morgen mit zum Park? Wir wollen Rollschuh laufen.
**Birgit:** Leider nicht. Meine Rollschuhe sind kaputt.

**Frank:** Macht nichts, du kannst meine haben. Sie sind ganz neu. Ich trage die von meinem Bruder. Er braucht sie morgen nicht.

11 **Birgit:** Ich weiß einfach nicht, was ich machen soll. Meine Noten in der Schule sind so schlecht, ich kriege andauernd Vieren.

**Frank:** Das wird schon wieder gut werden. Vielleicht wenn wir den neuen Klassenlehrer bekommen.

**Birgit:** Und dann habe ich gerade mit meinem Freund Schluß gemacht. Ich habe einfach keine Lust auszugehen.

12 Unser Urlaub war ganz fantastisch. Wir haben einen Campingplatz gefunden – fast direkt am Meer. Und einen tollen Strand auch.

13 – Wir haben am Wochenende eine tolle Party bei uns zu Hause gehabt.
– Was haben deine Eltern gesagt?
– Nichts. Sie waren bei Freunden eingeladen und sind erst gegen Mitternacht nach Hause gekommen.

14 Also, dieser Platz an der Uni ist für mich ganz wichtig, wenn ich später mit Computern arbeiten will.

15 Doch, ins Ausland fahren können ist für mich sehr viel wert. Daher möchte ich Fremdsprachen weiterstudieren.

16 – Unser Sommerurlaub ist also fast ins Wasser gefallen.
– Was ist denn alles passiert?
– Der erste Campingplatz war total voll, und man hat morgens für eine Dusche Schlange stehen müssen. Das Meer war nicht weit, aber es waren dort nur Felsen. Der zweite Strand war ziemlich weit zu laufen. Also habe ich beschlossen, zum nächsten Campingplatz zu fahren, aber ich habe vorher nicht angerufen, und es war voll ausgebucht.

Am Abend sind wir in einem Gasthaus an der Küste gelandet, wo wir zwei schöne Zimmer bekommen haben. Mit Blick aufs Meer, das war große Klasse. Und wir haben nicht selbst kochen müssen, denn das Essen dort war ausgezeichnet.

– Also, Ende gut, alles gut.
– Das kann man wohl sagen. Selbst das Wetter hat mitgemacht. Es war kein einziger Regentag in den vierzehn Tagen.

## Answers

1 C    2 D    3 B    4 B

5 B    6 C    7 C    8 C + E

9
> Lieber Herr **Blum**,
> Frau **Tiegel** hat für Sie angerufen.
> Sie kommt erst um **17** Uhr.
> Treffpunkt: **Im** Rathaus

10    D    11 B    12 B
13    bei Freunden
14    Weil sie später mit Computern arbeiten möchte.
15    Weil sie gern ins Ausland fährt.

16 **a)** It was very crowded./Queuing for a shower./There was no beach close by./The nearest beach was quite far to walk to.
   **b)** To try another campsite.
   **c)** That campsite was full, too.
   **d)** They found good rooms (with great views of the sea/good food). They had good weather all the time.

## Examiner's comments

1 You have two times to understand for the mark, and both phrases use the word *halb*, which often proves tricky.

2 *Bescheid sagen* comes directly from the passage, but you might be distracted by the word *Schlüssel* which appears in two options.

3–6 These contain only standard weather vocabulary, nothing difficult, although you don't need all of it for the answers.

7 *Wassersport* is obvious, but which one? *Segeln* is one of the few sports which is not a cognate word, i.e. the same word as in English.

8 **A** must be discounted because one group is visiting a museum.
   **B** is tempting, but only two of the three groups are visiting these places.
   **C** is correct.
   **D** is tempting because you hear *Park* in another context.
   **E** is correct.

9 Two names to get right, one time on the 24-hour clock and a wrong preposition. All crucial to the successful transmission of the message.

10 The intonation of Frank's speech will tell you how generous he is being, in offering Birgit his own, new roller skates.

11 Again, you hear someone who is obviously 'down' about school, and about having finished with her boyfriend.

12 *Fast* is the key word. Almost directly by the sea is not directly by the sea. C and D will distract those who have not learned to discount the masculine *See* which means 'lake', as against the feminine *See* which does mean 'sea'.

13 This answer can be lifted from the text providing you have understood the preposition *bei* correctly.

14 The *warum* of the question really needs a *weil* to start the answer. Again the words are directly from the text.

15 Begin again with *weil* and watch the subordinate clause word order. However, you can't lift the answer from the text on this one.

16 *Voll* is very straightforward but *Schlange stehen* is a bit more demanding. You would be unlikely to know *Felsen* (rocks), but *ziemlich weit zu laufen* should be easy enough.
   The word 'decide' leads you to the phrase following *beschlossen*, and *voll ausgebucht* again should present no problem.
   The three good things to come out of staying at the guest house have obvious positive words, like *schöne*, *große Klasse* and *ausgezeichnet*, and the comment about the weather – *kein Regentag* – is spelt out clearly.

---

## CHAPTER 15  SPEAKING

### TRANSCRIPTS OF RECORDINGS FOR CHECK YOURSELF EXERCISES

*Check yourself 2*

**Q2** a) Was war drin?
 b) Seit wann haben Sie das?
 c) Wie kommst du morgen in die Schule?
 d) Wo möchten Sie sitzen?
 e) Was brauchen Sie?

*Check yourself 3*

**Q2** a) Haben Sie schon in einem Laden gearbeitet?
 b) Was gibt es hier in der Nähe zu sehen?
 c) Können Sie die Frau beschreiben?
 d) Wo bist du letztes Jahr gewesen?
 e) Welche Schuhgröße hat dein Vater?

## SAMPLE STUDENTS' ANSWERS TO EXAM PRACTICE AND TRANSCRIPTS OF RECORDINGS

### Transcript

**1** **Im Hotel**

**Teacher:** Guten Tag. Kann ich Ihnen helfen?
**Student:** Ja. Wir möchten drei Zimmer, bitte.
**Teacher:** Für wieviele Personen?
**Student:** Zwei Erwachsene und vier Kinder.
**Teacher:** Möchten Sie Zimmer mit Bad?
**Student:** Nein, mit Dusche, bitte.
**Teacher:** Wie lange wollen Sie bleiben?
**Student:** Fünf Nächte, bitte.
**Teacher:** Geht in Ordnung.
**Student:** Was kostet das insgesamt?
**Teacher:** DM 927,00. Aber Sie brauchen noch nichts zu bezahlen.

### Examiner's comments

At Foundation level it is not always necessary to use a full sentence answer – a phrase will sometimes be sufficient. For the first and last utterances it would be difficult to avoid a sentence, however. *Drei Zimmer* to begin with would simply not be sufficient.

### Transcript

**2** **Im Café**

**Teacher:** Guten Tag.
**Student:** Guten Tag.
**Teacher:** Was darf's sein?
**Student:** Einmal Bratwurst mit Pommes und ein Käsebrötchen, bitte.
**Teacher:** Und zu trinken?
**Student:** Ich hätte gern eine Limonade, und mein Freund möchte einen Kaffee.
**Teacher:** Einmal Limo, einmal Kaffee. In Ordnung.
**Student:** Wo sind die Toiletten, bitte?
**Teacher:** Hier gleich um die Ecke.
**Student:** Danke schön.

### Examiner's comments

You should expect to start with a greeting every time. It certainly doesn't hurt to begin politely. The obvious *ich möchte* is omitted from the next utterance and this is perfectly acceptable, especially as the candidate goes on to use *ich hätte gern*. It is as well to have the two phrases ready, in order to avoid repetition. The last comment is obvious but don't forget it!

**3** **In der Bank**

**Teacher:** Was kann ich für Sie tun?
**Student:** Ich möchte Reiseschecks einlösen.
**Teacher:** Was für Reiseschecks haben Sie denn?

**Student:** Ich habe Sterling Reiseschecks, fünf mal Zwanzig Pfund.

**Teacher:** Wohnen Sie hier in Düsseldorf?

**Student:** Ich wohne bei einem Brieffreund in Bilk.

**Teacher:** Ach so. Darf ich Ihren Paß sehen?

**Student:** Leider nicht. Ich habe meinen Paß zu Hause gelassen.

**Teacher:** Dann kann ich Ihnen leider keine Schecks einlösen. Es tut mir leid.

**Student:** Na gut. Bis wann haben Sie heute auf?

**Teacher:** Heute haben wir bis 18.30 Uhr auf.

## Examiner's comments

The unpredictable element in this role-play is very easy, but remember to look at the examiner when you are expecting the question. Notice the use of the adverb *leider* for the idea of 'I'm sorry' when the candidate says he's left his passport at home. B*is wann* is absolutely appropriate in his last utterance, but he could just as easily have asked *Wann machen Sie heute zu?*.

## Transcript

**FOUNDATION/HIGHER**

**4** **Am Bahnhof**

**Teacher:** Ja, bitte.

**Student:** Wann fährt der nächste Zug nach Bonn, bitte?

**Teacher:** Um 10.24 Uhr.

**Student:** Eine Rückfahrkarte nach Bonn, bitte.

**Teacher:** Um wieviel Uhr wollen Sie zurückfahren?

**Student:** Erst heute abend, so gegen 7 Uhr.

**Teacher:** In Ordnung, dann ist es etwas billiger.

**Student:** Muß ich umsteigen?

**Teacher:** Nein, der Zug fährt direkt durch.

**Student:** Ich danke Ihnen.

## Examiner's comments

You may have learned E*inmal hin und zurück nach* B*onn* and that would be fine, too, as a way of asking for a return ticket. Again, the unpredictable question is very simple. *So gegen 7 Uhr* is a stylish colloquial phrase, worth remembering as an alternative to *um*. If you forget *umsteigen*, you can of course ask *Fährt der Zug direkt (durch)?*.

## Transcript

**HIGHER**

**5** **Teacher:** Also. Wie kann ich Ihnen helfen?

**Student:** Ich habe diese Hose gekauft und sie ist nicht in Ordnung.

**Teacher:** Was ist damit los?

**Student:** Die Hose ist gerissen. Hier, sehen Sie.

**Teacher:** Oh ja. Ich glaube, sie ist nicht richtig genäht worden. Wann haben Sie die Hose gekauft?

**Student:** Erst gestern. Ich habe sie noch gar nicht getragen. Was kann man machen?

**Teacher:** Ich gebe Ihnen gern das Geld zurück, oder Sie können sich eine neue Hose aussuchen. Was möchten Sie lieber machen?

**Student:** Ich hätte gern die gleiche Hose wieder in derselben Farbe.

**Teacher:** Mmm. Es tut mir leid. Wir haben diese Hose nur noch in Rot oder in Braun.

**Student:** Dann nehme ich sie in Rot, bitte.

**Teacher:** Gut. Und weil Sie zweimal fahren mußten, gebe ich Ihnen die Hose zu einem günstigeren Preis.

**Student:** Danke schön. Das ist sehr nett von Ihnen. Auf Wiedersehen.

## Examiner's comments

The difficulty with this sort of role-play is the constant need to stay 'on the ball', and concentrate on the unpredictable elements which come at you from the examiner. However, you should be able to think through many of the possibilities beforehand, which will cut down the unlimited nature of the exercise. You know, for example, that a shopkeeper is obliged to offer money back or exchange of goods in such a situation, so you can prepare for this choice. Similarly, you might guess that the shop might have no more of that particular article in stock. What do you do? And so on.

Taken at this level, the role-play is quite straightforward.

## Transcript

**6** **Teacher:** Also, erzählen Sie mal etwas über die Deutschlandreise.

**HIGHER**

**Student:** Wir haben uns vor der Schule getroffen und sind schon um sieben Uhr in Reading abgefahren. Wir sind auf der M4 nach London und dann weiter über die Autobahn nach Dover gefahren.

**Teacher:** Und wann sind Sie dort angekommen?

**Student:** So gegen halb elf. Und dann mußten wir etwa eine halbe Stunde warten, bis wir auf den Zug fahren konnten. Wir sind also mit dem Shuttle durch den Tunnel gefahren. Wir fanden es alles ganz toll. Es war sehr interessant und ging ziemlich schnell. Wir sind schon um fünf vor zwölf in Frankreich aus dem Tunnel gekommen.

**Teacher:** Und was haben Sie die ganze Zeit im Bus gemacht?

**Student:** Wir haben uns gut unterhalten – Karten gespielt, Musik gehört und Witze erzählt. Die Lehrer waren alle gut gelaunt, und es war ganz lustig. Wir sind dann durch Nordfrankreich und Belgien nach Aachen weitergefahren, wo wir an einer Raststätte haltgemacht haben. Es war kurz vor drei Uhr. Dann haben wir zum ersten Mal Deutsch gehört.

**Teacher:** Und? Haben Sie etwas verstanden?

**Student:** Eigentlich, ja. Ich bin ins Restaurant gegangen und habe ziemlich viel verstanden. Dann waren es noch drei Stunden, bis wir in Düsseldorf angekommen sind. Die Gastfamilien haben schon vor der Schule auf uns gewartet.

**Teacher:** Was haben Sie dann gemacht?

**Student:** Wir haben uns natürlich begrüßt und sind mit dem Auto nach Hause gefahren. Wir haben zu Abend gegessen. Bratwurst mit Pommes. Ich hatte Hunger, und es hat gut geschmeckt. Dann habe ich nach Hause telefoniert und bin ins Bett gegangen. Ich war todmüde.

**Teacher:** Das glaube ich Ihnen. Es war ein langer Tag. Danke schön.

## Examiner's comments

The candidate does the basics well and adds some stylish phrases to make a really good impression. For example, the first verbs are all straightforward and correct, but again, the addition of *so gegen* is very good to start the second phase of the narrative. The two modal verbs in the imperfect – *mußten* and *konnten* – are also worthy of merit, as are the other imperfect tenses in this section, which describe the feeling and mood.

The candidate's confidence is shown by the style in the next section – by not repeating *haben, haben, haben*, the verbs stand out even more. The mood of the teachers and the atmosphere of the coach are rightly in the imperfect. Then the long journey to Düsseldorf and the subsequent actions are covered by verbs in the perfect.

Don't be worried that you can't remember a piece as long as this. Your narrative may only need some of these features in order to convince the examiner of your competence.

## PRESENTATION AND DISCUSSION

### Transcript

**Teacher:** Und worüber wollen Sie mir erzählen?

**Student:** Ich werde meine Familie beschreiben. Also, ich habe zwei Brüder und eine Schwester, die alle älter sind als ich. James ist schon 26 und Anthony ist 22. Sie arbeiten beide bei Firmen in Southampton. Meine Schwester, Elizabeth, ist fünf Jahre älter als ich und arbeitet in der Bibliothek in der Stadt. Sie ist sehr glücklich dort, denn sie liest sehr gern.

**Teacher:** Und Ihre Eltern?

**Student:** Mein Vater ist gestorben, und meine Mutter arbeitet halbtags in einem Geschäft. Wir sind nur noch vier zu Hause, denn mein ältester Bruder hat letztes Jahr geheiratet. Und meine Schwester will nächstes Jahr heiraten. Ich komme mit meinen Geschwistern sehr gut aus. Ich glaube, das kommt daher, daß ich so viel jünger bin. Wir haben uns nie um das Spielzeug gestritten, weil wir selten miteinander gespielt haben, als ich jünger war.

**Teacher:** Und wie kommen Sie mit Ihrer Mutter aus?

**Student:** Eigentlich ganz gut. Nur manchmal, wenn ich spät nach Hause komme, wird sie mit mir böse. Und das dauert auch nicht so lange. Meine Mutter ist ganz in Ordnung. Sie versteht viel Spaß und mag gern Witze. Ich glaube, wir sind überhaupt eine lustige Familie.

Wir wohnen in einem Zweifamilienhaus am Rande der Stadt. Ich wohne sehr gern hier, weil wir sehr nah am Wald sind. Ich habe als kleiner Junge sehr viel im Wald gespielt, und ich gehe immer noch gern dort spazieren.

Wir haben einen großen Garten und ziemlich viel Gemüse. Ich helfe meiner Mutter damit, denn es wäre für sie alleine zu viel Arbeit. Meine Schwester mäht den Rasen, und ich pflanze die Kartoffeln an. Es macht mir eigentlich Spaß im Garten zu arbeiten.

**Teacher:** Danke schön. Das war sehr interessant.

### Examiner's comments

This candidate is well prepared, has covered the tenses required (the future is handled by *will*), and has demonstrated a good variety of structure. He uses *denn* several times, which allows him to continue with the simpler word order through the clauses. When he's talking about his brothers and sisters, the phrase *das kommt daher, daß* ... is well prepared, as is the use of *sich streiten um* .... The feelings and emotions are well handled, and the use of *es wäre* is also quite impressive at this level.

It is noticeable that the overall portrait of the family is a happy one. This leaves a positive impression on the examiner.

## GENERAL CONVERSATION

### Transcript

 **a) Teacher's questions**

Wieviele Unterrichtsstunden gibt es hier an der Schule?
Was sind Ihre Wahlfächer?
Was wollen Sie nach der Schule machen?
Wie groß ist Reading?
Gibt es hier viel Industrie?
Was gibt es zu sehen und zu tun in Reading?
Was haben Sie letztes Wochenende gemacht?
Wie helfen Sie normalerweise zu Hause?
Was haben Sie nächstes Wochenende vor?

 **b) Conversation**

**Teacher:** Wieviele Unterrichtsstunden gibt es hier an der Schule?

**Student:** Es gibt fünf Stunden, jede Stunde ist 60 Minuten lang. Wir haben vier am Vormittag und eine am Nachmittag. Nach der zweiten Stunde gibt eine kleine Pause von 20 Minuten.

**Teacher:** Was sind Ihre Wahlfächer?

**Student:** Geschichte, Erdkunde, Französisch – und Deutsch natürlich. Ich mag die Fremdsprachen besonders gern, weil ich gern reise.

**Teacher:** Was wollen Sie nach der Schule machen?

**Student:** Ich will zuerst Fremdsprachen studieren, vielleicht eine dritte Fremdsprache wie Russisch, zum Beispiel. Dann möchte ich eine Weile im Ausland arbeiten.

**Teacher:** Wie groß ist Reading?

**Student:** Die Stadt hat ungefähr hundertfünfzigtausend Einwohner, aber ich glaube, sie wird immer größer, denn man baut hier viele neue Siedlungen am Rande der Stadt.

**Teacher:** Gibt es hier viel Industrie?

**Student:** Nicht so viel. Es gibt viele Bürogebäude, aber weniger Fabriken. Viele Leute fahren auch jeden Tag nach London, um zu arbeiten.

**Teacher:** Was gibt es zu sehen und zu tun in Reading?

**Student:** Es gibt die Ruinen von der Abtei, die sehr berühmt sind. Und Reading liegt auch sehr schön an der Themse, also kann man schöne Dampferfahrten machen, aber so viel gibt es nicht für Touristen.

**Teacher:** Was haben Sie letztes Wochenende gemacht?

**Student:** Ich habe Hockey in der Schulmannschaft gespielt, und wir haben gewonnen, was sehr gut war. Und am Nachmittag habe ich meine Freundinnen in der Stadt getroffen, und wir haben zusammen einen Schaufensterbummel gemacht. Danach sind wir in die Pizzeria gegangen.

**Teacher:** Wie helfen Sie normalerweise zu Hause?

**Student:** Also, wir sind vier Kinder zu Hause, und jeder von uns hat seine Arbeiten zu machen. Ich decke den Tisch jeden Tag morgens und abends, und ich halte mein Schlafzimmer sauber.

**Teacher:** Was haben Sie nächstes Wochenende vor?

**Student:** Also, nächstes Wochenende ist etwas Besonderes. Wir werden eine Grillparty bei uns haben, denn mein Vater hat Geburtstag. Er wird vierzig. Wir haben viele Leute eingeladen, und viele seiner früheren Schulkameraden werden auch da sein.

### Examiner's comments

Every question is answered fully here, with interesting details in many cases. It's clear that the candidate has prepared thoroughly and that none of the questions comes as a great surprise. This is as it should be.

Much of the material is provided in earlier chapters of this book, and you will no doubt have practised similar language already with your teacher. When it's all put together like this, it makes a very strong impression of a competent candidate. There is more than enough material here to gain an A* Grade and you will not be expected to score all these points. However, you should make sure of at least some answers of this quality in order to assure yourself of the highest grade!

## CHAPTER 16 READING AND RESPONDING

### Answers (Foundation)

**1** D  **2** C  **3** D
**4** B  **5** B  **6** A
**7** i) Falsch;  ii) Richtig;  iii) Falsch;  iv) Richtig;  v) Falsch
**8** B
**9** i) B;  ii) A;  iii) B + F;  iv) D;  v) A

### Examiner's comments

These Foundation Level questions are all straightforward multiple choice questions and should pose no problems.

### Answers (Foundation/Higher)

**10** i) C;  ii) F;  iii) A;  iv) E;  v) B
**11** i)  Brieffreunde
     ii)  über Weihnachten
     iii)  hat keine Idee
     iv)  ist nicht so gut in Bio
     v)  sind gegen
     vi)  weiterlernen

### Examiner's comments

The small ads in Question 10 are a typical transition task to help you into the beginning of the Higher Level. The connection between the person and the appropriate advertisement is simple enough, but is not usually direct.

In Question 11, the passage requires you to make a greater degree of deduction. It is self-evident from the whole letter that those involved are *Brieffreunde*, and it is fairly straightforward to infer that the *Winterurlaub* must have been in the Christmas holidays. (Don't forget that you need to know the German for Easter and Whitsun as well!) Questions iii) and iv) are paraphrases of the text, whereas v) is an attitude betrayed by what the parents say. *Biostudium anfangen* is simply expressed as *weiterlernen* for vi).

### Answers (Higher)

**12 a)** Richtig;  **b)** Falsch;  **c)** Falsch;  **d)** Richtig;  **e)** Richtig;  **f)** Richtig

### Examiner's comments

Beware statistics! Don't begin to imagine what they might say when you read what the survey was about – they may have been designed especially for your exam! *Eine Umfrage* (which you have probably conducted at some time in your German classes) is simply a device for introducing opinions and preferences.

As mentioned elsewhere, you need not worry about your statistical competence when setting about these questions. Very little is asked of your maths skills except to recognise that 70% could be described as the majority (a), or that 12% is more than 5% (d). You can arrive at the answer for b) by two different methods: either by understanding the third sentence *Sie [Die Umfrage] zeigte auch …*, or by contrasting what young men used to want to do with their current ambitions. The third paragraph brings in the concept of job security for e) and the last paragraph gives an easy answer to f) in the word *flexible*. (Remember that this is *flexibel* normally, but drops one 'e' when it gains the adjective ending -*e*.)

**13 a)** D;   **b)** J;   **c)** H;   **d)** C;   **e)** E;   **f)** G

**Examiner's comments**

The difficulty with such a passage is that you have longer descriptions of places to read and a small amount of overlap between all the charming, historical places with wonderful views or things to look at. However, the questions are crafted to eliminate certain of the options while directing your attention to others.

**a)** *Das Weinstädtchen Königswinter* would be more appropriate than simply any other *Gaststätte*.
**b)** The phrases *mittelalterliche Fachwerkhäuser* and *historische Gaststätten* give a fair indication where mother would be happy.
**c)** *Spaß* is quite easy to spot but don't expect such information to be in chronological order when the exercise is multiple choice – for obvious reasons!
**d)** Again the words *Gaststätte* and *herrlichen Ausblick* signal the answer.
**e)** This is much more difficult because you need to realise that *des ersten Bundeskanzlers* puts you in the realms of history, even before you connect with *Museum*, which should confirm your choice.
**f)** The word *weit* might draw you to the answer, contained in *ältere Leute … herrlichen Gärten … ohne weit gehen zu müssen.*

## CHAPTER 17  WRITING

### 1  *Sample Student's Answer*

| | |
|---|---|
| 1 | Brot |
| 2 | Butter |
| 3 | Obst |
| 4 | Aufschnitt |
| 5 | Käse |
| 6 | Limonade |
| 7 | Orangensaft |
| 8 | Tischdecke |
| 9 | Geschirr |
| 10 | Tennisschläger/-bälle |

**EXAMINER'S COMMENTS**

● *The food and drink list must be the easiest of all to do quickly. Try to add one or two items which are not edible. Put yourself in the picnic situation and see what else you can come up with easily – sun cream, sun hat, swimming costume, etc.*

- Notice the adverb phrase in each activity to say when, with whom, how or where. The verb is the essential starting point for each diary entry.

| | |
|---|---|
| Sonntag | : schwimmen im Freizeitzentrum |
| Montag | : ins Museum gehen |
| Dienstag | : Oma besuchen (mit der Straßenbahn) |
| Mittwoch | : abends mit Jeff und Patrina in die Disco gehen |
| Donnerstag | : große Party in der Schule organisieren |

**3** *Sample Student's Answer*

- When writing a postcard, there is almost too little time to get started. This is only Foundation, but the occasional adjective or adverb does stop it becoming too bare.

Liebe Cornelia, Lieber Uwe,
Wir wohnen hier in einer bequemen Pension. Das Wetter ist hervorragend sonnig. Gestern wollten wir segeln, aber leider war gar kein Wind. Heute sollen wir hoffentlich nach Marseille fahren. Am Samstag fahren wir schon nach Hause zurück.

(41 words)

**4** *Sample Student's Answer*

- You need not use the subject for your verb each time, as long as it is clear who is intended. You couldn't omit the last Du kannst, for example, otherwise it might suggest that Bernd is going to ring up. A simple but clear message. Full marks.

Hallo Georg,
Bernd hat angerufen.
Kann heute abend nicht ins Kino kommen.
Muß seine Oma besuchen.
Er plant eine Party am Wochenende.
Du kannst deine Freundin und ihre Schwester mitbringen.
Du kannst morgen abend anrufen.

## 5 *Sample Student's Answer*

Bristol, den 26. Mai

Sehr geehrte Herren,

Ich werde im August mit meiner Familie nach Düsseldorf fahren, und zwar vom 14. bis zum 18. Ich möchte drei Zimmer mit Bad reservieren, wenn Sie noch Platz haben. Wir sind sechs Personen - meine Eltern, meine Großeltern und wir zwei Kinder.

Was gibt es in der Nähe zu sehen und zu tun? Ich habe viele Broschüren gelesen, und es scheint recht viel los zu sein. Wir möchten gern wissen, welche Sehenswürdigkeiten mit dem Auto zu erreichen sind, da meine Großeltern nicht mehr so gut laufen können.

Ich wäre Ihnen sehr dankbar, wenn Sie uns einen Stadtplan schicken könnten.

Vielen Dank im voraus für Ihre Bemühungen.

Ihr

Richard Sweeney

(114 words)

**EXAMINER'S COMMENTS**

- The introduction is a standard one for booking rooms, and the second paragraph uses the same sort of question which you might ask of the tourist office. The ending, too, is one you can use again and again. It is particularly polite and stylish.
- As far as the language goes, it is accurate and fulfils the requirement to cover both future and past time. There are also longer sentences containing subordinate clauses.
- This answer would easily gain a Grade C.

## 6 *Sample Student's Answer*

Für die Schülerzeitschrift 'Spieglein, Spieglein'

*Viele Grüße aus der Prospect Schule!*

Es sind etwa neunhundertfünfzig Schüler und Schülerinnen hier an unserer Schule. Wir haben ein ziemlich modernes Gebäude und viele Computer, die uns alle faszinieren. Wir haben schon viel damit gemacht, und im kommenden Jahr werden wir auch unsere Hausaufgaben damit machen können.

Die Lehrer und Lehrerinnen sind ziemlich in Ordnung, und verstehen viel Spaß. Wir treiben viel Sport nach der Schule, und von drei bis fünf Uhr kann man auch Nachhilfestunden an der Schule bekommen.

Wir haben seit einem Jahr ein neues Sprachlabor an der Schule, wo wir vier verschiedene Fremdsprachen lernen können.

Im großen und ganzen macht es mir Spaß hier, auch wenn wir manchmal meckern.

(118 words)

**EXAMINER'S COMMENTS**

- The greeting at the beginning is quite a nice touch.
- The facts which follow are uninteresting but you would expect to give them.
- The sentence which includes both past and future tenses is somewhat contrived but does the job.
- The comments about the friendly staff and the extra after-school lessons give a nice, positive feel to the passage.
- The details about the language laboratory, including the subordinate clause, are worthy of credit.
- All in all (im großen und ganzen) the passage is of a sound Grade C standard.

## EXAMINER'S COMMENTS

- Again, the opening is straightforward and can always be used in responding to an advert from a newspaper.

- The following sentences deal with the past and future respectively and adequately. Notice the use of habe vor to introduce the intention.

- The longest sentence, with two main and three subordinate clauses, is well under control and scores good marks for linguistic adventure.

- The final sentence is a nice, polite way to end an application.

- This letter is of a good Grade C level.

(108 words)

### 7 *Sample Student's Answer*

> Nottingham, den 30. Mai
>
> Sehr geehrte Herren,
> Ich habe Ihre Annonce im heutigen 'General Anzeiger' gelesen und möchte mich um die Stelle in der Bäckerei bewerben.
> Ich arbeite schon seit zwei Jahren in einem Supermarkt hier in der Stadt und ich glaube, daß mein Arbeitgeber mit mir ganz zufrieden ist. Ich habe vor, die ganzen Sommerferien in Bonn zu verbringen, und möchte daher eine Arbeit finden.
> Ich glaube, daß die Arbeit in einer Bäckerei sehr früh am Morgen beginnt, was mir sehr gut passen würde, denn ich bin ein Mensch, der gern früh aufsteht.
> Ich würde mich sehr freuen, eine positive Nachricht von Ihnen zu erhalten.
> Ihre
> Michelle Duncan

## EXAMINER'S COMMENTS

- Excellent. All the major points in the pictures are covered, as are the past and future tenses.

- In this case, the candidate has used the conventional imperfect tense very well, but he/she might equally have given the account in the perfect tense, remembering to leave feelings, circumstances, etc. in the imperfect.

- What stands out about this passage is the extent to which the adverbial phrases tell the story: aus dem Park, über die Straße, etc. give plenty of detail.

- The opinion is expressed by ich glaube, and the expression which follows has been specially learned to replace the usual böse.

- Notice that the speech is described in four different ways using sagen, schimpfen, erklären and reden. This makes a very strong impression on the examiner reading the script.

- The pluperfect in hatte geschlafen and the passive in wurde geweckt are particularly welcome inclusions at this level.

- This is undoubtedly at least a Grade A candidate.

(160 words)

### 8 *Sample Student's Answer*

> Ich ging gerade am Park vorbei, als ich den Hund sah, der vor mir aus dem Park schoß und einen Ball über die Straße jagte. Der Wagen, der gerade die Straße entlang fuhr, mußte scharf bremsen, und fuhr über den Gehweg, durch einen Zaun und in den Vordergarten eines Hauses.
> Der Autofahrer stieg aus, schein nicht verletzt zu sein, und schaute sich seinen Wagen an. Der Vorderteil seines Autos war ziemlich kaputt, und ich glaube, er war außer sich vor Wut.
> Dann kam eine Frau aus dem Park und über die Straße. Sie lief mit der Leine in der Hand auf den Autofahrer zu und erklärte ihm, daß es ihr Hund war, der den Unfall verursacht hat.
> Dann kam der Hausbesitzer an. Er hatte geschlafen, sagte er, und wurde vom Lärm geweckt. „Ich werde die Polizei anrufen" schimpfte er, und ging ins Haus zurück. In zwei Minuten war ein Streifenwagen da, und alle drei Leute redeten mit beiden Polizisten.

**9** *Sample Student's Answer*

Wir haben uns schon um acht Uhr dreißig vor der Schule getroffen, und sind gleich losgefahren, sobald die ganze Klasse da war. Wir wollten zwei Museen in York besuchen und sind um Viertel nach zehn am Heimatsmuseum angekommen. Es war etwas später als geplant, weil der Berufsverkehr so stark war.

(50 words)

Wir fanden das Museum ziemlich interessant, und kamen mit einigen Souvenirs wieder heraus, die wir dort gekauft hatten. Wir wollten gleich zu Mittag essen, aber unsere Lehrer hatten andere Pläne. Wir sind wieder in den Bus gestiegen, und in zwanzig Minuten waren wir in einem anderen Museum, und zwar in einer Kunstausstellung. Meine Freunde und ich fanden es teilsweise ganz toll, denn wir machen einen Leistungskurs in Kunst in der Schule, aber andere Schüler fanden es nicht so gut.

(79 words)

Zu Mittag haben wir unseren Picknick im Stadtpark gegessen, und danach haben wir ein bißchen Fußball gespielt. Es war übrigens ziemlich warm, und wir waren alle sehr froh, als unsere Lehrerin vorgeschlagen hat, in die Eisdiele zu gehen.

Als wir um fünf Uhr wieder in der Schule waren, waren wir alle sehr müde.

(53 words)

- This started as a very promising piece of writing, and indeed all that has gone into it by way of language and structure is very good.

- However, the candidate has broken a 'golden rule'; he/she has not planned sufficiently well, and has written more than is required. Why is this considered a mistake, you may well ask?
  – Firstly, there is no future tense, so far. Perhaps the candidate was going to use the ploy of looking forward to next year's trip in the last line.
  – Secondly the candidate has not mentioned the boating on the lake, which appeared to be a major activity of the afternoon.
  – Finally, the candidate has realised that he/she is overrunning, and has tried to round off quickly, but in doing so has finished with a rather tired and weak sentence.

- The lesson of this piece is that even the best linguist can come unstuck, if he/she does not plan adequately.

- It would be a good exercise for you to re-read the passage and go through the process of reducing the word-count, making sure that you finish with a sentence as strong as the rest of the passage.

# ACKNOWLEDGEMENTS

Published by HarperCollins*Publishers* Ltd
77–85 Fulham Palace Road
London W6 8JB

www.**Collins**Education.com
On-line support for schools and colleges

© HarperCollins*Publishers* Ltd 2001

First published 2001

ISBN 0 00 711199 1

Ken Wheeler asserts the moral right to be identified as the author of this work.

All rights reserved. No part of this publication may be reproduced, stored in a retrieval system, or transmitted in any form or by any means, electronic, mechanical, photocopying, recording or otherwise, without either the prior permission of the Publisher or a licence permitting restricted copying in the United Kingdom issued by the Copyright Licensing Agency Ltd, 90 Tottenham Court Road, London W1P 0LP. This book is sold subject to the condition that it shall not by way of trade or otherwise be lent, hired out or otherwise circulated without the Publisher's prior consent.

British Library Cataloguing in Publication Data

A catalogue record for this book is available from the British Library.

Edited by Sue Chapple

Production by Kathryn Botterill

Language consultant: Claudia Bergthaler and Birte Twisselman

Cover design by Susi Martin-Taylor

Book design by Rupert Purcell and produced by Gecko Limited

Index compiled by Yvonne Dixon

Printed and bound by Bath Press

**Acknowledgements**

**Photographs**
AKG: 45; Tim Booth: 2, 10, 28, 30, 66, 75, 100;
Sabine Oppenländer: 4.

**Illustrations**
Sally Artz, Roger Bastow, Kathy Baxendale, Harvey Collins, Richard Deverell, Hilary Evans, Gecko Ltd, Sarah Jowsey, Lorna Kent, Joe Little and Nick Ward

Every effort has been made to contact the holders of copyright material, but if any have been inadvertently overlooked, the Publishers will be pleased to make the necessary arrangements at the first opportunity.

**Audio CD**
The audio CD was recorded at Post Sound Studios, London and was produced by the Language Production Company with the voices of Claudia Bergthaler, Olivier Hess, Michael Hulsmann, Philipp Kunze, Birgit Leitner, Sarah Sherborne, Gertrude Thoma, Elisabeth Wellerhaus.

Production by Marie-Thérèse Bougard and Charlie Waygood.

Music by Nigel Martinez and Dick Walter.

You might also like to visit:
www.**fire**and**water**.com
The book lover's website